"This is unquestionably the best, ___ ___
up-to-date, accessible, and accurat___
—David R. Godine, David R. Godine Publisher Inc.

"One of the best books on all aspects of book publishing . . .
a must for every writer. Fair, detailed and commonsensical."
—Bill Henderson, Pushcart Press

"Clear-sighted, practical advice . . . unveils the mysteries
of the publishing world . . . valuable, informative, readable."
—*Publishers Weekly*

"Filled with useful, practical advice."
—*John Barkham Reviews*

"Essential reading for all writers—beginning and
advanced. There is no better overview of the publishing
process."
—Nick Lyons, Lyons & Burford, Publishers

"An absolute 'must' for anyone who wants to write a
book . . . a tremendous service to all writers and authors."
—*Omaha Metro*

"I hate to admit I have more to learn about the
publishing business, but Rick Balkin's *Writer's Guide to
Book Publishing* proved it."
—Richard Curtis, author of *Beyond the Bestseller*

RICHARD BALKIN is a well-known literary agent and
proprietor of his own firm, The Balkin Agency. He lives in
Amhurst, Massachusetts. NICK BAKALAR is a New York–
based book writer and editor.

A WRITER'S GUIDE TO
BOOK PUBLISHING

RICHARD BALKIN

Revised by Nick Bakalar and Richard Balkin

Two chapters by Jared Carter
Revised by Trent Duffy

A PLUME BOOK

PLUME
Published by the Penguin Group
Penguin Books USA Inc., 375 Hudson Street,
New York, New York 10014, U.S.A.
Penguin Books Ltd, 27 Wrights Lane,
London W8 5TZ, England
Penguin Books Australia Ltd, Ringwood,
Victoria, Australia
Penguin Books Canada Ltd, 10 Alcorn Avenue,
Toronto, Ontario, Canada M4V 3B2
Penguin Books (N.Z.) Ltd, 182–190 Wairau Road,
Auckland 10, New Zealand

Penguin Books Ltd, Registered Offices:
Harmondsworth, Middlesex, England

Published by Plume, an imprint of Dutton Signet,
a division of Penguin Books USA Inc.
First Edition published by Hawthorn Books.
Second Edition published by Elsevier-Dutton Publishing Co., Inc.

First Printing, Third Edition, August, 1994
10 9 8 7 6 5 4 3

The article entitled "A PUBLISHING FABLE" by Lachlan P. MacDonald originally appeared
in the 1980 issue of *Publishing in the Output Mode*, a newsletter issued by Lachlan
MacDonald's Padre Productions, San Luis Obispo, CA 93406. Copyright © 1980
by Lachlan P. MacDonald. Reprinted by permission.

Ⓟ   REGISTERED TRADEMARK—MARCA REGISTRADA

LIBRARY OF CONGRESS CATALOGING IN PUBLICATION DATA:
Balkin, Richard.
    A writer's guide to book publishing / Richard Balkin.—3rd ed., rev. and expanded,
Rev. / by Nick Bakalar and Richard Balkin.
        p.   cm.
    "Two chapters by Jared Carter, revised by Trent Duffy."
    Includes bibliographical references and index.
    ISBN 0-452-27021-9
    1. Authors and publishers.   2. Publishers and publishing.
I. Bakalar, Nick.   II. Title.
PN155.B3 1994
808′.02—dc20   93–46730
                                                                    CIP

Printed in the United States of America
Set in ITC Century Book
Designed by Leonard Telesca

To W.H.Y.H.,
who taught us both,
among many other things,
that publishing is more
than a business.

Contents

---

*Written by Jared Carter/revised by Trent Duffy.

Preface

On a trip to Manhattan recently with my two daughters, I stopped in at the new Barnes & Noble "superstore" on Broadway near 81st Street. It was initially not the sort of bookstore either I or my daughters felt comfortable in: too big, too brightly lit, too much a suburban supermarket—it was almost as if Kmart or Wal-Mart had gone into the book business. The whole layout seemed to discourage the kind of quiet contemplation I'd always thought necessary to the purchase of exactly the right book for my mood. And yet, there was a larger selection of titles than any of us had ever seen in a single store—some 150,000 in all. I looked for books by a novelist I like and found not one but six of his titles, including one I thought was out of print. The sports section contained entire subsections on baseball, football, basketball, even ice hockey, and a half-dozen books on squash. And the prices were right: Almost everything was discounted, some books selling at as much as 30 percent off list price. The cafe on the second floor, which at first seemed the work of a manic young interior decorator in league with a trendy Columbus Avenue restaurateur—a pathetic attempt to lure people who are uninterested in books into a bookstore—was actually quite a pleasant place to have a cup of coffee and a long browse. In short, the store was, even for those of us who love tidy, quiet little bookstores, a success. And we bought more books than we'd intended to.

Our experience is reflected in the financial reports of Barnes & Noble, the leader in the trend toward these gigantic bookstores. The number of B&N superstores rose from 88 to 168 between 1992 and 1993, an increase of 91 percent. Sales increased by 112 percent. At the same time, sales decreased by 12 percent in B&N's mall stores, while the number of those stores decreased by 3 percent. If you were president of Barnes & Noble, what kind of store would you open next? At least for now, however you may feel about it as a reader and buyer of books, the superstore looks like the future of bookstores.

If the way books are sold is evolving as we enter the twenty-first century, then so are the books themselves. Computers have now entered every area of publishing, from the computer disks authors now routinely deliver to publishers along with (and sometimes instead of) a typescript, to the compact discs on which thousands of books are now being encoded, with computer-driven typesetting, photo reproduction, printing, warehousing, and distribution in between. Electronic rights have become a serious source of profit, and publishers, agents, and authors now vigorously negotiate those clauses of the contract that deal with them, even while both parties struggle to figure out which of the half-dozen or more electronic rights formats they wish to retain, exploit, license, option, or ignore. While the traditional book in hardcover format seems in no danger of disappearing, publishers are discovering that for many works of nonfiction, especially large reference titles, digital formats work best. Few are prepared to proclaim the death of the printed word, but no one doubts that the electronic media will vastly change our reading habits over the next decade.

Business and reference titles are now the first to be widely distributed and read in electronic form. Most publishers feel that a kind of critical mass in the number of CD-ROM–equipped home computers will soon be achieved, and at that point encyclopedias, dictionaries, travel books, gardening titles, and business books will begin to look rather quaint in hardcover format. Children's books, science fiction, and cookbooks are also likely candidates for digitalization.

Some optimists feel that books in electronic form will enlarge the market—that multimedia compact discs can be sold, in addition to the traditional formats, to an even wider audience. Already publishers—and authors—are benefiting from the sale of rights to software publishers, and recently a company called The Online Bookstore has been set up to allow readers to download texts of books—for a fee, of course—to their personal computers. Several of the large houses have hired editors who specialize in electronic publishing, and agents and publishers discuss the sale of electronic rights now with an enthusiasm previously reserved for discussions of paperback or foreign rights. Publishers and authors have something the computer companies cannot do without: the software that makes the magical hardware worth using.

None of this is lost on companies like Microsoft and Sony. Microsoft recently bought 26 percent of Dorling Kindersley, a British publisher that specializes in illustrated reference books. William Gates, president of Microsoft, has said that within the next ten years, electronic publishing could be a $1 billion business, and he clearly intends for Microsoft to get its share. But this means another market for writers, since only writers can produce the material that Microsoft and Sony will encode on compact discs for use in computers.

While compact disc multimedia formats are a preoccupation now of publishers and the publishing trade press, another, much older, non-print medium has quietly grown into a highly profitable sector of the business: audiobooks, in both tape and CD formats. There have of course been recorded books for decades, dating back to books recorded on vinyl and played on turntables (remember Dylan Thomas's *A Child's Christmas in Wales* recorded by Caedmon Records?). But tape cassettes and now compact discs have vastly expanded the market for them. "Reading" a best-selling novel, or even an unabridged version of *Moby Dick*, while driving to work, jogging around the neighborhood, or lying on a beach with one's eyes closed is a pleasure widely enjoyed, and there is no doubt that sales of books in recorded form will do anything but increase over the coming years. Some large publishers produce and publish their own tapes and CDs. Companies like Dove and Books on Tape buy rights from publishers. In either case, writers stand to profit from these sales, and now the audio clause in a contract is one no author or agent can afford to ignore.

Over the years since the publication of the last edition of this book, the life of the book editor has undergone considerable change. The average book editor now works for a large "entertainment" conglomerate, making the editor a small cog in a very large corporate wheel. Random House, for example, now encompasses not only Random itself but also Alfred Knopf, Crown, Ballantine, Fawcett, Pantheon, Schocken, Villard, and Vintage.* The increasing concentration of the book publishing business in the hands of these companies is a phenomenon of the 1980s whose results the publishing world now lives with in the 90s: A dozen or so large hardcover houses plus another dozen mass market paperback houses dominate the market in bookstore sales, and two large book clubs account for more than half the sales through that channel.

Inside publishing houses, the concentration on the "big book" has not diminished over the decade. These "potential" best-sellers—such as Colin Powell's memoirs, sold to Random for a $6.5 million advance—still eat up the lion's share of the authors' advance and promotion budgets, and a remark from a marketing director that "this would be just a midlist book" can often spell rejection for the author. In many houses, the editors, the publicists, the advertising and sales personnel all get the message: Pay attention to the book with best-seller potential, and think about smaller books some other time. Literary fiction and seri-

---

*With gross sales of $1.1 billion in 1992, they lead the pack, but Paramount (which is the parent company of Simon & Schuster, and which bought Macmillan in 1994) nips closely at their heels, as do Bantam Doubleday Dell and HarperCollins.

ous nonfiction with a narrower audience suffer in a climate like this, and there is no indication, at least in the half-dozen or so major houses, that this situation will soon change. The result is a narrower range of reading matter from the largest commercial trade houses, with fewer serious works of nonfiction, more concentration on brand-name best-selling novelists, and more books on popular psychology, dieting, getting rich quickly, and improving one's love life. There are many subjective judgments to be made here, but there is a growing feeling among authors and agents that serious books are now harder to place with publishers, particularly the largest publishers, than ever before.

Ted Solotaroff, a retired HarperCollins editor, recently made this point before a meeting of The Authors Guild. He told a story of his bringing in a proposal for a biography of Henry Miller to an editorial board meeting. The proposal was excellent—well written, well organized, vivid in all the right places as a Miller biography ought to be. He listened to the marketing people discuss the idea—Miller's written so much about himself already, who would buy a book on Miller that isn't written by a familiar author, Miller's dead and no one especially cares. Solotaroff was able to fend off these objections, but then came the clincher: One of the marketing people opined, "I don't think she can write the kind of book we can sell." Solotaroff replied somewhat angrily: "I am very interested in what you have to say about the market for the book, but I really don't want to argue about whether this author can develop this project, because that's my job. That's what I've been doing for thirty years." The incident illustrates a trend in hardcover publishing: Editorial tradition no longer drives large houses, and editors take a backseat to marketing people when it comes to decisions about what to publish. And what marketing people want is the big book.

The big-book, conglomerate-dominated atmosphere inside publishing houses continues to take its toll on editors. Now fewer editors are handling more books, and the pressure to acquire and publish best-sellers is unrelenting. Editors do less and less actual manuscript editing—it is not uncommon for a book to pass through the editor's hands and directly to the copyeditor's desk after receiving little more than a perfunctory ·

glance. So difficult has the editor's job become that a large and experienced editorial staff could be made up just of editors I myself know who have been laid off over the past few years, or who have simply said, "I'm quitting. I just can't take it anymore."

Economic realities outside the control of publishers continue to bedevil the industry. In a generally recessionary economy, books, particularly hardcover trade books, must seem to many people an indulgence easily resisted. While the average price of a hardcover book has of course increased over the decade, books are still a bargain compared to other forms of entertainment. It has not been easy to convince people of this, even if it is true.

But before we despair that real editors have disappeared, that book publishing is dead, and that books have become extinct, the victims of inflation, conglomeration, and the proliferation of VCRs and personal computers, let's look again. The American Booksellers Association and the Association of American Publishers recently undertook a sophisticated statistical study of consumer book-buying habits covering the period April, 1991, through March, 1992. It discovered that 65 percent of U.S. households bought at least one book during the year—822 million adult books sold, an increase of 7 percent over the previous year. Unit sales in trade paperbacks were up 11 percent, trade hardcover up 8 percent. None of this will make the average venture capitalist reach for his checkbook, but these are hardly the numbers of an industry in its death throes.

Finally, while the few big houses get bigger, there is a large and growing number of smaller book publishers that should provide a measure of optimism, particularly for a first-book author. It has always been hard to crack the top two dozen houses, and while that problem has now intensified, the other end of the spectrum in publishing—the small, independent, regional presses—is flourishing. Although there is definitely less opportunity here to make much money from writing books, there is clearly now a greater possibility of seeing your book in print. For this reason, the sections of *A Writer's Guide* on small presses may prove for some readers the most important part of the book. Poets and literary novelists will find these sections helpful, because these are the writers small presses attract. The sections on el-hi and college text publishing, professional and reference books, university presses, "special sales," book distribution, and paperback originals will also be of interest to writers trying to find the best publisher for their books outside of the big trade houses. Trent Duffy has attempted to keep up with the mushrooming use of computers in the areas of editing, composition, and book manufacturing, by adding updated information on technical developments, and especially on what they mean for the author. So much is taking place so fast that it is impossible to be au courant by the time this book appears in print (that is one area of book publishing that has not changed—it still takes about nine months after manuscript delivery to make a book).

Within all the other phases of book publishing, I have attempted to supply recent statistics, information, and examples, and have added materials on current trends or developments. To try to authoritatively encompass the entire field of book publishing—even concentrating just on what I think authors want to know—is a presumption, and I must beg the reader's indulgence for errors or omissions.

Acknowledgments

My education in publishing has been immeasurably enriched by a number of fine articles and books written by dedicated book-men and book-women, without whom this book would not have been written. I have frequently dipped into their storehouse of knowledge for facts and explanations. Only some are mentioned in the Bibliography; many others have been mined for information used here and I apologize for their anonymity but thank them for their contributions. *Publishers Weekly* has equally been a constant source for information and statistics; I salute the men and women who are responsible for maintaining its excellence.

During the preparation of this revision a number of people were kind enough to read portions of it and to make useful suggestions and comments: Ted Nardin, Jerry Gross, Oscar Collier, Mike Larsen, Gerry Helferich, Gary Luke, Richard Curtis, Herb Addison, Tom Flynn, Judit Bodnar, Lisa Jacobson, John Hunt, Dan Zincus, Kate Hartson, Jo Hoffman, Steve Lewers, MiHo Cha, xviii / Acknowledgments

Alan Andres, Len Fulton, Richard Morris, Bill Henderson, Dan Poynter, Liz Hadas, Morris Phillipson, Colin Jones.

Chapters 5 and 6—originally written by Jeb Carter—were exclusively revised by Trent Duffy; the two of them bear all the credit for the informed and lucid explanations in these chapters.

For their assistance in updating these chapters, Trent Duffy would like to thank Jeanne Palmer, Kim Lewis, Meta Brophy, Nancy Clements, Madelaine Cooke, Karen Dubnow, Pat McCormack, David Frost, Anne McCoy, Angela Palmisono, and Meg Blackstone.

Nick Bakalar, friend, confidant, and colleague, has done more than help me with this revision; he has made it possible and is in large part responsible for it. Thanks are inadequate, but they will have to do. My wife, Felice Swados, has again sympathetically put up with all the grouching and assorted tantrums that many writers indulge in when working at their computers. I am grateful to her for this, and for so much more.

Nick Bakalar would like to thank the following for their generous assistance: Cliff Becker, Paul Bresnick, Deb Brody, Colin Day, Arnold Dolin, Steve Fischer, Jim Fitzgerald, Rachel Ginsburg, Alex Hoyt, Barney Karpfinger, Rachel Klayman, Ed Knappman, Jim Landis, Alan Lang, Jim Menick, Susan Milmoe, Lisa Queen, Bonnie Roesch, Susan Schwartz, John Thornton, Gladys Topkis, Len Vlahos.

Introduction

John Creasey, a noted mystery and detective-story novelist who died in 1973, had received—according to his obituary—744 rejection slips before his first work was accepted for publication. To add to this *Guinness Book of World Records* statistic, he wrote and had published 560 novels during his lifetime. Though you may have some doubts about the authenticity of the first figure, the second is a matter of record. The moral of this story is not "you are bound to get published sooner or later"—for many books will never make it to the printer's, and both the industry and the reading public, in most instances, will be grateful—but, rather, "don't give up too quickly." A few rejection slips do not mean your book proposal or manuscript is a complete flop and that editors sit at their desks laughing at it before they ask their secretaries to send you a polite but standard rejection letter.

Much of the seemingly inherent conflict between publishers and would-be and published authors (95 percent of whom can regale you with their publishing horror stories) is the result of ignorance about the various stages between the submission of a proposal or manuscript and the receipt of an author's first royalty check. It is usually the author's ignorance, but sometimes—in this age of specialization, expansion, and technological change—the editor's as well.

But this is a guide primarily for authors, and it is called a guide because it presumes to contain most of what an author or a potential author might want to know about publishing. There are, however, several qualifications. This is not a book about how to write a book. Many of these are available, from the humblest high school grammar to the most sophisticated style manuals, not to mention the many informal, anecdotal "how to's" turned out by both successful and unsuccessful writers. Nor is this book specifically concerned with the technical aspects of publishing, such as design, printing, and manufacturing; nor the internal aspects of publishing, as, for example, the economics of running a publishing house, new uses of technology in publishing, or the general administrative process.*

The decision on what to include in this book grows out of 25 years of experience communicating with writers, both as an editor and as an agent. There are seven main areas of the publishing process that particularly interest writers, and they comprise the bulk of this book: how does a writer approach a publisher; what are the methods and criteria publishers use in evaluating proposals and manuscripts; how does a writer prepare a "final" manuscript; how does one read, understand, and negotiate a book contract; what is a publisher actually doing with the manuscript during its nine- to twelve-month gestation; how does the publisher promote and sell the book; and, finally, what alternatives are open to the writer of a "noncommercial" book. No one can expect to be an expert, or even well informed, in all phases of publishing, and I do not pretend that *all* you wish to know will be found here. In fact, I have ignored several areas of publishing completely, such as Bible publishing, standardized texts,

---

*John P. Dessauer's *Book Publishing: The Basic Introduction*, 3rd ed. (New York, Continuum, 1993), successfully and amply explores this realm.

encyclopedias, and subscription sales—of the Time-Life variety—which taken together comprise a hefty portion of total U.S. book sales. I have little experience with them, and they are far afield of the average writer's concerns.

This book focuses primarily on general trade books (both cloth and paperback), but includes many references to and tips for writers of textbooks, mass market paperbacks, professional books, juvenile books, and other specialized areas of publishing. I have not distinguished religious books as a separate category, even though most of them are published by religious book publishers and distributed and sold primarily by the 8,000 or so religious bookstores in the United States and Canada. Every other distinction is more or less immaterial, and they can be considered trade books as far as the writer is concerned—except that, obviously, a writer is generally advised to approach religious publishers if the book fits into that genre. The ground rules for these other areas are much the same: You have to write the book, you have to find and interest a publisher, and the publisher has to produce and sell the book—that's the A, B, and C of it.

Both trade and textbooks are covered in *A Writer's Guide*. There is an increasingly murky distinction between the two markets, though what defines a textbook from a publisher's point of view is that texts are sold to stores at roughly 20 percent discounts, while trade books are sold at discounts of 40 to 50 percent. Trade books sell well in college bookstores—according to a survey by the Association of American Publishers, more than 33 percent of the books sold in college stores were general trade books. Probably most of those books are directly related to college course use; in other words, trade books are often adopted for use in courses. Many mass market titles are also used in courses—something paperback publishers realized long before *The Autobiography of Malcolm X* sold more than a million copies over a two-year period in college adoptions. So many trade publishers devote considerable time, money, and personnel to expanding and catering to the high school and college market: For certain titles, such as fiction by Steinbeck, Faulkner, and Hemingway, course adoptions can form the largest part of the market.

As a consequence, trade publishers and authors keep their eyes on the educational market, and many teachers and professors are writing less technical and more trade-oriented books. The more scholarly the book, the more difficult it is to find a publisher (and this is especially true now for university presses, who are increasingly pinched for funds). This is not to say that textbooks or scholarly books are on their way out, only that more caution is exercised in signing and publishing them, and you as a potential textbook author will feel this competitive crunch.

But finding a publisher who agrees to publish your book is not the end of your worries. When you consider that less than one out of every four books published earns a pretax profit for a publisher, and consequently not much in royalties for the author, you can understand why three out of four published authors are openly vocal about their gripes, and overtly hostile toward their publishers. The publisher is the easiest target for the writer whose book doesn't sell. Surprisingly, though, you don't find the publisher maligning the author for the lack of sales, even though three out of four books don't pay their way.

The reason for these low sales is simple in the abstract: Either the book wasn't of sufficient interest to a large enough group of book buyers, or the publisher didn't "handle" the book properly. Practically speaking, and in most cases, it's a much more complex set of problems and there is no definitive answer to them. Publishing will remain a giant lottery, and perhaps that's the way it should be, so don't expect advice on how to turn your book into a best-seller.

What this book offers instead is a realistic description of the publishing process, from the initial idea you have for a book to the receipt of your first royalty check. By describing all the phases in between, I hope you will not only develop a certain amount of respect for and understanding of the publisher's world, but also improve your chances of finding a publisher, getting a "good deal," and becoming the one-out-of-four authors whose books earn a profit—for the publisher *and* you.

Most of the people in publishing, especially those engaged in editorial work, are underpaid, especially if one compares their education, skills, and experience to those of people in other industries. Most of them go into publishing because of an authentic interest in books and ideas, certainly not to get rich. They are not the enemy; quite the contrary, they are turned on by nothing so much as the first few pages of a fresh manuscript that they immediately feel must be published. Many a battle may have taken place about your book in an editorial meeting where it was "shot down" for reasons that have nothing to do with the quality or even sales potential of your book; or it could have been turned down as a result of a five-to-four decision.

So, don't be easily discouraged by a rejection slip; you never know what the next editor's reaction will be. Two years ago I rejected a manuscript from J.M.—it wasn't "commercial" enough for an agent—but I encouraged her to make the rounds of smaller publishers because I felt her book was well written, worthy, and addressed an important issue: how communities can effectively resist unwanted governmental or commercial intrusions, such as an unnecessary dam, a fast food restaurant, or a nuclear disposal site. In her own words, here's what happened:

My quest for a publisher spanned the time period from June, 1992, to July, 1993. I sent out 5 separate batches of letters to a total of 114 publishers; 89 editors responded. The longest reply time was 13 months, but with each batch of queries, I received most responses within 4 to 6 weeks. Two of the publishers I contacted called me up to ask if I would be interested in writing *other* books for them. Twelve requested sample chapters or the whole manuscript. About half said "no" in very encouraging ways. I had long conversations with three of them; two really liked the book but couldn't get it to fit with the marketing slant they used for their other books. The third was S———; the time from query letter to verbal contract offer was about three months. My "pub. date" is June, 1994. The people at S——— have so far been prompt, businesslike, and considerate, even delicate in their dealings with me . . . but I will feel much better when I can hold a copy of the book in my hands.

1

How to Approach
a Publisher

> It circulated for five years, through the halls of fif-
> teen publishers, and finally ended up with Van-
> guard Press, which, as you can see, is rather deep
> into the alphabet.
>
> —PATRICK DENNIS commenting on *Auntie Mame**

Publishers are always on the lookout for a good book. This is
something to keep in mind no matter how discouraging the pros-
pect of finding a publisher is, no matter how many rejection
slips you get, and no matter how overwhelming the odds seem.
And the odds *are* discouraging since unsolicited manuscripts,
known as over-the-transom submissions, are put into the "slush-
pile"; an optimistic guess is that only 1 out of every 3,000 books
in the slush pile is eventually published.

There are some legendary cases of best-sellers that were
turned down by a dozen or more publishers, and probably an
equal number of tales of best-sellers plucked from the slush pile.
Zen and the Art of Motorcycle Maintenance, it is said, collected
some 120 rejection slips before it was published and went on to

---

*This and several successive epigraphs are gratefully borrowed from *The Writer's
Quotation Book*, edited by James Charlton ($14.95, Pushcart Press, 1991).

become a best-seller. *Ordinary People* was found in the slush pile at Viking by an editorial assistant. And almost any editor you talk to will admit (or brag, depending on the personality) that he or she once turned down a book that went on to appear on a best-seller list for some other publisher.

The reasons for turning down books are often more subtle than negative answers to "Do I like it?" and "Will it sell?" even though they are the basic considerations. For instance, "it doesn't suit our list" is a very common reason for rejecting a proposal. A house that has not published cookbooks is unlikely to start with yours, though you may never find this out, since most form letters of rejection are vague about the reasons behind the rejection. And where that reason is expressed, it may just be a polite way of saying maybe you should consider cutting out paper dolls for a hobby instead of writing. Most editors have no desire to dent a stranger's ego just for the hell of it; where they are unsure of or unimpressed with the writing style in a manuscript, they will rarely present that as an explicit reason for rejection.

Rejection letters are usually vague for three additional reasons: Since the number of proposals coming in each week is staggering, most editors or readers do not have the time to respond personally to each manuscript's problems—it's simpler just to say thanks, but no thanks. Another reason is that most negative decisions about a "maybe" book have been made after considerable reflection, and the editor feels it's time to go on to the next proposal. She doesn't wish to stir up correspondence with the author, who will probably try to counter or rebut any detailed analysis of the flaws of the manuscript, the small market, and such. There just isn't time for this kind of Ping-Pong, and anyway a good editor can usually spot a diamond-in-the-rough. The third reason is illustrated by a tale I heard from a seasoned editor-in-chief who resolved at the beginning of his career to be absolutely candid with authors whose manuscripts he rejected. He held to this policy until the day he read of the suicide of an author who had just received from him a brutally frank opinion of his work.*

---

*If you're skeptical about this tale, so am I.

The point is, whether an editor takes a week or six weeks to turn your book down, you may never know exactly why, so it is senseless to jump to the conclusion that your book is awful, or that the editor is a fool for not recognizing a masterpiece. The reasons may be complex and varied, or it may just be as haphazard as the fact that the editor put too much sugar in his coffee that morning and it's affecting his judgment. Since many books make the round of many publishers before they get signed up, and since factors beyond your ken may be responsible for any single publisher rejecting it, the moral is keep trying. Remember that editors do want to buy manuscripts, and that in general they much prefer to find a way to publish a book than a way to reject it.

If the editor feels the proposal or manuscript is sound and is interested in the book for his list, but thinks certain substantive changes in the form or content need to be made, he will say so. Then you have as options to revise and resubmit, to ask for a commitment before you make changes, or to go elsewhere. But it bears repeating to say that the market, the number of copies a publisher expects to sell in the first year or more is usually more important than the answers to such questions as: do we like the book; is it a solid, important, interesting, necessary, well-written book?

In 1992, in the United States alone almost 49,000 books were published—an astounding figure.* If you have something worth saying, can write well, and have chosen a topic of interest to a book-buying audience of more than, say, 7,500 people (or 5,000 for a first novel; even less for university presses, scientific, technical, and reference publishers), your chances in this lottery aren't as dismal as the huge slush piles would lead you to think. What is required is just persistence, and maybe a bit of luck. The suggestions I have to offer in this chapter should narrow the lottery for you, since many writers are either haphazard in their preparation of a proposal or in their choice of publishers.

---

*This figure also includes more than 13,000 paperbacks, both reprint and original.

Use Your Contacts

My first suggestion is to exploit any possible contacts you have, however distant, in the publishing industry. Friends, relatives, acquaintances, teachers, colleagues, someone who knows someone, are all possible links, no matter how tenuous, to that editor or agent who may become interested in your work. Though your work has to stand on its own, overcoming the anonymity of the unsolicited, over-the-transom manuscript will often result in your proposal or manuscript getting a serious review. In any publishing house, with proposals constantly flowing in and out, a flag—something that will induce the editor to look more closely at your proposal—may be just the added nudge that will result in a contract. So do not hesitate to ask someone to call or write and establish a contact for you, or do it yourself by referring to the relationship: "my cousin, who published a book with your company ten years ago," and so forth.

Selecting the Right Publisher

One of the major reasons most beginning authors get enough rejection slips to paper their walls with is their choice of publishers. They start with Random House, Simon & Schuster, or HarperCollins, and work their way through the biggies, the two dozen or so largest, best known, and most glamorous publishers. Since agents and successful writers are beating at the same doors, the competition is fierce. The largest publishers receive thousands of unsolicited manuscripts every year, out of which maybe two or three are chosen for publication. Unless your book is absolutely ideal for their list—fills an obvious vacuum, fits into a series, or perfectly complements one of their titles— skip them. There are approximately 2,000 trade book publishers; you are thus left with 1,975 or so likely publishers. *Literary Market Place* has almost all of them listed. (And this number does not include most of the independent smaller publishers— more than 5,000 of them—who are listed in the twenty-first edition of *The Small Press Record of Books.*) If this is your first book, you will improve your odds by avoiding the giants.

Though some of the larger houses publish in almost every field, most do not. It is important to understand that there are specific divisions in many houses, for instance, trade, college text, el-hi, juvenile, business, religious, technical and reference, scientific, law, and medical. As a very broad guideline, if it appeals to the general reader, it's a trade book; if it has a special audience, it may belong in another division. Each division usually has a separate editorial staff, and you should direct your proposals to the appropriate division. An additional limitation is that most publishers, even the large trade houses, have one or more areas in which they concentrate, for instance, history, biography, Americana, natural science, and how-to, even though many are nevertheless eclectic enough so that they will take on any trade title they want. You might also consider the 100 or so "religious" book publishers that account for 5 percent of the book industry's $6 billion annual sales. Though they are primarily interested in books with religious themes, whether they be fiction or nonfiction, many of their books—such as Oliver North's *Under Fire*—fall into the general reader category, and they are not as overwhelmed with submissions as are many trade houses. Finally, there are many smaller houses that publish almost exclusively in one field, for example, psychology, military history, or gardening. Again, *LMP* or *Writer's Market* can supply you with all these distinctions.

Since you should already know which publishers are doing books in the area you wish to write about, they may be the logical choices to approach first. Editors and publishers have both commercial and personal interests, as evidenced by their choice of subject areas, series, and titles. By looking at your own shelves, writing the publisher for their current catalog,* and

---

*Almost all publishers print a fall and spring catalog; get the address from *Literary Market Place* and request a catalog from the Publicity Director, or see *The Publisher's Trade List Annual* at your library. It contains the seasonal catalogs of many university presses and trade houses, as well as those of some independent and regional presses.

browsing in several local bookstores and the library, you will be able to identify the publishers that are more likely to be receptive to your proposal.

If you are proposing a book that directly competes with a book on a publisher's list, you may think that the publisher will not wish to compete with it. This is true in some cases—a biography, a specific hobby craft, or a translation, for example—but not true in others. Publishers seem to vary in their attitudes toward the ethics and commercial wisdom of publishing a new book that directly competes with a previously published one of their own. If the market is large enough, say American history, business management, or introductory textbooks, most publishers will consider a directly competitive book. If the market is smaller, for instance, for a guide to the restaurants of San Francisco, the publisher probably will not consider a competing book. For translations, reprints, certain types of anthologies, and upper-level textbooks, you are obviously better off approaching a publisher that does not have a directly competing book on its list. Most new trade books, however, although they may compete for the same book buyer's attention, are more likely to complement rather than exclude or replace existing books on the publisher's list, and are thus fair game for consideration.

Why Prepare a Proposal?

No matter what field or subject you are writing about, and no matter what category of publishing your book fits into—trade, text, reference, scientific, technical, religious, juvenile, law, medical, or business, you are going to need a proposal or prospectus. This is an outline, preferably accompanied by a sample chapter or two, plus a description not only of the projected or completed manuscript, but of other factors of interest to the publisher, such as the audience and the competition. The proposal is a more manageable document for an editor than a complete manuscript, not only because it is shorter, but because other people at a publishing house are normally consulted in the final decision-making process: an editor-in-chief, a sales manager, or any number of others depending on the particular house and its *modus operandi* and hierarchy. While an editor usually has the time and interest to scrutinize all the material you send her—besides, it's her role as an editor—the others involved may only skim it. However carefully they read your submission, obviously a concise presentation simplifies their task, and since the amount of written material circulating at any publishing house is huge, a proposal is more functional than a complete manuscript; it is virtually a necessity. Fiction is the only exception, for neither an editor nor anyone else in the house will normally sign up a first novel unless at least one person has read the entire manuscript. And here, a synopsis accompanying the manuscript can perform the function of an outline.

The Query Letter

One of the conventions in approaching an editor or an agent is called the query letter, which is basically the same as the covering letter we are about to describe. A query is merely a one-to-two-page letter that permits the editor to decide quickly whether or not she is interested in pursuing the idea any further. If she is, she can then ask to see a proposal or manuscript. My recommendation is to submit a complete proposal with sample chapters, if it is a book rather than an article you are working on. If you follow the guidelines of this chapter, you will be choosing your target very carefully, so why waste time in adding another step to your first contact with an editor? If your covering letter excites her, she's got the material right there to decide whether you have been successful in turning conception into execution.

The Proposal

Basic Requirements. Whatever the nature of your proposal, it should generally include a covering letter, a résumé of your previous publications and qualifications (if it is pertinent), a contents page if it is suitable (obviously you won't need a contents page if you are submitting a novel or proposing a new translation of Plato's *Republic*), an outline, and several sample chapters, particularly if this is your first book. Always type the complete proposal: Double-space the material not included in your covering letter, use decent margins, and check the spelling carefully. The proposal should be as neat as a letter sent to request employment or to a foundation requesting a $10,000 grant. Be sure your name is on all material in addition to your covering letter; it can easily go astray if you are using paper clips. While these suggestions may seem self-evident, an amazing number of proposals violate one or more of these basic procedures. Many editors will read no further than the covering letter if that is handwritten, littered with spelling errors and faulty punctuation, or marred by a flabby style.

Following these principles may not make the difference between an acceptance or a rejection, any more than they might make the difference in your getting a job or grant; but *not* following them certainly won't help, and since you are, in effect, urging a publisher to invest anywhere from $15,000 to $60,000 in publishing your proposed book, you can at least assure her of the seriousness of your intentions by *not* sending in a sloppy proposal.

If you are submitting a novel, your covering letter need only include your previous publications, if any, and any pertinent biographical or vocational information, such as the fact that your novel about life on a submarine was inspired by a ten-year stint in the navy, or that the setting of your novel, Lapland, achieves its verisimilitude from your many years as a reindeer shepherd. Otherwise, just say hello and goodbye, but always submit a finished novel, unless you have already published one or more successful novels (meaning you earned back more than your advance). Partially completed first novels generally don't stand a chance, unless perhaps you are halfway through a 600-page commercial saga or romance, in which case the first 300 pages will do, or if you have an extremely novel novel idea with a hefty sample (A genetic mutation in a pig belonging to a dirt-poor farmer in the western part of Georgia appears to make the animal immune to the effects of aging. But there's one small problem with the pig . . .). And, as mentioned, also include a two-to-four-page synopsis of the novel—when we discuss what happens to your proposal (or novel) at the publisher's, you will see the advantage of the synopsis.

I used to warn authors never to send photocopied cover letters with their proposals (although the proposals themselves can of course be photocopied). In these days of computer-generated mail-merged letters and ink-jet and laser printers, there is probably little temptation to send such photocopies, so a warning against them may be superfluous. In fact, it is often almost impossible to tell the difference between a good photocopy and a laser-printed original. It is enough to say that the more individualized a cover letter looks, both in content and form, the better. You know how you feel when you get a form letter in the mail— your eyes wander toward the location of the nearest wastebasket—and you can assume that an editor's reaction will be similar.

The Covering Letter. The information an editor finds useful in a covering letter includes: a brief description of the book, the reason you think the book ought to be published, why you have chosen that particular publisher (this is not expected, but for obvious reasons is useful), your own special qualifications to write or edit the book, the audience and competition (or lack of it) for the book, and the approximate length and special requirements for it.

The Description. A brief description of the book is simple enough. Consider it a kind of synopsis in which you describe the relevant features in one paragraph. For further information the editor can turn to your more extensive outline, contents page, or preface or introduction. Whether it is a guide to flowers of the Northeast, a "how-to," a psychological self-help book, a sociology textbook, or a study of American Indian sign language, you are approaching your topic from a specific point of view and can explain this in a paragraph. Avoid jargon in your description.

Why Publish It? The fact that you are writing or editing a book implies that there are reasons that the general reader, the professional, the antiques collector, or the novice macramé enthusiast may want to buy it or read it—or, specifically for a textbook publisher, that other teachers or professors will want to use it in their classes. If you are breaking new ground, that is, treating an area previously not explored—say, multimedia software—explain it. If you are applying a certain model (e.g., Freudian, Hegelian, or deconstructionist) or taking a particular point of view for a topic already treated in other ways, justify it and explain its unique relevance. A new translation? Why is it necessary and superior to those already in print? If you wish to edit a book that is out-of-print, why do you think that now is the time for reissuing it? If you are putting together an anthology, what is unusual about your coverage or approach? If a proposed monograph fills a vacuum in the literature of a scientific or scholarly specialty, explain its topicality. There are scarcely any subjects you can think of that have not been treated in book form in one fashion or another. If your previous publications and reputation in that area are not sufficient in themselves to prompt a publisher to offer you a contract, then you will have not only to submit a well-written sample, but make a good case for it as well.

Your Unique Qualifications. It follows, then, by reason of either your own personal experiences, vocation or avocation, previous publications, research, the courses you teach, prior education, or current interests that you have some special competence to write the book. Whether you include a résumé or list of publications or not, you can and should describe in a paragraph what unique expertise and resources you bring to the book.

Why That Publisher? If your book fits in with their current list, or into one of their series, or seems to fill a gap on their list, point this out and explain why you think this is the ideal publisher for your book. If you have bought or read or are impressed with the books that they have published and this has influenced your decision to write to this publisher, let them know it. Editors are not immune to praise or recognition of the success of their decisions. Choosing the right publisher can save you a lot of time and effort and will definitely increase your chances for publication; many publishers turn down books because they aren't right for their list. It will also decrease your chances of receiving a form letter of rejection.

The Audience. In most instances, the audience for your book is obvious: either just a general audience (as for a biography or a novel) or a readily identifiable specific audience (such as for a coin collector's manual), but in some cases it is broader than an editor might recognize at first glance, or otherwise difficult to ascertain. For instance, a general book on laptop computers might have an audience that ranges from high school students to engineers. You undoubtedly know which audience(s) will be interested in your book. It can do no harm to point this out to the editor, even though her knowledge of the market may be equal to your own. Some textbooks—this is true in the social sciences particularly—may fit into several disciplines. If this is the case, the sociology editor, for example, may wish to consult the psychology editor to see if the book fits into both areas.

Many publishers have several divisions: trade, textbook, reference and technical, religious, and juvenile, as well as their own book club(s). If you think your book would have a secondary market for one of the other departments, that is, would also interest the clergy, doctors, scientists, or business executives, then mention this. Obviously a technical or narrowly focused or jargon-laden monograph will not have "trade appeal," nor will a standard textbook, nor will most juvenile or young adult books. But you may have reasons to think that your book will interest both the general public and a more specific but not obviously identifiable special segment of it, and you should point this out. The various divisions of a publishing company sometimes collaborate on a book (depending on the company), and they may decide to produce a trade cloth edition and a college text paperback, for example. A number of other options are possible, and an editor will try to exercise them if the book warrants it.

Many authors make blanket generalizations about the huge

audience for their books. They project a grandiose and unrealistic estimate of the potential market and sales for their book. It is wise to restrain any impulse to make this sort of estimate. Textbook authors, for instance, often mention "guaranteed adoptions" or anywhere from 100 to 5,000 copies at their own school, but this has limited value because of academic mobility. Still, there's no harm in putting a *conservative* estimate in your letter. The editor not only has at her disposal the accumulated knowledge and intuition of her years in the business, but she will be aided by other editors, sales marketing specialists, and reps in estimating potential sales. Your exaggerations will be suspect; your realistic projections can be useful and may provide additional ammunition for getting your book approved at the weekly editorial meeting. (More about this later.) And beware of overkill; publishers do not welcome "instructions" on the size of first printings and other similar matters which are their domain.

The Competition. If your book competes directly with one or more already published, you should be able to list the distinctive merits of your own book, as opposed to the leading competitor(s). Your book may have a unique perspective, a broader or more detailed coverage, a particular thematic structure, unusual organization, or just be more up-to-date. Whatever the distinction, you should favorably compare your own book, especially if you think that a book buyer is going to have to make a choice between your book and another. Mentioning the leading competing books and pointing out the important differences and improvements of your own will not only show the editor that you have considered this carefully in your decision to send a proposal, and that you know your field well, but will inform her of additional merits in your book which neither she nor her colleagues might otherwise be aware of. Perhaps current developments, discoveries, or research in the field render certain competing books obsolete; translations may be old-fashioned; "how-to's" can quickly become dated; some textbooks will no longer be suitable because of changing curriculum patterns. Whatever the reasons, you can place your book in the context of competition, especially if it provides new information and consequently has no real competition but is, rather, *related* to books in the same category. Of course, the book may just be a new entrant in the field. Some fields are so competitive or the market potential so great that competition is much less relevant. Nevertheless, it is likely that there are some significant differences between your book and others that you are aware of that can and should be described. It isn't necessary to put down the competition—just explain how your own book is different, or better, or both.

Size and Special Features. Whether you have finished writing the book or are merely outlining it—in which case you should state the completion or delivery date—some estimate of its size and special features should appear in your proposal. It is best to give the editor an approximate word count (including introduction, preface, appendixes, and even footnotes, if they are going to be plentiful), which she can translate into printed pages. If there are to be illustrations, charts, graphs, maps, or other sorts of "artwork," indicate the kind and number. The cost as well as the price of the book, obviously, will vary in direct ratio to the length and special requirements. Length should be considered carefully, particularly if your book may be a long one (e.g., more than 75,000 words). Mounting plant, paper, and manufacturing costs now make it quite expensive to produce a book. Such costs will often have an influence on the publisher's decision to accept or reject the proposal. The longer your book, and the more artwork it requires, the more cautious the publisher's decision. This information will be needed sooner or later, and you can save yourself some unnecessary correspondence by providing it sooner. If you don't know approximately how long your book will be, you may not be ready to propose it to a publisher.

An average single-column page of text contains approximately 320 to 360 printed words, versus the 220 to 250 on a double-spaced typed manuscript page: A manuscript of 75,000 words will produce a book of roughly 224 pages (most books are published in multiple units of 16 or 32 pages, called signatures). Any manuscript between 50,000 to 75,000 words is considered normal to a publisher; between 75,000 and 125,000 words the publisher begins thinking about the higher cost estimate. (See Chapter 2 for a discussion of cost estimates, print runs, and pricing.) Above this amount is the beginning of mild indigestion, and any manuscript over 160,000 words can be a cause for an ulcer. Of course, this can be mitigated by several factors: the type of book, the extent of its coverage, the audience, the market, and the author's willingness to cut the manuscript. Most manuscripts have fat on them.

Selections for an anthology may require the payment of permissions fees to the various copyright holders, as may a translation, a book with artwork, or a reprint of an out-of-print book, provided the material for these is not in the public domain.* If your book requires the use of previously published material, it will be necessary to write to the *original* publisher or present copyright holder, describe precisely what you wish to use, and determine whether or not there is a fee for permissions. Many anthologies have extremely high permissions costs. An anthology of contemporary poetry or drama could cost upward to $20,000 in permissions alone. Every editor will consider these costs before making a decision, and they will definitely influence the final verdict on whether or not to sign up the book. From experience, an editor, or someone else in the house, can make a fairly accurate estimate of total permissions costs. There is no point in writing for permission until you have a contract, as you will see in Chapter 4 where both permissions and copyright are discussed in detail.

Résumé, Contents Page, Preface, Introduction, Outline, Sample Chapters. Most editors would like to know some facts about your personal or academic background (insofar as it pertains to your book) and your previous publications. A brief résumé, if you have one, is the simplest way to provide this in-

---

*Copyright law is quite complicated, but to be both practical and cautious, you should assume that anything published and less than 75 years old is in copyright unless you can prove it isn't. You can get a copyright search done—the cost depends on the complexity—by calling the Library of Congress at 202-707-6850.

formation, even though you may have mentioned some of it in the covering letter. It is particularly appropriate for textbooks and scientific, technical, or reference books. If you have published a book before, it will lend some weight to an editor's decision—articles too, but not quite as much.

In most cases, whether you are preparing a nonfiction trade book, textbook, a scholarly monograph, or an anthology, you should as a matter of course include a contents page. The other ingredients—preface, introduction, outline, and sample chapter(s)—will depend on the book itself and your own judgment.

Most nonfiction book proposals ideally should include an introduction, a preface, or an extensive outline and at least two sample chapters. If both your previous publications and rank in your field are sufficient to have garnered you a "reputation" of sorts, you may be able to get a contract without sample chapters; enclose relevant samples of earlier published work. An outline of a book could either mean a one-paragraph synopsis of each planned chapter, or a two-to-six-page description. For a translation, you can include a sample of 10 to 20 pages. For an anthology, I would recommend including either a finished introduction, or a precise outline of the introduction, with some indication of how you plan to introduce the sections and the individual selections. Several representative sample selections should be included as well. For a reprint, an introduction (or outline of it) should suffice—or a preface, if an introduction already exists. If you are putting together an original collection (i.e., an anthology of hitherto unpublished essays by several authors), you definitely ought to include a synopsis in which each selection is described in a paragraph or two. If you are planning this kind of collection, you must have informal commitments from the contributors *in advance*; many of these proposals are planned and submitted without consulting the proposed contributors (sometimes listing second and third choices for individual selections). This kind of optimism is unwarranted; publishers know it and may not seriously consider such a proposal.

Each book is unique. It is impossible to generalize about which combination of these materials you should include. The main distinction between the covering letter and the proposal is that the latter fleshes out the former; don't be reluctant to repeat yourself, provided you are giving more detailed information. Whatever you decide to include, unless it is a novel, do not send a complete manuscript if your submission is unsolicited. Editors or readers who are examining 25 or more proposals a week will generally not read entire manuscripts. A sample is sufficient either for a contract or for a decision to request more of the manuscript.

When to Send a Proposal. Should you send a proposal before, during, or after you have completed a book? Many of the proposals publishers receive that do not come from agents are for books that are already completed. But that does not mean you have to wait that long. If you have not published a book before, and have published only a few articles or none, an editor or publisher will wish to see at least a partial manuscript before the house makes a decision.

I would discourage an author from completing a nonfiction manuscript without a contract. Since almost all publishers (some university presses are an exception) will contract a book based on a sample or half a manuscript, it seems to me an exercise in unwarranted optimism to spend six months to five years completing a book that may not find a home. If you have previously published a book, you may be able to get a commitment from a publisher without sample chapters, but even this is not always true, especially if you are approaching the publisher, rather than vice versa.* If your first book was a financial success, by all means let the editor know; if it got good reviews, include up to a half-dozen of them.

For most books, a sample of 20 to 25 percent should be sufficient, though exactly how much of a completed manuscript you may need for a contract depends on several factors: past publications, how much the proposal interests the editor, the

---

*Be sure to check the fine print on your first contract; the publisher may have an option on your next book.

kind of book you propose, the reputation or expertise you have in your area, and the whims of the individual editor or publisher. In any case, an editor who is interested in your proposal will let you know how much more of the manuscript he or she wants to see in order to make a decision; some will insist on a complete manuscript. You can decide whether to do more writing or whether you want a publisher's commitment before you go further.

Who Gets Your Proposal. At most houses, editorial assistants read unsolicited manuscripts and over-the-transom proposals, so no matter whom you address the letter to, it will probably be read by someone. Very few over-the-transom proposals are addressed to a specific editor, but if yours is, there is a decent chance that he or she will try to respond to it personally, if only to recommend the appropriate publisher if the house is not interested or to comment on the proposal's strength or lack of it. At many of the major houses, queries not personally addressed to an editor are generally returned with a form letter stating that only submissions by agents are being considered.

It is not difficult to get the name of an editor to address a proposal to. Though form letters may be the most common response, it is still always better to address a proposal to an editor. Find a book similar to yours, and—if the name of the editor is not mentioned on the acknowledgments page—call the publisher to ask who the editor was. Usually the managing editor (who, in a book publishing house, is not the boss, but the person responsible for scheduling and trafficking) will be the one who can most readily supply this information. Then address your proposal to that editor. It may even be useful to refer to the book in your cover letter: "Since you are the editor of such-and-such, I thought you might also be interested in my book. . . ."

Do *not* try to pitch your proposal on the phone with an editor; they resent it unless you have a specific entrée, that is, someone who knows the editor has paved the way for you with a phone call or letter. Even then, writing is better than calling; until an editor knows whether you can write a decent paragraph, you are just a distraction. Most of the writers who call me are less articulate and persuasive on the phone than in writing, and so I am much more inclined to say "no thanks" than "send it along."

The bible for the publishing industry, *Literary Market Place (LMP)*, a Bowker publication, is updated every year and contains a listing of key personnel at almost all publishing houses, as well as listings of agents, advertising agencies, jobbers, distributors, and a host of other services and personnel. Small presses have their own catalog, the *International Directory of Little Magazines and Small Presses.**

Writer's Market 1994 also has an up-to-date listing of publishers, though it is not as extensive or accurate as that in *LMP*. On the other hand, *Writer's Market* provides information, such as the kind of books a house is interested in, that is sketchy in *LMP*. You can find at least two out of these three reference tools at your local library. Unfortunately, they sometimes do not identify the editors by name, often listing only the editor-in-chief, executive editor, and other executives.

Instead of writing to "Fiction Editor" or "Nonfiction Editor" or "Sociology Editor," you are better off addressing your letter to the vice president, editor-in-chief, or executive editor of the appropriate division—trade, text, or professional. This person will reroute it to the right individual, who will usually give it the attention it deserves. In using *LMP* or *Writer's Market*, you will secure up-to-date information and frequently save yourself some time and energy, though because of musical chairs in publishing and rapid changes of ownership, these guides are already somewhat out-of-date upon publication.

Multiple Submissions. Many authors will send proposals to more than one publisher at a time. One can scarcely blame them, considering the treatment most over-the-transom proposals get: no response, a very tardy response, or a standard rejection letter. If you prepare your proposal carefully and send it to the right publisher, you will generally get a polite response

---

*This handy annual is available in paperback for $26.95 from: Dustbooks, P. O. Box 100, Paradise, CA 95967. It is particularly useful for poets and short-story writers, for whom commercial markets are scanty, to say the least.

within a month. Nevertheless, I believe it ethical to submit a proposal to more than one publisher at a time (not with novels, though) provided you make it clear in your proposal that you have done so, both to keep your conscience clear and to be fair with the editor. Many authors submit to more than one publisher. A proposal is a probe, and since it could take you a year or more to get an offer if you were to submit it to one publisher at a time, you ought to have the opportunity to find out in less time than that if anyone is interested in your book.

One disadvantage to a multiple submission is that many editors feel only successful authors or agents are justified in following this procedure and even then only for a "hot" book. So your proposal may be turned down without consideration.

If an editor or publisher is interested, she may respond by saying that she wants to examine your proposal or manuscript carefully, but wants some assurance that you will not make any other commitment until she has a chance to "check it out" and make an offer. This is only fair, considering that the editor may engage the services of readers, consultants, or outside specialists, not to mention investing her own time and effort.

Current Fashions in Proposals. Certain subjects of topical interest become popular for a year or two. Then they either become permanent features, such as ecology, maintaining a long life, or they abruptly fade into obscurity. The publisher, during the period of intense interest, receives scores of proposals from authors who attempt to jump on this bandwagon, though many of these are hastily conceived proposals (often for anthologies and reprints) that arrive too late to be of real interest. In the past few years health and nutrition, feminism, pollution and ecology, and psychological self-help have been subject areas heading the fad list. While such topics may deserve the consumer and publishing attention they get, the average publisher can be overcontracted in those fields by the time the topic is nationally popular, or feel that the wave has crested.

There is always room for the serious, carefully researched, and well-written book that has permanent value, but many of the proposals that come in to publishers are one to three years out-of-date. For example, over the past few years I have received a number of proposals for books about on-line computer services, the breakup of the Soviet Union, rap music, home mortgage refinancing, incest and other forms of childhood sexual abuse, and recovery from alcoholism. They usually arrive just around the time that *Publishers Weekly* announces the imminent publication of half a dozen books on each of these topics. Even though the marketplace can support several editions of certain classics (there are at least a dozen paperback editions of *Moby Dick*), or even 50 books on vegetarian cooking, it is unlikely to be able to do so for most books. If you are planning a book in an area that is currently "hot," it has to be very original.

Tips for Academics

In the field of academic publishing, whether elementary, high school, or college textbooks, the writer has certain advantages and disadvantages.*

One advantage is that agents and "first readers" scarcely operate here, so that even though your proposal may be coming in over-the-transom, it will get more serious attention than will an over-the-transom submission at a trade publisher; the slush pile here is a more likely source of textbooks, and the editors usually specialize in a discipline and are more familiar with your field and hence the market for your book. You also have several other potential contacts not available to trade book authors: consulting editors (professors who read, evaluate, and recommend manuscripts), college travelers (textbook sales reps), academic conventions, and colleagues. Each or all of these can be a source for an editor's name, what kinds of books publishers are currently pursuing, what areas they are lukewarm about, a possible formal or informal (by letter or phone call) introduction, and information on whether a publisher is expanding the

---

*For an informative, free 12-page booklet, *Author's Guide to College Textbook Publishing,* write to: The Association of American Publishers, 220 E. 23rd St., New York, NY 10010.

list or cutting back. Pursue any or all of these potential contacts rather than sending in an unsolicited proposal.

Incidentally, a scholarly convention is no place to peddle a book; don't walk around to every booth trying to hand an editor a proposal or manuscript. Either write the editor before the convention and try to set up an appointment, or merely make an editor's acquaintance and ask whether you may send in your proposal.

A current disadvantage for textbook authors is that many houses are cutting back their lists and concentrating strictly on comprehensive textbooks for basic courses. Trade paperbacks have become more and more popular as texts, and though this trend has put only a small dent in high school and college textbook sales, it has decreased the number of supplementary and corollary books that text publishers are signing up. You can take advantage of this by going directly to the publishers of quality paperback lines, many of whom are devoting some attention to the educational market, for instance, Penguin, Touchstone, Anchor, Delta, and Vintage (all are paperback lines for major houses, as are many quality paperback lines). Even here, though, there has been some tightening of belts lately, and your book should have considerable trade appeal. If the book is strictly for classrooms, these publishers won't consider it. Anthologists should note that almost all trade and textbook publishers are now up to their necks in anthologies and are extremely selective about taking on any new ones.

Most teachers and professors are bombarded by catalogs, mailing pieces, and "exam" copies; this should make it easier to keep track of which publishers might be interested in your book.

Professional and Reference Books

This genre actually consists of books in a wide variety of fields, though it sometimes falls under one or two umbrellas at large houses, such as McGraw-Hill and Paramount Publishing (the parent company of Prentice Hall and Macmillan, which publish, respectively, their professional and reference books), or may exist as a separate division or be the sole output of a smaller house. "Professional" usually refers to books for specialists or academics in the field of the humanities and the social sciences: Books in psychology, for instance, will be sold not only to professors, but also to clinicians, researchers, social workers, and others. Libraries are also a prime market for these books. "Professional" is also sometimes used to describe divisions or houses that publish books in architecture, law, business, medicine, real estate, and other disciplines. A sprinkling of these titles will also be suitable as graduate-level textbooks. "Sci-tech" refers to books primarily for professionals in the hard sciences, scientists, engineers, technicians, et alia.

The list price tags are high, and the first printings are usually low, but the rewards for the author can often be more generous than you might think. Handbooks, source books, or reference books in any of these fields may go into multiple editions over a period of 5, 10, or 20 years—for instance, a television repair manual for service technicians. If the book lists for $49.95 and the discount averages 25 percent and the author gets a 15 percent-of-net royalty (i.e., $5.62 a copy), then a modest sale of even 5,000 copies adds up to a royalty check of $28,097. Though the production and start-up costs for reference books are quite high, even small sales mean big profits for publishers, as did Houghton Mifflin's recent best-selling *American Heritage Dictionary*. Consequently this is an area that is now booming, and many editors are clamoring for more titles in virtually any field. Editors here are not at all intimidated by a project that may run to 200,000 or even 400,000 words; in fact, the bigger the book, the higher the list price, and the happier the publisher.

Just as with trade books or textbooks, you should provide a detailed outline and sample. Editors will look more carefully at your credentials; you may have to qualify as a certified expert in the field in order to get a contract. Moreover, a slim sample, with an estimated manuscript size of 250,000 words and a completion date of three to four years, generally stands less of a chance than a book that is half-written and will be completed in one to two years.

Elementary and High School Texts

Approximately 15 el-hi publishers, many of which are divisions of larger houses, account for the bulk of the publishing and sales in this field. Many of the ideas for books originate "in-house," with the editor approaching a teacher, soliciting an outline, and then carefully supervising the writing of the text at each stage. A further refinement of this process is the "managed" text (now becoming more common in college text publishing as well), in which the publisher hires a professional writer who either works with the teacher or transforms an extensive outline into a finished book. Incidentally, many of the editors in this field are former teachers.

Books are commonly coauthored by two, three, or even four teachers, primarily to capitalize on the unique geographical marketing situation that el-hi houses face. Twenty-one states now have blanket adoption policies: A committee chooses the text for a course or grade level for the entire district, county, or state. California or Texas, for example, may purchase as many as 100,000 to 300,000 copies of a high school text (and even more for elementary school readers). It is clear to see the potential advantage to the publisher of having at least one coauthor from one of these states if it is trying to secure the "adoption" (sale).

With the stakes so high, the start-up costs so great, and the minimum sales expectations so large—at least 40,000 copies a year, with a first printing of perhaps half that amount—the el-hi publishers are very cautious about their decisions and conservative in their editorial policies, and have recently come under some fire for the blandness of their texts.

To be successful, a high school text has to sell at least 100,000 copies over a five-year period, and for an elementary school text, upwards of 300,000. Net profit margins match the high stakes, however; they run to approximately 16 percent, which is more than double the margin for trade publishers.

Successful books are generally revised every two or three years, depending on when big-state adoption decisions are made, which is also about the time it takes for students to demolish a book. As with college text publishers, "travelers" sell the books, and their efforts are supplemented by the mailing of brochures, advertising in appropriate journals and magazines, and appearances at the yearly regional and national el-hi teacher conventions.

Whereas you may approach an el-hi publisher with a proposal and sample, the decision to offer a contract, or to actually publish the book, may be postponed until a final manuscript is delivered.

Children's Books

A major branch in many publishing houses, both large and small, is the juvenile or juvenile/young adult division, though there are houses which publish children's books exclusively. The audience, however, is fragmented. One informal and flexible breakdown, based on reading levels and supplied by The Children's Book Council,* suggest five general categories: babies and prenursery schoolers, nursery school and kindergarten (ages 3 to 5), early school years (6 to 8), older children (9 to 12), and teenagers or young adults. Presumably you will identify one or more of these age groups as your audience when conceiving, writing, and submitting a children's book.

Virtually all that has already been said about submissions applies equally to children's books. One distinction to keep in mind, particularly for heavily illustrated "picture books," is that the publisher normally chooses the illustrator and does so *after* a manuscript has been accepted (usually with the writer's advice and consent). If your forte is writing, control the urge to send in your own or your wife's or husband's sketches. You run a greater risk of rejection if the illustrations don't go over—they can always be brought up if you get a serious nibble or an offer.

---

*They will send you, if you enclose a $1 bill and a self-addressed, stamped #10 envelope, an informative small pamphlet: *Writing Children's Books*. Write to: The Children's Book Council, 568 Broadway, Room 404, New York, NY 10012.

If you haven't read any children's books since your own pre-pubescence, you are in for a surprise. There are scarcely any taboos left, and many books, both fiction and nonfiction, are candid and realistic about unmentionables as well as mention-ables. A would-be author might innocently surmise that a chil-dren's book can be polished off in a long weekend; it isn't quite so simple. If you have had a vague urge to turn your hand in that direction, it might help to read one of the four books listed in the Selected Bibliography which discuss the writing and publishing of children's books.

Children's books have been hard hit by inflation and reces-sion: Rising production costs have joined with a declining birth-rate and taxpayer revolts—such as Proposition 13 in California, which cut drastically into public and school library budgets, the major source for children's book sales—to force publishers to adopt some strict measures. According to James Giblin, the former publisher of Clarion Books, many houses during the early 1980s used less color and thinner paper, ordered smaller first print runs (which raised unit-costs), let low-selling books go out of print, and cut back on staff. But the market for chil-dren's books has improved over the past decade, and it is now one of the fastest growing segments. Between 1986 and 1991, net sales of children's books doubled from $546 million to more than $1.1 billion. Part of this growth can be attributed to the publication of more pop-up books, game books, and tie-ins with TV programs and movies. Increased sales may also come from tie-ins with home videotapes based on children's books. But dis-tribution has changed, too. Libraries now account for about 70 percent of sales, somewhat less than they did in the early 1980s, and publishers have increased· penetration into the consumer market via sales in supermarkets, toy stores, and variety stores. Moreover, a growing number of bookstores now sell only chil-dren's books. In 1985, there were 215 children's bookstores in the United States; today there are more than 500. All of these factors have combined to boost revenues for publishers and au-thors alike.

Poetry

In trade houses, the reception to unrecognized serious poets—excluding humorous, sentimental, or "popular" versifiers—is more than dismal. Most houses will not even read a manuscript unless it comes highly touted by some distinguished literary figure or similar luminary. In commercial publishing, roughly 60 books of poetry are published each year, and of this number only about two are by new poets. One reason that so little poetry is published by trade houses is that very few editors have a serious enough interest in poetry, or are adequate judges of it, to take on or feel comfortable with such a responsibility. Publishers, many of whom do maintain an old-fashioned commitment to literature (and may feel a bit guilty because of current accusations of crass commercialism), would perhaps be willing to break even or take a small loss and publish poetry, but they are unable to find a suitable or willing editor within the house. Unlike decisions about other projects in a trade house, that for signing a book of poems generally rests exclusively with one editor; other decision makers are usually not interested in evaluating poetry or just don't know enough about it.

When collections of poems are published, they tend to average 64 to 72 pages in length, are published simultaneously in cloth and paper, and have a first print run of 2,500 to 5,000 copies (the latter only for a poet with a reputation and track record). Most of the sales are to libraries, college bookstores, and from readings by the poets (this latter generally separates the red from the black).

In fact, trade houses that choose their poets carefully and wisely don't usually lose money on poetry. With small first printings and high list prices, they will often sell out their stock in two to three years. One continuing source of revenue (and sometimes profit) is from second serial rights; that is, when poems are selected to be reprinted in anthologies, primarily for high school and college textbooks. These "permissions" fees can add up to a tidy sum for poet and publisher alike. Occasionally British rights are sold, but foreign translations are rare.

It seems clear that it is an exercise in futility for poets to attempt to break in with trade houses (or try to get an agent, for that matter: Poets such as Lowell, Berryman, Bishop, and Moore didn't have one, and times haven't changed). Most poetry in the United States is published by independent and university presses, and those are the places to try.

Fiction

The case for literary fiction and first novels is not quite so grim, but considering the large number of novels coming in over-the-transom and the smaller number of novels published by trade houses each year, there is scant reason for a major in creative writing to conclude that he can support a family by writing novels. Fewer than 100 first novels are published yearly (not counting category fiction—mysteries, westerns, science fiction, romances, etc.). A number of these first-novel writers have already made a name for themselves in some other way, or published nonfiction, such as Scott Turow, William Safire, or Anna Quindlen. Of course there are some astounding first-novel successes—*The Joy Luck Club*, *The Secret History*, *Kitchen*, *Less Than Zero*, and others—but these are needles in haystacks. For better or worse, the best-seller lists, over the decades, generally contain repeated familiar names: Stephen King, Ken Follett, Danielle Steel, Dick Francis, John Grisham, and others.

Figures for the total clothbound fiction published are more reassuring, with an average of about 5,000 novels a year, but it follows that nine out of ten were by previously published novelists. And most don't fare as well as you might think, since the fanfare about best-selling novels and huge paperback rights sales tends to skew the realities of the economics of publishing novels. Most novelists, even those who publish a book every two years or so and have five or more under their belts, fail to sell out their first printings (which only average 5,000 to 6,000 copies) and don't have their books picked up by paperback reprinters.

The big ones pay for the small ones: 10 percent of any trade house's fiction list pays for the other 90 percent. Novels, unlike nonfiction, have to be priced competitively. Even a long novel cannot carry the list price it should, in order to make a modest first printing pay for the book. Therefore some publishers calculate that in order just to break even, a clothbound novel has to sell 15,000 to 20,000 copies, which rarely happens. Yes, but what about subsidiary rights? In fact, a first novel has about one chance in five of being taken by a paperback house, even for a modest price, and the figures are not much better for repeat fiction. (Actually, almost the entire first-print run of first novels is sold to library wholesalers; not only won't chain stores carry first novels, but most of the 9,000 standard book outlets won't either.)

There was a time when houses could generally count on a small percentage of their novels selling to mass market reprinters for six figures or more (which the author and publisher usually split 50/50). These few rights sales usually financed the balance of the novels on the list—as did a few books that sold very well in cloth or were selections for major book clubs—and turned in a profit as well. But those days are gone. Six-figure sales have declined substantially, and trade publishers have not only cut back somewhat on publishing novels, especially serious or literary ones, but they now realize the need for, and may concentrate on, better promoting the novels they do publish. Moreover, most major houses now have their own mass market imprint and buy "volume" rights: that is, hardcover, trade paper, and mass market rights.

The mass market houses have increased their own lists of paperback original fiction, not only category fiction and romances, but both commercial and literary fiction too. They have reduced the number of modest books, novels by unknown authors and six-figure blockbusters that they were buying, and prefer to concentrate on developing their own list of respectable and bestselling novels.

A little more bad news: Close to two-thirds of first hardcover novels don't sell more than 2,500 copies, are ordered or sit on bookshelves for an average of six to eight weeks after publication, have heavy returns of one-third, and when remaindered, bring in to the originating publisher an average of 10 to 25 cents a copy (whereas remainders by best-selling authors are "auctioned" off, and can recoup as much as $4 or more for the publisher).

If I have painted a thoroughly bleak picture, take heart, it is not really that hopeless: Interest in commercial or popular fiction is still high—suspense thrillers, "faction" novels, and historical romances head the list. Second, there are the paperback houses; there, fiction outsells nonfiction by three to one (these figures are reversed for cloth), and, as I pointed out, these publishers are increasing their lists of original literary fiction, both in mass market and trade paperback formats. Moreover, the university presses continue to increase their own output of serious fiction, and this is even more encouraging for those writing short stories. Several university presses now publish one or more collections a year (the universities of Pittsburgh, Illinois, and Missouri now head the list), and the small presses, which are explored in detail in Chapter 8, are always looking for a good literary novel.

It seems clear, though, that the author of a literary first novel will have a very difficult time finding a hardcover trade publisher in spite of the fact that most editors are very interested themselves in good literary fiction, and more often than not came into publishing for that very reason. But the economics are brutal, the conglomerates totally unsympathetic to the notion of nurturing authors for their first few novels—the first two or three books by many successful authors, such as John Updike, sold modestly—and so the outlook remains pessimistic. If you do submit a literary first novel, nine out of ten houses will expect a completed manuscript, not sample chapters. Your chances of having your manuscript read and carefully considered—by an editor *or* an agent—are more than doubled if you had a story or a chapter from the work "in progress" printed in a national publication, or if you can secure a letter of enthusiastic recommendation from a known writer, distinguished mentor, or creative writing teacher.

But whether or not your novel will actually be given more then a perfunctory glance is questionable. Consider the following anecdote reported by Douglas Peters, a professor of psychology in an article from the September 1980 issue of *The Sciences:*

In 1977, the publishing process of the literary world was tested in a unique way. Jerzy Kosinski, the Polish-born author of the 1969 award-winning novel *Steps,* allowed Chuck Ross, a Los Angeles free-lance writer, to resubmit a typed manuscript of *Steps* as though it were the work of an aspiring but unknown author. Ross changed the title and substituted a pseudonym for Kosinski's name. He sent the disguised manuscript to 14 major publishers requesting that they consider it for possible publication. What prompted this charade was concern about the difficulties that face unknown writers in getting their work published. It was strongly suggested that even if unknown authors were to write novels of the caliber of *Steps,* they would have difficulty finding a publisher because their names were not recognized in literary circles.

Remarkably, the editorial consultants for the publishing houses failed to detect the deception. None realized that the manuscript which was sent to them for review was actually a verbatim copy of Kosinski's novel, which had won the National Book Award in 1969. What was even more surprising was that every publisher returned the manuscript with letters of rejection. The biggest shock of all, though, was that one of the publishers who rejected the manuscript, Random House, was actually the original publisher of *Steps.*

Original Paperbacks

To help steer us through the maze of paperbacks, some general definitions are in order. A "mass market" or rack-sized paperback is approximately 4¼ inches by 7 inches and will fit into those racks found in drugstores and airport lounges. A "trade" or "quality" paperback is roughly in the 5½ inch by 8 inch format, give or take an inch either way. An "outsized" or "oversized" paperback ranges from 8½ inches by 11 inches upward. Most hardcover houses have trade paperback lines, as do most of the mass market publishers. Either of them can, and will on occasion, put out an oversized paperback. Most of the mass market houses are now owned by, or are subdivisions of, hardcover houses (which in turn are owned by a conglomerate), and some have developed their own hardcover division, as have Warner Books and Pocket Books. St. Martin's and HarperCollins have both started mass market paperback divisions during the past few years.

In two decades, mass market publishers such as Avon, Bantam, Dell, Warner, and Fawcett have increased their output of paperback originals (which comprises up to 60 percent of their lists). For various reasons, such as the increasingly high prices of hardcover books (and consequent consumer reluctance to buy them), a decreasing resistance to reviewing paperbacks, the greater consumption of paperbacks as texts in high school and college, and the frequently high prices and occasionally extravagant auctions for paperback reprint rights—Warner paid more than $3 million for Scott Turow's *Burden of Proof*—paperback houses have stepped up their quotas of original titles.

Paperback executives now cite additional reasons for this phenomenon. Hardback houses traditionally "lease" the mass market rights for seven to ten years, and then can demand a better deal (or new advance) if the book has become a successful backlist title, whereas an original remains with the house for the full copyright term, or at least so long as they keep the book in print. Also, some hardcover houses "take the money and run," failing to adequately promote and publicize the book they sold to the reprinter for a half million dollars, perhaps even before publication date, and the reprinter may have to devote an additional huge sum to this task. Or perhaps the book will fail to live up to expectations, garnering only mediocre or poor reviews and/or selling poorly in hardback, and will have these strikes against it when the paperback salespeople go out to sell stores the book.

The paperback houses realize they can just as successfully spend six figures to promote and advertise a paperback original, using money they didn't spend in an auction. And they have the option—now more frequently exercised—to make a "reverse" rights sale; that is, to lease hardcover rights and to withhold paperback publication for a season or a year, or even to publish the book simultaneously in both cloth and paper. Most mass market houses now have their own hardcover lines in order to have the flexibility to market a book according to what they feel will be the ideal strategy. All of these factors have made it harder for trade cloth publishers to sell mass market paperback rights, even for books that have had good reviews and were written by authors whose first book(s) was successful.

This ongoing trend is good news for novelists, especially of "category" fiction (science fiction, mysteries, romances, etc.), since this is a major area of growth in originals. But it is true with both general fiction and nonfiction. If you feel your book has a potentially broad readership (most paperback houses won't sign a title unless they estimate sales of 50,000 to 75,000 copies in a period of 12 to 18 months), you may be better off going directly to a mass market house. So far, agents and established authors still concentrate on getting published by hardcover houses first, so the competition from pro's and even over-the-transom is not quite as keen. In the long run, if your book is successful (goes back for another printing), you may earn more money for it, since you will not have to split your paperback royalties with the hardcover publisher (50/50 is the common arrangement). Recently, however, mass market unit sales have slightly declined, probably because the median price for a paperback is close to $6, and with inflation, consumers are cutting back on impulse purchases. My optimism, then, has to be tempered by the realization that mass market houses are also concentrating their attention on the "leaders," that is, the big books.

Still, a paperback original is worth considering, provided your book potentially has a "mass" market, that is, a broad readership. Here again, you may be better off skipping the top seven or eight houses and approaching one or more of the dozen or so less glamorous paperback houses, such as Zebra, Leisure Books, or Harlequin. Many of the smaller paperback houses concentrate on certain areas, such as science fiction (or pornography— always doing well!), which you can ascertain by bookstore browsing or writing for a catalog. They have the same ground rules for proposals.

If a publisher of trade paperbacks can estimate a sale of 10,000 to 15,000 copies or more over a 12-month period, they will seriously consider your proposal. They will often simultaneously print a small number of clothbound copies, say 1,500 to 3,000, to catch some library, professional, and mail-order sales, and for those people who are not happy unless they have a clothbound book (and also because the chances of getting reviewed are still considerably increased by having a clothbound edition).

The Bottom Line

Intangibles like friendship, contacts, editors' idiosyncrasies, parent corporation's interests or caprices, and acts of God can also have an effect on the acceptance or rejection of your proposal; ideally, they have a minimal impact. If you have a good idea and can execute it well, you should be able to find a publisher even if it takes a while. The unpublished author is often too quickly discouraged and gives up after receiving several rejections (although some authors *never* give up); the next submission might mean a contract. The number of proposals sent to publishers each year is huge, but the number of books that are published each year is even more astounding.

An unplanned or hasty or impulsive decision as to the choice of publishers is bound to increase the number of rejections you get. Correspondingly, a calculated effort to determine the "right" publisher can pay off in time saved and heartache—no one gets totally hardened to rejections, not even agents. The more subtle distinctions, such as which publishers will do a better job of promoting and selling your book, are very difficult for the unagented author to take into account in selecting a publisher.

Every editor or publisher is enthusiastic, encouraging, and often full of promises when signing up your book. Unfortunately, there's many a slip twixt cup and lip, and numerous authors become dissatisfied with the "handling" of their book, though often their complaints stem from unrealistic expectations. All I can offer is some suggestions for hedging your bets in the contract itself (in Chapter 3) and some suggestions in the chapter on marketing that can help you maximize your participation in the publisher's fulfillment of "adequate performance," that is, ideally fulfilling the role as producer and marketer of your book.

Do You Need an Agent?*

There is no disputing that a good agent is not only worth her 10 to 15 percent commission—beware of any agent who charges more than that; this is the conventional fee for agents—since she can not only generally negotiate a more lucrative contract but can also, by virtue of her experience, contacts, and authority, help see to it that your book gets the treatment it deserves, and place it with the ideal editor and the ideal house for that particular book. But the ideal is not often achieved, and not every agent is a good one—nor are even good ones miracle workers. The variety of steps and factors involved between the submission of your proposal and the appearance of the book in a store are often governed by people and forces beyond the agent's circle or control, which may prevent her from being completely effective. If you have just had a best-seller and are now working on your next book, then a good agent can virtually call the shots. A lot of money has been made on your book, and a battalion of other publishers—not to mention your own publisher—are eager and willing to be as cooperative and generous as you could possibly want. So your agent can then write the ideal contract. But how many of you have just had a best-seller?

Two associations of literary agents, The Society of Author's Representatives and the Independent Literary Agents Association, merged in 1991 to form the Association of Authors' Repre-

---

*Several books and annuals are good sources of information about and listings of agents; see the Bibliography.

sentatives. This new organization has more than 260 members. It is a voluntary organization of literary agents whose members subscribe to certain ethical practices. They publish a list of their members, a canon of ethics, and a brochure describing the role of a literary agent, all of which you can obtain upon request.*

Their description of an agent's functions includes: negotiating the sale or licensing of certain rights to publishers; retaining certain rights for later disposition, such as magazine or film rights;† examining contracts and negotiating modifications; recommending approval or rejection of a contract; examining royalty statements; checking on a publisher's handling of a book, such as advertising and publicity; and checking on copyright. In addition, a good agent will act as an editorial adviser both with the proposal and occasionally with your book, article, or short story, though agents tread lightly when it comes to substantive editing, since their recommendations may be in direct contrast to those of an editor—and it is the editor who buys the manuscript. Finally, the agent acts as a buffer between you and rejection slips, saves you the time and hassle of dealing with publishers, and acts as a dispassionate arbitrator in the event of problems—and they do occur. All in all, the advantages are sufficient to recommend getting an agent, *provided you can*, and provided he's a good one—there's the rub. About half of all literary agents belong to the Association of Authors' Representatives (there's no particular stigma in not being a member of that establishment) and a virtually complete list of agents appears in *LMP*. There are approximately 450 agencies with more than 600 agents who represent writers, and the procedure for approaching an agent is about the same as for a publisher—that is, a letter and a proposal. Getting a good agent may be almost as hard as getting a

---

*Association of Authors' Representatives, 10 Astor Place, 3d floor, New York, NY 10003. All three publications can be had if you send them a check for $5 made out to A.A.R. and a self-addressed stamped envelope with 52 cents postage on it.
†British and foreign translation rights are handled by an agent's overseas agent, so the commission typically increases to 20 percent. Virtually all publishers have a subsidiary rights department of their own to handle these additional markets for your book, in case you do not have an agent.

publisher. Most agents want to represent "professional" writers, that is, people who either make a living as writers and thus can be counted upon to keep churning out publishable work, or writers who have proven through prior publication that their work is commercial and that it is worth an agent's time and efforts to handle it. (Selling your article to a specialized magazine at 5 cents a word is not what I mean, since an article that grosses $150 for you means a $22.50 fee for the agent.) Thus, agents concentrate on professional and previously published writers. Not that they don't occasionally take on new writers, but it doesn't occur with any more frequency than publishers take on new writers. As you can imagine then, agents have their own slush piles and send out a stream of rejection letters.* If you have a contact—a friend, relative, teacher, writer, etc.—who can or will pave the way for you, then it's worth a try. If not, why spend the time and effort soliciting the intermediary when you can go directly to the source?

If you feel that you really do need an agent, since you expect to be quite active as a writer and not just a weekend scribe, then find a commercial publisher who wants your book (by *commercial* I mean a trade publisher who will pay an advance and a royalty), and then call or write an agent and present her with a *fait accompli*, asking her to negotiate the contract for you. Don't think this means she will necessarily grab the bait; it will just increase your chances, and with persistence you will probably get a nibble. But the agent will still want to see your work first, and it's no guarantee you will be hooking a good agent.

I can't tell you how to judge a good from a mediocre agent; it's like trying to judge a good shrink—you can't tell until you get your head shrunk a little. If at all possible, meet him or her and don't spare the questions. From the quality of the answers and your reliance on your own instincts, you should be able to make a judgment, and time will tell whether it was a good one.

---

*One reason is that many agents do not handle all genres; most will not take on children's books, for example, and virtually none will consider poetry. I don't handle fiction, but half the queries I receive are about novels. *LMP* and the sources listed in the Bibliography indicate agents' particular interests.

A good agent cannot always sell your writing, nor can she see to it that your book doesn't die on the shelves. She earns her commission because she cares and she tries.

There are one- and two-person agencies, and then there are big ones that employ between 5 and 25 representatives, some of whom are specialists in selling certain rights: film rights, British rights, first serial rights to magazines, and such. These larger agencies often combine literary and dramatic agents under one roof. A disadvantage at a big agency for a writer who hasn't yet "made it" is the position of a small fish in a big pond. What is most important is finding someone who appears to believe in you and your writing and doesn't act as if he or she is doing you a favor.

Be cautious of the "agencies" that advertise in writing magazines and charge a fee for evaluating and editing or improving your manuscript. Both practices are frowned upon by established agents and editors. On the other hand, there are freelance editors and writers who will help get a manuscript or proposal into shape for a fee, and their services can be useful; an extensive list of them can be found in *LMP.* Shop carefully, ask for references, and be sure the services you expect and the prices are spelled out in writing. An agent can be helpful here. If she thinks your work has potential but needs the attention of an editor before submission, she can help you find the right person. A good agent—or a good book doctor—will also tell you if your work won't benefit from the services of a freelance editor. If a piece of work is genuinely unpublishable, no freelance editor, no matter how talented and well-intentioned, can make it otherwise.

Some authors employ an attorney both to negotiate the major terms of the contract and to scrutinize the small print for potholes and mines. Attorneys will not find a publisher for you; their meter only starts ticking when you have a buyer lined up. But they can negotiate every aspect of the contract and will usually attend to seemingly minor but important details that might escape your attention. However, you would be well advised not to have your local or family lawyer negotiate or vet the contract, but rather to hire one who specializes in intellectual property law (also known as entertainment law). A list of more than 300 firms that offer these services throughout the country is found in *Literary Market Place*. (Impecunious writers may contact Volunteer Lawyers for the Arts, branch offices of which are found in a dozen or so major U.S. cities. Through VLA, writers may engage the services of these same specialists at very reduced rates. As with a low-cost dental clinic, though, be prepared to wait before your case is taken up.) Attorneys without practical experience in this specialty are just as likely to create more problems than they resolve.

One major advantage to using an attorney rather than an agent is that, having paid the onetime charge (ranging from $250 to $1,000, depending on the hourly fee and the amount of time devoted to completing the task), you will not be sharing 10 to 15 percent of your book's future revenue. Conversely, an agent stays the course with you and is there to oversee, troubleshoot, and advise through the long, arduous, and occasionally problematic gestation of your book.

In sum, the answer to the question, do you need an agent? is no, you don't *need* one, though it would be useful to have one eventually. Once you have a book published by a recognized publisher, you will probably find agents are more receptive to your work. But by following the guidelines in this chapter for approaching a publisher and carefully reading through the chapter on contracts, you will know enough to represent and protect yourself adequately. Sure, you may not squeeze out that extra $1,000 in advances, but if your book sells, you will get it later anyway. Keep this in mind if you find the "small print" in Chapter 3 putting you to sleep.

2

How a Publisher Evaluates a Proposal or a Manuscript

> From the moment I picked up your book until I laid it down, I was convulsed with laughter. Someday I intend reading it.
>
> —Groucho Marx on S. J. Perelman's first book

The procedure for reviewing and evaluating proposals and manuscripts differs considerably from house to house, as do the procedures for almost everything else in publishing. What follows is the "typical" procedure for the "average" publisher.

At most houses when a proposal or manuscript is first received it is logged in so that its arrival and location can be monitored. At that point a short note or postcard may be sent to the author indicating the material has arrived and will be considered "shortly."

The Editorial Assistant

In many trade houses, the first step on the editorial ladder is an apprenticeship as an editorial assistant. The editorial assistant works for a senior editor, largely taking care of secretarial tasks, but also acting as the first reader of unsolicited (and sometimes even agented) manuscripts. Of the unsolicited manuscript, the editorial assistant may be the only reader—he or she learns early on what kinds of books the house considers automatic rejects, such as cookbooks, mysteries, or poetry—genres this house never publishes—and gradually develops a sense of what is immediately rejectable even among the kinds of books the house does publish. The assistant may read the submissions of agents as well before the editor sees them, but in general, an agented manuscript will be at least skimmed by the editor as well. Outside of trade and juvenile publishing—in textbook divisions, professional books, law, and such—it is not the convention to have editorial assistants read manuscripts, and editors at these houses usually go through the slush pile themselves.

An editorial assistant may provide a short memorandum, usually a page or less, describing the book to the editor and offering an opinion about its publishability (or lack thereof).* This type of memo from an assistant may be the editor's closest contact with many of the proposals that come into her office. If the editor has an experienced assistant whom she trusts, a rejection by the assistant may be the end of the process—back it goes to the author. More commonly, the editor will take at least a quick look at a proposal, and almost always will skim proposals that come from agents or other contacts. Sometimes, something will catch her eye in a proposal an editorial assistant has judged negatively, and she will read it carefully and decide that her assistant was mistaken. If she is unsure herself, she may pass the proposal on to another editor, informally, for a second reading.

Some houses circulate a weekly list of the manuscripts and proposals that have arrived in-house, so that any editor who may be interested in that topic (or author or agent) can request a copy of the proposal. But to get on a list like this, the proposal must have at least passed muster with an editorial assistant, or have some other obvious reason for further attention.

---

*See the Appendices for a memo suggesting the rejection of the book you are reading.

The Editor Bites

An editor will usually read carefully a proposal that an editorial assistant is enthusiastic about to decide if the material interests him or perhaps would be suitable for another editor. The editor may of course at this point decide that the editorial assistant was too optimistic, and reject the proposal before going any further. He keeps certain considerations in mind as he reads: Is the book well written? Does it have a clearly defined audience? Will it sell? Is it suitable for the house? Are there publicity possibilities in the book or the author? Is she "promotable"? Does he have time to work with the author on this book (editors are usually working on a half-dozen manuscripts at any given time)? Is there sufficient material here to make a decision? Does the book have any potential for subsidiary rights sales (especially paperback reprint, book club, and foreign)? The income from these rights is often crucial for a trade house and may mean the difference between profit and loss for the publisher. If the answers to most of these questions are positive, and the editor is interested in going on to the next stage, he may—at some houses—photocopy the material and circulate it to one or more colleagues, both to enlist their support for the weekly editorial meeting (sometimes called the pub board or the acquisitions committee, which is where the final decision is made), and to have the benefit of their opinions and advice: Perhaps they know that another house has signed up or is already producing a similar book, or that a certain book club would probably take it, or that the author is "difficult," or that the sales manager is dead set against another cookbook for next year because they already have two under contract.

Usually, people in marketing, promotion, and rights are consulted informally for their opinion at this stage, as well as later on a more formal basis at the editorial meeting. Marketing input on acquisitions has become so important that it is virtually impossible to sign up a book without support from that department.

Editor's Checklist

Most publishers have a form that editors must fill out for each book they wish to contract. This is usually called a checklist or proposal form, and sometimes houses have their own unique names for them. At Doubleday, this was always referred to as a "blue form," even long after the paper it was printed on had been changed to plain white. The form normally covers five basic areas of evaluation: marketing, costs, contractual, editorial, and price. This form can range from two to six pages, or it may just be a memo typed up by the editor. Whatever the name, size, or arrangement, it is an attempt to analyze and estimate the potential costs and income for that book. In addition to these five areas, the editor will usually provide a 50- to 100-word description of the book. This checklist, with or without the author's proposal, may be circulated to other editors, the editor-in-chief, the sales manager, the publicity director, the subsidiary rights director, and anyone else who either plays a role in the weekly editorial meeting or has a say in the determination of whether or not to sign up the book (at many houses the publisher or president must approve all new contracts).

Marketing Evaluation. This usually contains an analysis of the author's previous publications: date(s), title(s), number of copies sold and subsidiary rights sales, and any other marketing information provided by the author or secured from other sources (though most publishers are *very* reticent about releasing any kind of sales information). It estimates the prepublication sales, known as the sales rep's "advance,"* as well as the first year's sales, and sometimes the second and third, if it is the kind of book that will have a shelf life (e.g., a how-to gardening title). Many trade books have a shelf life of six months or so (although in the past few years some bookstores and chains are returning books within two or three months after receiving them, if they are not "moving" from the shelves), while most success-

---

*See Chapter 7 for a discussion of advance sales.

ful texts, juveniles, reference, and technical books have a life of at least three to five years. The sales estimate may project low, medium, and high figures. Subsidiary rights possibilities, particularly reprint and book club, are projected, as is the book's potential as a house trade or mass market paperback, provided the house has its own paperback line(s). Recommendations for advertising, publicity, and promotion may be suggested, both the type and budget, as well as any other pertinent marketing information, such as: The author is promotable on radio or TV, the book should be brought out quickly because of its topicality or potential competition, the book is particularly suitable for mail-order sales, and so forth.

Product Evaluation. The chief element of this evaluation is an estimate of the costs involved in producing the first print run. Since the estimated typesetting and manufacturing costs, determination of print run, and list price are crucial and complicated factors, they deserve a separate section; let's hold off for those with a taste for figures until the end of this chapter.

The product evaluation also contains your estimate of the length of the manuscript as well as the editor's estimate of the number of printed pages, the suggested trim size of the book, and the special features, such as photos, maps, charts, and an index. Naturally, a complete manuscript permits a more accurate estimate of the final costs than a proposal. If there are to be any additional costs, such as permissions fees for text, illustrations, or complete units (for an anthology), translation fees, libel readings, or index charge,* these will be listed.

Contractual and Editorial Evaluation. Here the editor estimates how much of an advance and what royalty percentage may be needed to get the book. If there is an agent, the editor may already know how much is being asked, though of course

---

*In most cases, if you don't want to do the index yourself, a publisher will subcontract it to a freelance expert, and deduct the cost from your first royalty check, or bill you for the cost. Some houses are now withholding a portion of the advance— say $500—to cover the index cost.

this is negotiable. If he is dealing with the author directly, he may or may not have discussed terms, but until the editorial meeting and the determination to take on the book, all outside discussions are tentative. He may estimate that he can get the book for a $7,500 advance but suggest going to $10,000 if necessary, that is, if the author or agent holds out for more than is offered, or if the book is being considered at another publishing house and will have to be "bid" on. (We will discuss this in greater detail in the next chapter.)

Unusual features of the potential contract are listed, such as any deviation from standard contract terms—for example, the agent wants a 60/40 split on paperback reprint rights instead of the normal 50/50, or a British publisher might share the production costs, or the author will clear permissions for the anthology only for North America or the English language (cheaper than world rights). Anything the editor has learned about the author and his or her relations with other publishers and editors may be recounted here, since it's a small enough industry for information and gossip to be passed around either casually or sometimes upon request. Will there be any special problems in copyediting the manuscript, and approximately how much time will it take? Finally, the competing books, if any, and the effect they could have on sales will usually be discussed. Here the editor may either rely on the author's discussion in the proposal and merely double-check the *Subject Guide to Books in Print*, or he may send an assistant to the library or, especially in a trade house, to a bookstore, or go personally, both to check the shelves and perhaps to scrutinize a few titles closely. He may call an authority in the relevant field and ask for advice or send that person the proposal or manuscript for a critique or a reading, which will not only compare the book to others in the field but will evaluate its general quality, coverage, and such. This is a very common procedure for textbooks, technical, reference, and scientific books, but is infrequent in trade publishing.

Price Evaluation. Based on the various costs, such as composition, paper, printing, binding, and the suggested number of copies for the first printing, a tentative list price for the book is given, which is calculated to recoup the publisher's investment after the sale of X number of copies, that is, after the "break-even" point, and earn a pretax profit on additional sales. The figures are broken down in various other ways: the book's potential contribution to the publisher's overhead (the "indirect costs"), the estimated gross income on the sale of the entire print run, etc. Other costs, such as royalties, are calculated to determine a profit-and-loss statement for that particular book.

Some of these estimates and calculations are, of course, based solely on an editor's past experience with other titles and hunch. Editors are handicappers, and a close examination of any editor's or publisher's list will show that they bat around .333 (if they are going to stay in business). About one-third of their titles earn back more than they cost the publisher to secure, produce, and market.

The editor's checklist is, as you can see, a densely packed document, whose figures must add up properly *before* the book is formally presented to the house for consideration. No matter how exciting, delightful, and important the editor may think the book is, if the cost of producing your 900-page full-color illustrated study of the Ojibwa Indians means the house either has to price the book at $95.00 for a first printing of 5,000 copies or sell 35,000 copies at $45.00 just to break even, they probably won't do it. This is not to say that expensive books aren't often published and sometimes profitable, but rather that as the investment increases so does the publisher's sense of caution. His instincts about the first year's sales or "guarantees" (e.g., a book club promises to take 5,000 copies) must be compatible with the realization that the bigger the wager, the better the odds must be. In the long run, though, most publishing decisions are still gambles, and it's part of the excitement and anxiety that gives editors, sales reps, and publishers both a sense of adventure and an ulcer.

The Editorial Meeting

Most houses hold a weekly or bimonthly editorial meeting in which, among other matters, the proposals or manuscripts that editors wish to sign up are evaluated, discussed, and then either rejected, held over, or approved. Provided your book has passed the first two hurdles (i.e., the editor wants to sign it and the figures add up), it now faces its roughest critics. Attending this meeting may be: most of the editors and their superiors, the sales manager and his or her superior, the marketing manager, the subsidiary rights director, the publicity director, the managing editor, and perhaps even the art director, advertising manager, production director, and others; it varies from house to house. At some places the editors are *not* in attendance—only the upper echelon of executives makes the final decision.

Normally, most of the staff in attendance will have had a chance to look over the checklist and perhaps the proposal as well. As the editor has merely estimated one of the crucial figures, namely how many copies the book will sell in its first year, he may find that his own enthusiastic guess will be tempered by more sober or pessimistic predictions. Other questions are raised and other opinions may be aired with respect to the market, the audience, the competition, the subsidiary rights potential, the suitability of the book for the house, the cost and number of copies for the first print run, the amount of the advance to be paid, the list price, and such. As a consequence, some of the estimates the editor has made may be modified. Gradually, the drift of the discussion will move toward the pro or the con, and the final decision is usually a consensual one rather than a specific casting of votes, though it may come to that on occasion. The editor, of course, will defend the project. He has already convinced himself that the book should be signed, and may be able to sway less optimistic voices. Depending on his clout, which is based on his age, experience, position in the hierarchy, and track record, he may prevail in spite of a generally skeptical attitude toward the book; though of course he is sticking his neck out, and several failures with "unpopular" projects will tarnish his clout.

It is possible for a final decision to be withheld at this meeting, to be put off until certain questions are answered or certain options explored. Is it true, for instance, that Random House is already planning to publish a book on the men's liberation movement on their spring list? Isn't there a book on the history of Indonesia that a British publisher has already promised us a first look at? Isn't that the same author who signed several contracts with some other publishers, yet never delivered the manuscripts? Perhaps we should wait to see a few more chapters before signing the book. Maybe we should get a reading from an expert in that field. Let's check out the book club or paperback reprint possibilities before we commit ourselves (either because the author or agent is asking for a high advance and the publisher wants to hedge its bet, or the book is very expensive to produce and only the assurance of a subsidiary rights sale can guarantee the recouping of the costs). These are just a few of the issues that may put your proposal on hold until satisfactory answers are found.

Presuming that there are no unanswered questions, however, a decision will be reached, though occasionally with some qualifications: We will only pay so much for an advance, the book will have to be shorter or longer, the maximum number of illustrations will have to be cut in half, etc. If the decision is a positive one, the editor will call or write to you and say those magic words, "We want to do the book." If the decision is negative, the editor will probably let you know why, in contrast to the vague rejection you may receive if the book never got past the first reader.

The editorial meeting is by no means the sole method of arriving at a decision to sign up a book. In smaller houses with only a single editor or two the decision may be reached merely on the basis of a discussion between the editor and the editor-in-chief, who will, nevertheless, have reviewed the proposal and checklist. In other divisions, such as for textbooks, the custom is to send the material up the ladder, attempting to get approval from the executives occupying higher rungs. The same would be true for most specialty types of publishing. In most houses, an executive such as the editor-in-chief, or even the publisher, continues to keep his hand in by signing and editing a few books a year (somewhere between 12 and 20 is considered a normal load for an editor). Such executives usually sign up books of authors they have previously worked with or books for which the major question may not be whether to sign, but how much of an advance they are willing to pay. Their projects may not require the editorial meeting hurdle. Editors who specialize in certain types of books, such as mysteries or cookbooks, or who edit series, such as travel books or ethnographies, may only have to get an okay from their superior. And again, some editors with clout, special arrangements, or their own imprint may have virtual carte blanche, though in almost every case a superior must approve advances above a given amount. Remember that a commitment to publish a book means a production investment of tens of thousands of dollars, not counting the advance, and the advance itself can escalate into seven figures for "hot" properties.

There are some companies whose evaluation procedures do not fit into this bell curve. At one end of the scale is a major publisher whose decisions seem to be made rather capriciously. I will phone the editor and explain the project in about two minutes. If she likes it, she tells me she will "try it out" at the editorial meeting. Tuesday afternoon, after the editorial meeting, she calls me and says, "They love it; we'll take it. How much do you want?" I send her the proposal then, and two weeks later I have a contract on my desk (not that she always operates that way). Mind you, the phone call is not for John Grisham's next novel, but for a midwestern professor's sociological study of long-distance marriage. Small and privately owned publishing houses still make snap judgments on occasion, but they make them less often now.

At the other extreme, sometimes the result of conglomerate takeovers, is the requirement of a five-year profit-and-loss statement, a complex and elaborate projection and analysis of the costs and sales over a five-year period, breaking down the figures so that each and every variable—even the $20 for copyright—is worked over in a number of ways. This mountain of bureaucratic paperwork seems to soothe the corporate breast, as if the piles of papers themselves will ensure the success of the project.

Finally, there are those deals concluded over lunches or on the telephone with an author or agent, in which the project seems so obviously a winner and the author's track record is so successful that any subsequent evaluation by the house is merely *pro forma*—that book is going to be signed.

Almost any financial commitment above the average, whether in production costs or advances, will almost certainly require the publisher's or president's approval. One expensive failure can rock the foundation of a moderate-sized company; equally, one huge success can put a small company on the map as *Life's Little Instruction Book* did for Rutledge Hill Press. The stakes can be high in publishing, so most decisions are not made on impulse.

As you will have concluded by now, the decision to contract or reject a book is not simple, nor does it usually hinge on an individual editor's tastes or whims. It normally depends on a number of factors and a variety of people, so that when and if your book is rejected, you ought not to jump to hasty conclusions—especially since you may never have even considered some of the factors weighed—nor should you be overly discouraged. Your next submission, even if it is your fifteenth for that particular project, may result in a contract.

For those of you who have a taste for figures, the following section will analyze in greater detail the mathematics that publishers use to decide on their list price and print runs (first printings). Since these decisions are tentatively made during the period in which your proposal is being considered, this is as appropriate a place as any to discuss this process, even though it will go through a more complex and careful refinement when your completed manuscript arrives in-house.

Cost Estimates, Print Runs, and Pricing

From a publisher's point of view, there are three vital factors in the creation of a book over which it has a measure of control: the production costs, the number of copies on the first print run, and the list price. Because the sales of many books do not warrant a second printing, the ideal juggling of these three variables is often the difference between profit and loss, so that the final decisions are made only after considerable caucusing and refinement of earlier estimates. The two basic stages at which these calculations are usually made are: before the editor presents the book at the editorial meeting, and after the final manuscript is delivered. Two subsequent events can change the print-run decision and sometimes even the price. The first is a subsidiary rights sale of folded and gathered sheets or bound copies to a book club or to a British or Canadian publisher, both of which are attempted before the book is "put on press." The second is a determination at the end of a sales conference (or even after the sales reps have made their first round of calls) that the original estimate of how many copies can be sold in the first six months or a year was too low or too high. So long as the plates are not yet on the press—and this usually doesn't occur until at least six months after your manuscript has been delivered—the number of copies to be run off can be increased or decreased.

Plant and Manufacturing Costs. A cost estimate is determined on the basis of two major expenses: the plant and manufacturing costs. Plant costs generally include the typography (normally called composition), the negatives and the plates, the jacket art and plates, any preparation and separation costs for illustrations, and for many publishers, the cost of copyediting and proofreading, which is sometimes assigned to each book on the basis of hourly rates. Naturally the editorial changes are very rough estimates if they are made on the basis of your proposal, since the manuscript (and the editorial problems it may entail) is often a year or more away from delivery. The plant costs are a onetime charge—that is, regardless of whether the publisher decides to print 10,000 or 50,000 copies, or has to go back for ten successive reprintings, the plant costs are a single charge, and they only have to be written off one time.

The manufacturing costs, primarily the paper, printing, and binding costs of the text, the cases or the covers, and the dust jackets, are costs reincurred for each successive reprinting. Hence, any calculations of the "unit-cost"—the cost of a single book—for the first printing means adding the plant and manufacturing costs together and dividing by the number of copies to be run off on the first printing. On the other hand, a second printing unit-cost can be roughly calculated by dividing only the manufacturing costs by the number of copies reprinted. It is apparent, then, that the publisher's total costs for the second and successive printings are reduced, and not only does their profit increase, but this accounts in part for the normal escalation of royalty percentages for the author (typically 10 percent of list price for the first 5,000 copies, 12½ percent for the next 5,000 copies, and 15 percent thereafter).

In order to arrive at a preliminary estimate of the plant and manufacturing costs, the editor must supply the production department—whose job it is to make these calculations—with the following information: the approximate number of words in the final manuscript, the approximate amount of artwork, the suggested trim size (the actual length and width of the printed page), and the ideal number of printed pages. This latter number may seem immutably linked to the number of words, but there is some flexibility because of the possible variation in the size of the printed page, the size of the type used, the amount of margin on the final printed page, the "looseness" or "tightness" of the design, and the amount of space devoted to illustrations. The editor usually does not suggest details for other variables which influence the costs, such as: the quality and thickness of the paper, the cases, the jacket, the method of printing, the manner in which the signatures are bound together—sewn or glued—and several other minor details. These are normally left up to the designer and the production manager, who are working within certain parameters of their own—for instance, the house prefers certain trim sizes, designs, qualities of paper, and so forth.

But the crucial figure in determining costs is how many copies to print. For this number, the editor has both a guideline and some leeway. The guideline is that the "normal" first printing of an average book for that house is 6,000 or 12,000 copies, and the leeway is that the editor can request a cost estimate for both figures for purposes of comparison.

Normal is a rather elusive term here. On any trade publisher's spring or fall list, well over 50 percent of the books are expected to have a modest to moderate sale. For this category of books, most trade publishers will have a first printing minimum of 6,000 copies and a maximum of 12,000. Less than the minimum will make the publisher's cost per unit too high for a "reasonable" list price, and more than the maximum may be too optimistic and leave the company with thousands of copies in the warehouse which will have to be remaindered at a fraction of their cost. So if we were to pick an "average" first printing for an "average" trade clothbound book, it would be 6,000 copies. For the sake of discussion, let's work with that figure, keeping in mind that first-print runs can range from roughly 2,000 copies (for reference, technical, university press, and other specialized books) to 100,000 or more for books the publisher believes are going to "take off." (Mass market paperback first printings normally range from 50,000 to 150,000 copies, sometimes escalating to more than a million for anticipated best-sellers.)

The editor, then, supplies the production manager with those figures and suggestions and from a day to a week later receives what is often called a "preliminary cost estimate." This gives the estimated cost for plant and manufacturing, broken down into the individual costs of each item, such as for typography, plates, covers, and so forth, as well as the individual unit-cost for both plant charges and manufacturing charges for each single book.

Let's take an average trade book with no illustrations that contains approximately 75,000 words and will print to 224 pages. The plant cost will be approximately $6,000, and the manufacturing cost for a first printing of 6,000 copies will be about $10,000. The unit-cost for plant is thus $1.00 per copy, and the unit manufacturing cost is $1.67 per copy—I just divided the 6,000 copies into each charge. The total unit-cost, then, of manufacturing and plant is $2.67. With this figure, the editor can now extrapolate further.

The List Price. Publishers normally determine the list price of a book on the "cost of sales," that is, the direct costs of plant, manufacturing, and royalties. But in order to figure in the cost of royalties, you need a list price to take 10 percent of, which places the editor in a cart-before-the-horse situation. Even though the author will be paid an advance against royalties— let's say $7,500 on this book—it is the actual royalty percentage on 6,000 copies that is used for determining cost of sales. Since this average book will disperse approximately 300 copies for publicity, reviews, promotion, goodwill, and author's copies, we will calculate the royalties on 5,700 copies. (For textbook publishers free "examination" copies are a major expense in advertising and publicity, and may be figured in as a cost of sales.) To get this figure the editor will try out a list price that seems reasonable, based on the plant and manufacturing costs, to see how it adds up. Let's say the editor assigns a tentative $17.95 list price. The royalties add up to $10,546 based on 10 percent of list for the first 5,000 copies, and 12½ percent for the next 700 copies. This gives an average unit-cost of $1.85 for royalties for each book. Thus, the unit-cost of sales is:

Plant	1.00
Manufacturing	1.67
Royalty	1.85
Total	4.52

That is, $4.52 per copy.

As a rule of thumb, most publishers use a formula that tells them to multiply this unit-cost by four, five, or six to arrive at a list price (that we have, in fact, tentatively calculated) that will not only pay for the direct cost and help contribute to his overhead, but will also earn for the publisher a pretax profit of roughly 15 percent, provided he actually sells that first printing.

This formula has been partly derived by figuring out on a yearly basis the average total costs of his other expenses, namely the "indirect costs," and apportioning them among the books he publishes in any single year. These indirect or "operating" costs consist of the publisher's normal expenses: salaries, promotion, publicity, advertising, travel and entertainment, sales reps' commissions, order processing, shipping, warehousing, and general and administrative expenses—rent and so forth—but let's not belabor the bookkeeping. Suffice to say that in addition to the cost of sales of each book, the publisher must somehow figure in his operating expenses, and this is normally compensated for by using the formula approach. Thus our average book, with the $4.52 unit-cost of sales, and the tentative list price of $17.95, is about four times the unit-cost.

From these figures the editor can now deduce a number of other figures that are needed in order to complete the product evaluation on the checklist and to see whether the figures add up.

It will be easier to visualize if we lay it out in the form of a chart (see Fig. 1), but first a word about discounts. Discounts are what publishers give to booksellers, and the average discount for a trade publisher is 47 percent: that is, the publisher only averages a net receipt of 53 percent of the list price of each book it sells (the details of marketing will be examined in Chapter 7). For our book, then, which tentatively lists for $17.95, the publisher will only receive $9.51 per copy.

FIGURE 1
Prepublication Estimate of Profit and Loss

Total copies printed	6,000
Total copies sold	5,700
Retail price	$17.95
Revenue per copy @ 47 percent discount	$9.51

Total gross revenue	$54,207.00
Plant costs	$6,000.00
Paper, printing, and binding	$10,000.00
Royalty	$10,546.00
Total cost of sales	$26,546.00
Break-even copies	2,791
Gross margin	$27,661.00
Operating expenses (roughly 45 percent of gross revenue)	$24,393.00
Net profit (before taxes)	$3,268.00

Notice one additional new term on our chart, the *gross margin* which is the amount left over by subtracting the total cost of sales from the total gross revenue. Does it look pretty good? The publisher has to sell only 2,791 copies—only about half the first printing—to break even. Even after allocating operating expenses there is still a small profit of over $3,200, if 5,700 copies are sold. But let's consider some problems. We haven't figured in returns (books returned for credit to the publisher by bookstores that have been unable to sell them), which, according to *Publishers Weekly*, average 30 percent throughout the industry. Even if we calculated the returns at only 20 percent, that would force us to subtract $10,841 from the gross revenue, giving us a net loss of more than $7,500. What's the solution to this dilemma?

First, the editor can increase the list price to $19.95; remember, she's sitting at her desk preparing a *preliminary* estimate and trying to make the figures add up—probably using the P&L template installed in her personal computer expressly for the purpose—so she's free to change the list price. That will add an additional $6,042 to the gross revenue and put her almost back in the black (although it will also raise the author's royalties by 25 cents per copy). Also, we have not considered the subsidiary rights, particularly paperback reprint and book-club sales.* Any kind of sale there is gravy and will immediately boost the potential income, but this contribution will not manifest itself until much later in the game, after the book has been set in galleys, so she can't fall back on it at this preliminary stage.

The solution, if you want to call it that, is this: While less than half of the publisher's list pays for itself, a certain percentage of titles will go back for reprinting and earn much more than their share of pretax profit. Don't forget that on a reprinting of, say, 5,000 copies, the publisher pays only the royalty and the manufacturing costs on each copy; the plant costs have already been written off on the first printing. For our book, this would mean his unit cost on the next 5,000 copies is about $3.52, though in reality the escalating royalty drives this higher. Also, subsidiary rights income averages about 10 to 20 percent of net revenue overall for many trade publishers, and can add up to a crucial amount in the profit-and-loss columns. Many trade publishers are in the black only because of that extra 10 to 20 percent; without it, they would go under. Finally, a certain number of books on the list become "back list titles," that is, continue to sell, even at a modest rate, for a number of years and earn their investment back more slowly, perhaps in two to three years.

But the reality is that in spite of the estimating that the editor does—and she must of necessity juggle the figures somewhat so that each book appears as if it will make a profit—she knows, as does the rest of the staff, that fewer than half of the books are going to pay the way for the bulk of them, and the editor often does not know in advance which are which.

The kind of bookkeeping that is hypothesized here varies from company to company in so many different ways that it isn't useful mentioning some of the alternatives. Also, I have simplified some of the statistics and calculations—there's only so much a writer wishes to know about the figures. But in the main the preceding example is a generally accurate portrait of the fig-

---

*A book-club sale may, paradoxically, cause the publisher to boost the list price, since book clubs want a significantly lower discounted price for their members, which is most profitably achieved by raising the publisher's list price.

ures, methods, and madness that go into determining the cost estimate, print run, and list price. Between the preliminary estimate the editor prepares her checklist, which will be a major determinant in the decision to reject or approve the proposal, and the final list price and print run, many a minor change will be made.

Once the manuscript is delivered, all these figures, except the estimate about how many copies will sell, can be refined so that the actual costs can be calculated, and the decision about the list price can be reviewed and changed, if necessary. The importance of the first-print-run decision cannot be overestimated. The difference between 6,000 and 7,500 copies is often the difference between profit and loss (with 1,500 copies sitting in the warehouse as proof), and many an editor, editor-in-chief, and sales manager has learned to temper his or her optimism the hard way; there is always the temptation to print more copies, since the unit-costs go down as the print order goes up. But the real pros are usually conservative; it's better to go back for a reprinting than to chance getting stuck with an overprinting. It's still guesswork, though, and there is no way in publishing to avoid this gamble.

Outside of trade publishing (i.e., for textbooks, technical and scientific books, and juveniles) there are certain variables and factors that change some of the ground rules; for example, lower discounts (textbooks normally sell to bookstores at a 20 percent discount), lower first-print-run quantities (professional books may have a first-print-run of 2,000 to 3,000 copies), or a longer shelf life (juveniles are expected to sell over a number of years). Thus the figuring may be different in certain dimensions, but publishers are still stuck with some of the same perennial gambles: How many should we print, and how many can we sell?

Many authors complain about the high list price of their book, often accusing the publisher—after the fact—of having priced their book off the market. Normally this just isn't so. Very careful planning supports some of these hunches, and the decisions are usually arrived at by a putting together of experienced heads: the editor, the editor-in-chief, the sales manager, and maybe others. Most publishers do, on occasion, consider "how much the market can bear" in figuring their list price, and the accusation that they are ripping off the public with outrageous prices is sometimes warranted, though this is more common outside of trade publishing. Some feel that the price of books isn't especially high in any case—in a world of $25 pro football seats, $65 Broadway show tickets, and $49 computer games, a $22.95 hardcover book may be a pretty good buy. But if prices are high, the reason is simply that this is what it costs to get a book written, printed, and published and make a modest profit while you do so. The pretax profits in trade book publishing are not the stuff that excites the imagination of a venture capitalist, and then after taxes . . . well, let's get on with it and turn to an item closer to home, the author's contract.

3

How to Understand and
Negotiate a Book Contract

Writing is the only profession where no one considers you ridiculous if you earn no money.
—Jules Renard

Most authors, surprisingly enough, pay very little attention to their book contracts. Having discussed an advance and a royalty with the editor involved—which often means that the editor has told the author what the terms are going to be—the author is normally content to sign the contract after a perfunctory glance to see that his or her name is properly spelled. Even considering the legalese in many contracts, this indifference does not seem reasonable, and a casual attitude at this point can result in more than the loss of money from sources obscure to most writers. There are legal and long-term ramifications to many clauses, some with a potential for causing headaches or grief. What may appear to be a minor issue now may turn out to be a major one later. A writer who can spend from one to five years finishing a manuscript can certainly spare a few hours to scrutinize a contract—and then try to negotiate it to his or her best advantage.

By and large, most publishers are not out to take advantage of your naïveté, but they are running a business for profit, in addition to their other motives, and your goods and services are the source of their profits. As a "partner" in this phase of the business, you will get a fairer share of these profits by making an effort to understand what the terms of the proffered contract mean, and by attempting to negotiate some of those provisions which are modifiable, since virtually all "standard" publishing contracts heavily favor the publisher.*

Just as horse trading is one of an agent's skills, so do many editors develop this knack by virtue of the same capitalist commandment that governs any other business: Buy cheap and sell dear. Since many commercial publishing houses are owned by—or are run as if they are owned by—conglomerates, "let's look at the bottom line" is taking precedence over any earlier publishing canons. The moral is that as the publisher is no longer a patron, the author is constrained to look after his own interests.

But in one chapter it would not be possible either to analyze a sample contract thoroughly or to make detailed recommendations for all the differing contingencies, clauses, and provisions that are found in the bewildering variety of publishing contracts in use today. I also realize that most authors have neither the will nor the desire to nitpick over every detail and that most professional writers expect an agent to provide this service. Therefore, I will only survey and interpret the most common and vital provisions in a contract.

I must stress that this chapter is a superficial view and interpretation of a contract. The 40-odd-page *Guide to The Authors Guild Trade Book Contract* (which accompanies its approximately 20-page "Recommended Trade Book Contract"), finds more gopher holes in the average contract than are found in all of Kansas, and even their analysis is far from complete. While the A.A.R., the National Writers Union, and the A.G. are making

---

*Both the Association of Authors' Representatives and The Authors Guild issue a recommended contract (the latter has been recently updated), but I don't know any house willing to accept them in toto. They are more useful as ideal manuals from which to mine specific favorable clauses or provisions.

inroads in changing conventions and "standard" clauses so that authors can more equitably share in the income from their books, almost every contract still contains so many covert twists and implications that a book would be needed to explicate the contract, analyze the pitfalls, and suggest the changes to request.* Even with such a book, the unagented author would be unable to take advantage of it: Unless you are a very successful author, or unless your book is virtually guaranteed to make it big, the publisher is sitting in the catbird seat and will not agree to the ideal contract, such as the one issued by the A.A.R.

Nevertheless, let's briefly consider some of the ways to improve your bargaining position to secure the best possible deal. You might hire an intellectual property attorney (as we discussed in Chapter 1) to negotiate the major terms and to scrutinize the contract carefully, including the small print. Or you might immediately join one of the major writers' organizations, such as the National Writers Union—which has been especially active in trying to redress the imbalance of power between writers and publishers—the American Society of Journalists and Authors, Poets and Writers, Inc., or The Authors Guild. All of them have useful materials available to members on the details of negotiating contracts, such as the *ASJA Handbook: A Writer's Guide to Ethical and Economic Issues.* (The addresses for all of these organizations can be found in *LMP.*) Alternatively, you can read one of the books mentioned in the Selected Bibliography, or you can read the balance of this chapter and try to implement some of my suggestions.

The First Encounter

If an editor has been successful in getting your proposal or manuscript approved by the editorial board, you will receive a phone call, or sometimes a letter, in which you are not only told

---

*See the Selected Bibliography for several books containing advice on contract negotiations.

the good news, but are extended an offer. Since editors assume, and rightly so, that authors are generally innocent about contracts and terms, the offer will consist of an advance against royalties and a mumbled reference to "our standard royalties." An advance is a payment made, usually prior to publication, which has to be earned back by the sale of copies of your book before any additional royalty payments are made. As an example, if the royalty rate is 10 percent of the list price of the book—for convenience' sake, let's price it at $20—then the author will receive $2 for every copy sold. If the advance is $8,000, then the book has to sell more than 4,000 copies before earning additional money for its author. However, if the book sells fewer than 4,000 copies, the author does not have to repay the difference to the publisher; it's for keeps, provided the contract describes the advance as "guaranteed," "nonreturnable," or "not repayable to the publisher," or unless the author defaults by not delivering the manuscript on time or breaks the contract in some other way. Most contracts make such a guarantee, and you should insist on this assurance.

As pleased as you may be by this phone call, you do not want indelibly to commit yourself to those terms or the unseen contract; you can express your delight and still ask for a chance to think it over. Meanwhile, you also want to ask for a blank copy of the contract or a rough draft with the terms penciled in, and the opportunity to examine it at leisure. Don't accept any excuses; you have a perfect right to look it over. Negotiating a contract once it has already been signed by or passed through executive hands is a much more awkward task, and an author is inclined to go along with it rather than request changes.

In the Appendices you will find a representative contract printed in its entirety. Since some of the clauses are negligible or self-explanatory, I have omitted a discussion of them here. Conversely, I have added some clauses here that do not appear in the contract in the Appendices, since they are common enough possibly to appear in your contract. Though most contracts identify each clause by an abbreviated caption in the left-hand margin, they do not necessarily conform from house to house either in their order of presentation or in their designation; nor does my order here conform to the order of the clauses in the contract in the Appendices. Nevertheless, you should have no trouble identifying each corresponding clause by comparing it with your own contract.

The least complicated contract that I have seen contained about 15 clauses; the prize for long-windedness goes to a major publisher with a 108-clause contract. The last clause reads: "Captions or marginal notes, and the table of contents of this agreement are for convenience only, and are not to be deemed part of this agreement." Amen.

The contract we are using for a guide is a representative one; it contains the basic and vital elements found in virtually all trade contracts. However, bear in mind that it is a *trade* contract; there are a few elementary differences in contracts for textbooks, juveniles, professional books, and mass market paperbacks, which we will discuss later in this chapter.*

If you read this chapter carefully, you may know as much about contracts, if not more, than many editors. Lawyers and agents pore over these documents, but some editors are surprisingly unacquainted with even their own company's contract. One consequence may be that an author will come to an agreement with an editor over the phone and then find that the document does not seem to fulfill the verbal agreement, albeit for harmless reasons—perhaps the editor did not understand your request. Obviously, you can return the contract and request the changes. But to prevent this kind of misunderstanding, you, the author— once you have scrutinized the contract and noted the changes you want—should write a letter to your editor detailing your requests and asking the editor to call once he has assimilated them. This will give the editor a chance to consult his superior or the appropriate executive(s), who may approve or reject your demands. Most decisions in publishing, as I have already pointed

---

*The publisher's printed contract, free of any negotiated items, and with some blanks to be filled in, is known as the "boilerplate." Many of its provisions are "house policy" (i.e., they are relatively fixed); many are not. Since policies vary from house to house, it is hard for an author to determine where and how much leeway there is; this is one instance in which a seasoned agent earns her commission.

out, are not made autonomously. Remember that the contract is legally binding, whereas verbal assurances are not. If you consider any demand vital to the success of your book, such as placement of a mail-order ad in a journal of mycology for your book on mushrooms of the Southwest, get it in writing, either as a clause in the contract or in a letter from your editor. So much time elapses between signing up a book and its appearance, and so many editors play musical chairs in publishing, that an author should not rely on a verbal assurance, however sincere the intentions of the editor.

Remember also that you are *negotiating* a contract. Be prepared to compromise, because you may not have all your requests honored. If you feel that you do not want to budge on a certain demand, such as the size of an advance, you are free to go elsewhere and try your luck. In 1975 I submitted the outline and two sample chapters for the first edition of this book to a house that offered me a $2,000 advance; I explained that $4,500 was closer to the figure I had in mind. The house offered no compromise; I went to another publisher. On the other hand, be wary of an editor who insists that his house's standard contract permits no deviation, and rejects all your demands. It just isn't so. If a publisher wants a book, they should and usually will compromise—up to a point, anyway. If they won't, *caveat vendor*.

For certain clauses, especially those that relate specifically to finances, there are conventional boundaries on either side of which you or the editor are over the line. For instance, on an unagented book the author/publisher split for foreign translation rights generally ranges from 50/50 to 80/20 (you get the 80). Some provisions are stickier, such as the size of an advance. The boundaries are hazy, so how does an author decide what her book is worth? After we examine the clauses, I will suggest some guidelines for these stickier provisions, but do not expect definitive advice, as it's still a horse-trader's game. It is a good idea to keep a sense of proportion in coming to an agreement with a publisher. At most, 3,000 writers in the United States earn their living from writing books and articles; the rest of us, say 30,000, enjoy the supplementary income, but are unlikely to join the ranks of full-time professionals and try not to fantasize too much about striking it rich in print. If you write a best-seller, or even a "successful" book, you will have no trouble getting yourself an agent who will negotiate a stiffer contract for you for the next one. The time and effort it normally takes to get an offer from a publisher usually discourages a writer from shopping around for a better deal. My suggestions in this chapter notwithstanding, to some extent you are still faced with playing it by ear. If the offer seems fair, and compromises are made, you should accept it.

Conventional Publishing Contract Features

Grant of Rights. Virtually all contracts begin with this clause, which delineates the territory in which your publisher has the exclusive right to publish, sell, and license rights for the book (commonly referred to in contracts as "the work"). The primary territory for a book publisher in this country consists of the United States, its possessions—the Virgin Islands, Guam, etc.—the Philippines, and Canada.* The secondary territories are the British Commonwealth—the British Isles, Australia, New Zealand, etc.†—and other foreign countries in which the book may be translated. Traditionally either your agent or the subsidiary rights department of your publisher licenses other publishers in these secondary territories to produce and market the work in their own countries, though this clause also grants your publisher the *nonexclusive* right to sell the English-language edition throughout the world, except for the British Commonwealth. In other words, your U.S. publisher and its British licensee may

---

*Some agents and authors are now separating out and retaining Canadian rights to license as a "foreign right," because writers unfairly lose royalties, which are cut to from two-thirds to half of those in the U.S. In addition, sales are often diminished by the customary half-hearted distribution arrangement most U.S. publishers adopt.
†Several years ago a court decision split up this traditional division of the English-language market, which was said to be monopolistic, but it is still frequently, though informally, observed.

compete for sales in, say, Denmark. Later in the contract a major clause spells out the disposition and revenue share of these secondary territorial rights, along with other subsidiary rights. Sometimes this first clause grants "world rights" to the publisher but will (or should) specify the author's share of revenue from the secondary territories in a later clause.

If you do not have an agent, the publisher will retain world rights, and—in essence acting as your agent—will attempt to sell or license these other rights.

Copyright. Most authors will ask that the work be copyrighted in their own name rather than in the name of the publisher, and publishers generally grant the request. Though having the copyright in your name does not give you ideal protection of your rights, as you are either licensing, giving, or selling them depending on the wording of your contract and what subsidiary rights are sold, it is a modicum of protection, and you should insist on it. Otherwise the contract should specify that the copyright is held in trust for the author and will be reconveyed upon request. It is most important to retain copyright or have it assigned upon publication if you publish an article, short story, or poem in a magazine. We will discuss the whys and wherefores in the last chapter.

This clause should also oblige the publisher to register the U.S. copyright and to make sure that copyright is registered in other countries where the book is licensed, sold, or translated. It obliges you to cooperate with the publisher in securing or signing any documents required to keep the copyright in force.

Incidentally, many authors display an irrational or excessive concern for protecting their unpublished work against plagiarization or piracy. While an idea or even an outline for a book may have dubious legal protection, a partial or complete manuscript is virtually safe by reason of "common-law copyright," which now asserts that all unpublished writings are protected from the moment of execution until 50 years after the author's death. There is no need or value to putting *copyright* on any page of the manuscript as some authors do.

Manuscript. This clause estimates the approximate number of words your final manuscript will contain, the number of copies you are required to deliver to the publisher—usually the original plus one copy and, more frequently now, a copy on diskettes—and the due date of your manuscript. A key phrase in this clause is "delivered in final form and content acceptable to the publisher." Almost every contract contains that phrase or words to that effect, and they are much more important than they seem. They give the editor or the publisher the right to reject the manuscript if for one reason or another it is deemed unacceptable. If you receive a contract on the basis of a complete manuscript, this won't apply unless you really botch up a suggested revision—the publisher knows what it is getting. But if the contract is issued on the basis of an outline or an outline plus sample chapters, and the editor decides that the execution of the project is severely wanting and beyond redemption (she doesn't think a revision can cure the problem or the requested revision is inadequate), then the publisher is customarily entitled to cancel the contract. If the issue is clear-cut, for instance, the final manuscript does not adequately coincide with the outline, the author is not in a strong position to argue with the publisher's decision or to sue. But rarely is the issue clear-cut. More frequently the reasons given are: poorly written, insufficient exploration of the topic, outmoded data, and so on. These reasons are sometimes open to question, and a reasonable editor will listen to your arguments, or may suggest that an unbiased expert(s) read the manuscript and submit a report on it, or the publisher may do this before notifying you of its own dissatisfaction. (Reader's reports are conventional in textbook publishing whether or not there are problems with the manuscript.)

Implicit in book-publishing contracts is a publisher's obligation to provide the author with guidelines for revising the manuscript in order to make it acceptable, and an opportunity to do so. Many contracts now spell this out in a boilerplate provision, detailing, among other issues, how much time the author has—usually 60 to 90 days. Several courts cases in the early 1980s—most notably *Goldwater* v. *HBJ*—set the legal precedent for this obligation. Thus, any author is now on solid legal ground when demanding both a detailed explanation of the reasons for having a manuscript rejected and a list of specific editorial guidelines for revising the book to make it "acceptable." The rejection of a novel, of course, is a stickier problem.

Sometimes the publisher's rejection of the manuscript on the basis of quality masks more cogent "commercial" reasons, which are not generally valid legally: The market has changed, a competing book appears, the book is no longer timely, and so forth. Nevertheless, these can be persuasive reasons for reconsideration on *your* part.*

Invoking the "acceptable manuscript" clause is an uncommon event, but it happens often enough to consider it here. If it happens, what recourse do you have? Authors have gone to arbitration or sued publishers over this issue. A number of years ago a major publisher contracted for what it knew would be a favorable biography of Richard Nixon and forked over an $83,000 advance on signing, with two additional equal payments respectively due on delivery of a partial and then completed manuscript. When the Watergate scandal arose, and with it Mr. Nixon's reputation declined, the author contended that the publisher's rejection of the partial manuscript on the basis of "quality" was actually disguising more commercial considerations. A financial compromise was reached between the author and publisher out of court, and the book was later published by another company.

As of now, there is no definitive legal ruling in cases like this, and they are either settled out of court, through arbitration, or in a suit, though the author is usually left holding the bag. If you feel that the publisher's arguments are flimsy or capricious, hiring a lawyer and attempting to pressure the publisher to publish the book may succeed, but most authors feel that if a publisher does not want their book, they will treat it as an orphan (and they will), so that it falls "stillbourne, as it were, from the press," as David Hume reported of his first *Treatise.* If you feel the publisher is wrong but sincere, try to persuade them with your own

---

*Note rider #28 on the sample contract, which addresses this possibility.

arguments, and suggest outside readers. If this fails and you still believe the book is sound, you are going to have to find another publisher (best to keep the brouhaha to yourself) or sue or both.

Conventionally, the publisher will insist on repayment of any money advanced only if and when you sell the book to another publisher. If they demand it immediately, write and inform them that you will repay the advance when you place the book with another house. If this doesn't work and you receive a letter that sounds like it means business, get a lawyer. Common publishing practice is on your side, and the publisher knows it, even though the outcome will depend on a legal interpretation of the contract. To avoid this pitfall, try to negotiate a rider such as #31 in the sample contract.

This is an uncommon event, however. If the publisher decides to cancel the contract for reasons independent of your book, such as changing the direction of its list, a general cutback in titles, or canceling a whole series, you are not legally obliged to return the advance, and in fact are justified in demanding or suing for the balance of any advance due. Most publishers in this situation, upon receipt of a strongly worded letter from an attorney, are very likely to offer a reasonable settlement.

Conversely, late delivery is a much more common problem, and publishers have become increasingly rigorous over this breach of contract, especially if the author has received a sizable advance. I estimate that 50 to 75 percent of the manuscripts an editor signs up are delivered anywhere from two months to a year and a half late, whereas approximately 10 percent are complete no-shows. At one time, publishers were more casual and tolerant of late delivery, but they have since begun to take a harder line, meaning that they can and sometimes will cancel a contract if the author is more than, say, three months late, particularly if the topic is faddish (and the competition is mounting) or timely. Editors are quite conscious that writers have blocks and other problems that delay a book, so they are accustomed to granting extensions. If you think you will exceed the delivery date, you should write for an extension at least two to three months beforehand; do not wait until the last minute. Also, it is best not to accept a verbal grant of an extension; politely request it in writing. The kind of letter that shows evidence of the author's progress and provides legitimate reasons for being late will find a more sympathetic ear. Since the majority of manuscripts *are* late, a publisher is not on firm legal ground if it cancels your manuscript a week after it is due. While there is no definite legal ruling on this point, you are entitled to a reasonable amount of time within which to deliver (say two to four months). Some contracts further stipulate that "time is of the essence," in which case your right to a reasonable extension is more tenuous. Without a written extension, you are on shaky ground after three months, even though you may not be called on it. A second extension is sometimes given on request, but any author passing this extension has put himself out on a limb and is subject to the mercy of the publisher. Incidentally, the house has the right to demand repayment of any advance if the contract is canceled for lateness or nondelivery.

Author's Guarantee (Warranty and Indemnity Clause). In this clause you guarantee the publisher that you have the right to sell the book: The contents are written by you (not plagiarized), and none of the material is used without permission if owned, copyrighted, or controlled by someone else or some other publisher. For example, if you are quoting original source material such as tapes, diaries, letters, or other material for a biography, you will have to secure written permission to use each item from either the author or the author's estate. It also implies that you cannot sell the same book to another publisher (don't think it hasn't been done). It further warranties that the book contains "no scandalous, libelous or unlawful matter," and indemnifies the publisher against any suits arising from this contingency. This last provision is one of the more unfair and unreasonable items in a publishing contract.

The author is here certifying that in the event of a claim or lawsuit brought against either the author or the publisher, the author must bear the full brunt of any payment of money that such a defense involves, which may include attorneys' fees, court costs, and any amount from a sustained judgment. Even if the claim or suit is not upheld in court, the author may still be liable for payment for costs up to that point. Some contracts modify this clause to splitting expenses, and a few hold the author financially responsible only if the claim is upheld or the judgment sustained (provisions you may want to request if they do not appear in your contract). But with most publishers one must call it an inequitable clause, if only for the following two reasons: Most authors could be financially ruined for years if they lost a suit and had to pay heavy damages, whereas most publishers could write the amount off as a business loss. Also, publishers not only retain their own literary lawyers who are supposed to know what is libelous, slanderous, or unlawful, but they are also supposed to try to avoid the problem by reading the manuscript before publishing it, that is, by authorizing a "libel reading" if the author or editor has any doubts about the material. Furthermore, many publishers carry "errors and omissions" insurance to protect them against expensive suits but fail to include the author under the umbrella.

However, long-term lobbying on the part of both the A.A.R. and The Authors Guild to include the author in the publisher's "media perils insurance coverage" bore fruit in the mid-1980s, so that most of the leading commercial houses now provide such insurance for their authors, according to a recent Authors Guild survey. The bad news is that the deductibles "have increased dramatically," and they can be potentially bankrupting; for instance, under the terms of one policy, the author shares payment of the first $50,000 or $100,000 or even $250,000 of a settlement or sustained judgment. Even so, the vast majority of publishers do not provide writers with such protection. Thus, agent nonpareil Richard Curtis says, "Caution is the best policy when writing a book."

The only preventative is to familiarize yourself with what constitutes libel, slander, and unlawful matter, and if you have any doubts at all about the work, I would suggest you have a lawyer examine this clause and advise you on what changes you should *ask* for and what changes you might want to *insist* on. Unfortunately, interpretations of libel, slander, and unlawful matter are so ambiguous that often it is only in a specific case that there is a decision on what they in fact mean. If you remain uncertain, advise your editor to authorize a libel reading when the manuscript is finished, a not unconventional chore that he is likely to undertake anyway if *he* has any doubts. It probably would not hurt to get an outside libel reading from a lawyer on your own. You might also try to negotiate this clause to state that the publisher will at least share equally in the defense and costs of any claim or suit, if it doesn't already read that way, and that your warranty is limited to the future earnings for that book. As a last resort, you can purchase libel insurance, which is now available to authors from several insurance companies.

Lest this all sound excessively alarmist, however, bear in mind that such suits are quite rare. Even when they do occur, publishers customarily reach into their own pockets to cover all expenses, and even the settlements, *provided* you did not knowingly, with malice aforethought, plagiarize, libel, falsify, or create quotations, and so forth; that is, act in bad faith.

Copyrighted Material. Permission must be secured to use extracts of copyrighted material (this does not apply to short "fair use" quotations) and the writer agrees to supply the publisher with the written consent of the copyright holder at the time of the delivery of the manuscript. See the following chapter for a detailed discussion of "fair use" and related copyright issues.

Material Supplied by Author. This clause details the author's responsibility to supply any matter other than the manuscript itself, such as tables, illustrations, or photographs—referred to as artwork—as well as the written permission to use them if they are not directly produced by the author. It is important that you state clearly in your proposal what type and amount of artwork is to appear in the book and then to decide in a discussion with your editor whose responsibility it will be to supply it. Normally the author is expected to supply all the artwork, but a variety of other options are common. For instance, you may supply rough drafts of charts, diagrams, or drawings to your editor, who will turn them over to an in-house or freelance artist to render "camera-ready" copy. You can negotiate that the cost of this could be tacked onto your royalty account, that is, deducted from future royalty payments. Sometimes the editor or the art director is both more experienced and more conveniently located to secure illustrations, and the house will provide all or some of them for your book.

Securing artwork may involve two types of expenses: the cost of preparation or reproduction and the permissions cost. For the latter your publisher might provide a budget or ceiling beyond which the house will not advance the money. The cost of supplying all of your artwork, as well as the method of paying for it—out of your pocket, out of the publisher's pocket, advanced by the publisher and deducted from royalties, or some combination of these three—is negotiable, whether the artwork or extracts are of minor importance or whether they constitute the bulk of the book. In most cases the publisher will pay outright for artwork it secures and pay all permissions costs upon publication, charging them to your future royalty account. But since each book is quite different when it comes to artwork and permissions, and since the arrangements are negotiable, it is quite important to discuss these details with the editor, to have decisions made prior to signing the contract, and to insert in the contract any modification or arrangement that deviates from the clause as it is written.

This clause also exonerates the publisher in the event that the manuscript or artwork is damaged, destroyed, or lost in the mails. Of course publishers exercise due caution, but be particularly careful with original or irreplaceable artwork. Send it by overnight Express Mail, Federal Express, or any of the other half-dozen courier companies. It may be worth the extra expense for you to have such items as old photographs reproduced locally, supplying the publisher with the new print and the negative. With respect to the manuscript, notify the editor that you want the original returned to you when the book is published, and see that you get it.

Publisher's Determination. In essence, the publisher has the right to determine the format of the book, the method of publication, and the manner in which the book is marketed, which includes the number of copies on the first printing, the list price, and such. In some contracts the publisher also has the right to alter the title—an unconventional provision—though no publisher is likely to force a title on an author. If the editor thinks the title is not catchy, informative, or suitable, he will ask the author to supply some possible alternatives, or he may supply some himself, and by mutual agreement a new title will be chosen.

Though most publishers are reluctant to permit the author a voice in the style or format of the book, he or she could ask for the following amendment to this clause, so that it reads (approximately): "Publisher will consult in advance with the author concerning the format and style of all trade editions, and concerning the text, graphic material, and style of the dust jacket and catalog." Most should agree to it, or will assure you, instead, of their intention to "run them by you . . . we always do." Even though many editors customarily do this, ask for a letter anyway; nobody remembers these promises a year or more later (and today's editor is often tomorrow's freelancer). Note that "consultation" is not the same as "approval," but since you have a right to ensure, at the least, that the description of your book is accurate (if not graceful), this written promise will suffice. Yet, even if nothing is put in writing, if pressed, the editor will agree to showing you the rough sketch of the dust jacket and the jacket copy. If you have recommendations for either, send them in with your final manuscript or author's questionnaire. Though you both have the same ultimate goal, the publisher's experience, cost limitations, and the conventions of that particular house usually outweigh an author's request on matters of design, style, and format.

On the other hand, you should know whether the house intends to publish the book in a cloth or paper edition or both. Perhaps you feel quite strongly that only a paperback will reach the prime audience for the book, and you wish the publisher to insert a phrase here that "guarantees" paperback publication within a year or two after the cloth edition (provided your publisher has a paperback line). Or maybe you feel that the publisher's paperback line doesn't get enough exposure in the places where your book is most likely to sell (college bookstores, for instance), and you want to make sure it attempts to sell paperback rights. These are negotiable issues, though the publisher's experience is generally a more reliable guide to follow for marketing strategy. Remember, well-intentioned verbal assurances, such as, "We have to wait and see what happens, but we'll do what's best for the book . . ." have no influence over its destiny: only commitments in writing give an author—or an agent— some leverage. Normally the publisher's desire for maximum sales and the author's desire for maximum dissemination of her work will not be in conflict, but they can be.

Advance Payments. Conventionally, one-half of an advance is paid upon signing a contract and the other half on delivery of the final or revised manuscript. Occasionally, when the work is a lengthy one or is not to be delivered within, roughly, 18 months, or when the advance is large, the publisher may want to pay the advance in three installments: on signing, on delivery of half the manuscript, and on delivery of the completed manuscript. More frequently now, publishers are making the last of three payments upon publication, but I recommend you strongly resist this alternative. Since the writer fulfills his part of the agreement by delivering a final manuscript, why should he wait another year for the publisher to ante up?

This clause further stipulates that the publisher may deduct any "overpayment," which means that if your first royalty statement indicates that the book has both paid off the advance and earned additional royalties, and there is a check enclosed or appears to be forthcoming, the publisher can deduct from the following royalty statement six months later any amount it has overpaid you because of interim "returns." When bookstores first order your book, all that are shipped and billed are listed as sold on your first statement, even though they are normally sent with a provision for "full" return privileges for up to a year or more. But the bookstores may not sell every copy. In fact, on a yearly basis, hardcover returns throughout the industry average 20 to 25 percent, ergo your publisher may have overpaid you by that much. However, in anticipation of these returns, many publishers commonly withhold 25 to 50 percent or more of your royalties from the first, second, or even third statement, pending returns, and may have a provision in this or a later clause which states that they can do so. Most publishers do it even if there is no such provision in the contract, because it is a conventional industrywide practice.

Book Royalties. Most publishers pay royalty rates for trade and juvenile books based on the list (cover) price, and an author should resist any deviation from this policy except for textbooks and professional books, which generally pay royalties based on the net receipts (we will discuss that later in the chapter). For clothbound sales in the United States, more than 50 percent of trade houses pay: 10 percent for the first 5,000 copies sold, 12½ percent on the next 5,000 copies sold, and 15 percent thereafter. However, other permutations, such as from 10 percent on *all* copies to 15 percent on *all* copies, or different steps for escalations—say, 10 percent to the first 10,000 copies—are not uncommon. Quality paperback royalties are a bit more flexible: The average rate is 6 percent of list for the first 15,000 or 20,000 copies, 7½ percent thereafter, though some contracts start at 5 percent, and some offer a flat 7½ percent, which is what you should ask for. Agents and established authors sometimes demand and get higher royalties or additional escalations. The quality paperback we are discussing is the one issued by *your* publisher. If the paperback rights are sold by the subsidiary rights department to another publisher or to a mass market house, you will generally receive 50 percent of the proceeds and your publisher will negotiate the royalty rate.

Royalties are normally reduced by 25 to 50 percent in the following circumstances: export sales, such as to Canada or overseas; direct sales to the consumer either by mail, radio, television, or in coupon ads (the cost of fulfillment—individually processing and shipping single orders—is the rationale for reduction); and copies sold at a discount of from 48 percent to 50 percent or higher. This is a tricky one; see clause #8 (1) in the sample contract. Because the discount offered to wholesale or retail booksellers by most publishers generally does not exceed 48 to 50 percent, only a small percentage of book sales (if any) ever fall under this provision. Some few houses, however, frequently give 50 percent or slightly higher discounts, and then pay the author on *net* receipts for these sales. This means the author receives almost half of normal royalties. In such an instance, if the book is successful, the author stands to lose a sizable amount of income. Ask your editor for what percentage of book sales this provision is normally invoked. If it is high, consider a provision limiting these high discount sales to no more than one-third to one-half of normal trade sales (or consider shopping for another publisher). A current wrinkle to ponder is that the book-publishing world is considering revising its normal "consignment" policy, in which all books sold to booksellers are returnable for almost full credit for up to a year or more. Under the new policy, books would be sold on a nonreturnable basis but for higher discounts above 50 percent, a practice now limited to special or premium sales. Authors and agents will scream bloody murder if they are not consulted before this policy is implemented, and will insist that some reasonable sliding royalty scale, pegged to the new, nonreturnable, discount sale, be adopted.

Copies sold as "overstock" or remainders pay anywhere from 5 to 10 percent of net proceeds. Note that most publishers have a provision regarding future printings of approximately 2,500 copies or less, which stipulates that royalties are decreased if sales do not exceed a certain amount within a 6- or 12-month period. The rationale is that the higher unit-cost of a small reprinting, plus the continuing costs of warehousing and keeping a modest-selling book in print, reduce the publisher's ratio of net income to—let's say—the amount of expended effort for your book. This kind of reasoning seems flimsy, but it is a common clause in many contracts. I would advise requesting a provision that permits a royalty deduction only if sales fall below 500 (or 750) copies in any given year.

Subsidiary Rights. Virtually every publisher has either a department or individual actively engaged in attempts to license (sell) these rights: In other words, the publisher will act as the author's agent. If the author has an agent, she would normally try to retain 100 percent of the following rights for her client: first serialization (prepublication of part, all, or a condensation of the book in a magazine or newspaper); British Commonwealth and foreign translation rights; motion picture, dramatic, radio, television, and audio and video rights, which are sometimes lumped together in one clause as "performance" rights. (For an extended discussion of the audio industry and audiocassette rights, see the section on subsidiary rights in Chapter 7.) If you think an audiocassette rights sale is a possibility for your book (certainly any novel is), you may want to include a provision that gives you approval over abridgments of the text (most sales are for two-cassette sets that are abridgments of books, resulting in scripts of roughly 125 double-spaced pages), which most publishers are comfortable giving. Most houses and producers will generally *not* want to use your voice for the recording, so don't insist on it; you may, however, be able to suggest appropriate actors. Fiction is usually read by a celebrity; nonfiction by a noncelebrity. Licensing of video rights is so uncommon—it is used primarily to adapt celebrity sports or exercise books, such as those by Jane Fonda and Richard Simmons—that it scarcely merits space here. The publisher retains and attempts to license the other remaining rights, the most important of which are for book clubs, foreign sales, and paperback reprints. Normally the proceeds are shared equally with the author.

Considering the total number of books published every year, only a fraction will earn revenue from a single subsidiary rights sale. Though the yield is higher for trade books, the odds are still against your book being sold to a book club or a mass market reprinter, the two most important subsidiary rights for a publisher. Nevertheless, the revenue from these rights is vital to trade publishers and may determine the difference between profit and loss in any given year. The small percentage of books that are successful can generate huge sums from subsidiary rights. The paperback rights for *Fatherland*, for example, a bestseller about what would have happened if Hitler had won World War II, were sold by Random House to HarperCollins for a $1.5 million advance. However, the majority of paperback reprint sales pay advances that range from $2,500 to $10,000, so do not let your fantasies run away with you.

Close Connections. Over the past ten years, several of the major houses have introduced mass market lines, as have St. Martin's Press and HarperCollins. Others have acquired them (Viking Penguin and Random House). And some have become related to them through mergers, as with Morrow's connection to Avon through its parent, the Hearst Corporation; Doubleday's connection to Bantam and Dell through Bertelsmann; or Little, Brown's to Warner through Time-Life. (Incest is now rife in publishing.) At the same time, traditional mass market houses, such as Ballantine, Bantam, Pocket Books, Warner Books, Dell, and New American Library, have started hardcover lines especially to attract brand-name authors of commercial fiction. They can thereby control and exploit the financial potential of blockbuster books from start to finish. (Danielle Steel, for example, is published in hardcover by Delacorte, then in mass market paperback by Dell, both now imprints of the Bantam Doubleday Dell Publishing Group, a subsidiary of Bertelsmann.) Consequently, these houses with hardcover and mass market capabilities are acquiring a much greater percentage of books for "volume rights" (often described as a hard/soft deal), for which they generally pay more money up front. They pay more yet again for "world rights"—the right to license British and foreign language editions—in order to apply the advances gained there against the author's own large advance, which is seen as an unearned balance until book and rights sales earn it out. General Schwartzkopf's autobiography, *It Doesn't Take a Hero*, for example, commanded close to a $6 million advance from Bantam for all except film rights, and Bantam may have recouped as much as half of this from licensing foreign rights even before the book was published in the United States.

The results of this trend are that fewer high-priced paperback auctions are held. Nevertheless, they still occur regularly, because some large commercial houses, such as Houghton Mifflin, Farrar, Straus and Giroux, and Henry Holt don't have mass market lines or affiliates. Also, there are a thousand smaller houses that occasionally publish best-selling auctionable books. Or sometimes the writer and the writer's agent insist that the mass market affiliate must participate in an auction just like the other potential bidders.

Since the sale of subsidary rights is a function of marketing, I will discuss the methods in Chapter 7. What an author can negotiate is for a greater share of the revenue from rights normally retained by an agent. If the film or television rights for a novel are sold, a difference of 10 to 30 percent in the split of these rights might cover a down payment on a house on Cape Cod right next to Norman Mailer's place. A nonfiction book can also be adapted for other media, even if less frequently. Whereas from many publishers you might receive half the "net compensation" from these rights had you not raised the issue, you are justified in asking for an 80/20 split on British and foreign translation rights, and a 90/10 split on first serial, motion picture, radio, television, and dramatic rights, as well as audiocassette and video rights (you are probably going to have to settle for less on some or all of these). Even though your book may seem a thoroughly unlikely candidate for any of these rights, there is no reason to give away more than you have to, just in case. For this book, for instance, a British edition or a translation is highly unlikely, since it is primarily about U.S. publishing practices, and written for U.S. authors. But portions of it are suitable for writers' magazines.

Other Subsidiary Rights. A variety of minor sub-rights are either spelled out in one or two clauses, such as "licensed special media" or merchandising or commercial rights (e.g., licensing the Jurassic dinosaur logo for T-shirts or cocktail napkins, or the Simpson family for dolls or toys), though they may be enumerated in several clauses.

Though these rights are rarely exercised, there is little justification from the publisher's side for retaining *any* part of these rights since there is generally no attempt made to exploit them. By custom, however, most authors still sign over 50 percent without even knowing what these rights are. Though you might not want to make a federal case out of it, you are justified in asking for a 90/10 split, especially if there's the slightest chance of their being exercised—a minor industry has grown from the exploitation of characters from the Ninja Turtle films, and from TV's *Sesame Street.*

Payments. Most publishers send out royalty statements twice a year (though a small percentage report annually) and will include a check if one is due. A statement is sent three to five months after the royalties are calculated for a given six-month period. That is, a statement received on April 1 will reflect sales from the preceding July through December, giving the publisher three extra months to prepare the paperwork and to calculate and deduct returns. Most statements fail to include important information, such as the size of the first and subsequent printings, or the amount of revenue that is being held as the "reserve for returns," and can be quite difficult to decipher even though The Authors Guild and the A.A.R. have labored for years—so far with limited success—to reform common practice. Usually the deficiency is in the lumping together of sales that carry different rates or the failure to clearly identify the different items. Be prepared to puzzle over your statement for half an hour with a pocket calculator and then to call or write your editor for an explanation. Many publishers will withhold 25 to 50 percent of earned royalties for two to four or even more years (and sometimes for the life of a book) to compensate for anticipated returns. If the royalty due is less than $25 to $50, you may not receive a statement or check until the following royalty period (though you will get both if you request them).

Author's Changes. These are usually called "A.A.'s," author's alterations. They refer to any changes the author makes in the galleys or page proofs that are sent to the author for correction after the manuscript has been set in type. Chapters 5 and 6 describe the actual bookmaking process from manuscript to bound books, so it is sufficient to note here that any rewriting, revising, or additions you make in the galleys will obviously generate additional expenses for the publisher, discounting correction of the typesetter's mistakes. Any changes the author makes that cost more than 10 percent of the typesetter's first bill will have to be paid by the author. She may be billed for them right away or have the cost of them deducted from her future royalties. Resist any deviation in your disfavor from this common 10 percent arrangement.

The author is responsible for the "completeness and accuracy" of corrections made in galleys, though someone at the house will simultaneously be reading and correcting galleys. But if the typesetter inadvertently omits a paragraph or an entire page and the proofreader fails to catch it, don't blame the publisher if the book appears with that omission; you probably didn't read the galleys carefully enough.

Editing by Publisher. This clause refers to copyediting (see Chapter 5); it assures the author that the publisher will not materially change the work.

Free Copies. Most contracts stipulate that the publisher will furnish the author with 6 to 12 free copies—ask for 10 to 20 copies of *each* edition; at this juncture of the negotiation editors usually feel generous—and will sell her additional copies at a discount of 40 percent or less. Because almost all authors buy many more copies for relatives and friends, they should insist on a 40 percent discount (which actually escalates to 50 percent or more, since they receive royalties on these copies, too). Less than 40 percent for a trade book would mean that a bookstore gets a better discount than the author.

Revisions. If the first edition of the book is successful, and if it is the kind of book that lends itself to a second edition, such as in updating a textbook, a travel guide, a how-to, or a contemporary history, then the publisher may ask the author to revise the book. Successful textbooks, for instance, are often revised every two to three years. If the author cannot or does not wish to revise it himself, he can negotiate with the publisher, at that time, the cost of having someone else do the work, since this clause is usually vague about the apportionment of costs. If not vague, the following arrangement is fair: The author (or his estate) should either suggest someone or be able to approve the publisher's choice and be prepared to have either a flat fee or an advance and share of future royalties deducted from the second edition. The royalty share ranges from 15 to 50 percent, depending on the amount of work involved in revising, but authors should resist signing away more than 20 to 33 percent of the future royalties. A negotiable advance to cover the cost of preparing a revised edition is commonly given, if requested, but a better policy is to build it into the contract, such as: "Publisher agrees to provide a reasonable advance against royalties when requesting a revision." Incidentally, our sample contract is one of the few I have seen that contains no revision clause.

Discontinuance of Manufacture. This clause is sometimes designated as the "out-of-print" or "termination" or "reversion of rights" clause. Some of the provisions are antiquated but have now become embedded in many publishing contracts. For instance, one conventional provision reads: "If at any time the book shall be out of print, and the author shall notify the publisher to this effect. . . ." In other words, *you* are supposed to tell the publisher when the book is out of print in order to reclaim the rights! In fact, stated or not, nine out of ten publishers will *not* inform an author when a book goes O.P. We can define *out of print* as "when copies are not available or offered for sale in the United States through normal retail channels in an English-language hardcover or paperback edition, issued by the publisher or by another publisher licensed by the original publisher, and are not listed in either publisher's catalog." I am paraphrasing a provision from The Authors Guild recommended contract.

Until such time as this antique is generally effaced from many contracts, I can only urge you to make sure that there is a clear provision for reclaiming *all* the rights (not just publication rights) and suggest some ploys for determining whether the book is still in print, as some publishers are less than forthright in proclaiming the book's demise—the order department may refer to it as O.S., out of stock, which could mean "T" (temporary) or "P" (permanently). In the event that a work goes out of print, the conventional clause instructs the author to write the publisher requesting either that the book be reprinted, or that the rights revert to the author six months after the date of the letter, provided the publisher does not indicate or follow through on his intention to reprint it, or license someone else to reprint it. Make sure that your clause has some *specific* teeth in it as this one does.

The rub is how to know when the work is out of print. A little sleuthing will do it. If two consecutive statements show negative sales (more returns than sales or no sales at all), or if you fail to receive a statement—they are all invariably late by between a day and a month—check the most recent *Books in Print*, write for your publisher's current catalog or order list to see if it is listed, and ask a friend to order five copies by mail. If all three of these actions indicate that your book is not available, then write to the publisher and request the rights. If your friend's request for copies results in a T.O.S. letter of invoice (temporarily out of stock), you have to follow up with a letter to your editor (or the president, if your editor is no longer there) demanding to know when copies will be available. T.O.S. is sometimes a gambit to permit the publisher to hold on to the rights, even though they are not selling the book and have no immediate intention to reprint it. Why do they bother, and why should you bother to get the rights back?

Works are occasionally rediscovered or exhumed and go on to become best-sellers: It happened to the author of *Fried Green Tomatoes*, Fannie Flagg. Her first book, *Coming Attractions*, originally published by Arbor House, was "discovered" by Warner Books after the publication of *Tomatoes* and republished as *Daisy Fay and the Miracle Man*. It has now sold more than 600,000 copies in a trade paperback edition. A more typical example took place recently when my clients' book *The Executor's Manual*, was declared out of print by Doubleday upon selling out its first printing of 1,000 in cloth and 5,000 in paper. I believed it could have a long life as a backlist title, and easily licensed the reprint rights (for a revised edition) to Consumer Reports Books. With a new title, *How to Settle an Estate*, it is now one of their leading books, and has sold more than 20,000 copies in hardcover during the past three years and is still going strong. A more likely possibility is that a reprinter, a publisher that specializes in reprinting out-of-print books in expensive hardcover editions, may come seeking the rights anywhere from 5 to 50 years after the book has presumably been laid to rest. And the rights will be worth an advance and royalty once again. Since it is impossible to predict what might happen, the author should have the benefit of the doubt. More to the point, you will not have to share the revenue 50/50 with your original publisher but will retain 100 percent of it.

You are also normally offered in the discontinuance-of-manufacture clause the right to buy the negatives or plates, if they still exist, and either the bound or unbound copies remaining in the warehouse, before the publisher destroys the plates and remainders the overstock. You will have little need for the former, unless you have rustled up a reprinter on your own, but you may want to stock up on some more copies at bargain rates.

Competing Work. As you might suspect, an editor or publisher would not take it kindly if an author were to write a book for another publisher that directly competed with the original. In most cases, common sense will provide the answer to what constitutes competition: Writing another introductory textbook in psychology for a different publisher would probably stimulate a lawsuit, whereas writing a juvenile version of a biography of Thomas Jefferson (provided you don't copy whole passages) would not compete with the trade edition. Many authors mine the same fields for several books. If in doubt, discuss the issue with your original editor before signing a second book; if you aren't satisfied with the answer, consult a lawyer.

Options. The option clause, which grants the publisher the first crack at the author's next book, made more sense in the days when publishers nurtured novelists, hoping to be rewarded for their faith by the financial success of the second, third, or fourth novel. However, nurture is in short supply nowadays (equally matched by most authors' tenuous loyalty to their publishers), even though almost every first literary novel loses money: Publishing them is both a sign of commitment to literature and a realization that the next generation's novelists have to come from somewhere. Though I urge nonfiction writers to try to delete this clause, because the publisher's case for it is a weak one, there is real merit to the argument for retaining it in the case of a first novel, a collection of short stories, or a book of poems. However, the clause should not be linked with the publication date of the first book, but rather state that you may submit your option book after *acceptance* of your first book, and the option should be contingent upon the publisher reaching a decision within 60 days of submission (for a nonfiction book, on the basis of an extensive outline or a sample chapter), and "acceptable terms to be negotiated" or words to that effect. This means that if you are not satisfied with the terms that are offered, you are free to go elsewhere, provided you do not accept an equal or lower offer. You will want to strenuously resist a commonly encountered tag on this clause that permits your publisher—if you reject their offer—to match, or to match and top by 10 percent, any other publisher's offer. It's an umbilical cord with unfavorable, constricting ramifications.

Entire Agreement. This clause protects both you and the publisher from any arbitrary deviations from the agreement, unless by mutual consent in writing. What should also be included or implied in this or another clause is "no *assignment* without mutual consent," signifying that the publisher cannot sell the contract to another publisher without the author's consent, except when most or all of the publisher's assets are acquired by another entity. Royalty income, however, can be assigned by the author at any time to a relative, heir, mistress, charity, or what you will.

Binding Effect and Assignment. This contract is binding upon your heirs, or their heirs and assigns, so long as the contract and copyright are in force. It is equally binding on the publisher or whoever succeeds or acquires the publisher. Hawthorn Books published the first edition of this book. E. P. Dutton and Co., which acquired Hawthorn, published the second edition, and Dutton Signet, formerly New American Library, which was acquired by Viking Penguin—as was Dutton—is publishing this third edition. We are both still bound by the terms of the original contract, signed in 1975.

Other Possible Contract Features

The number of clauses in a contract can range from 15 to 108, and it would be impossible—and tedious—to discuss in a single chapter the entire range and variation of individual clauses. Nevertheless, here are some additional common clauses or provisions that are common and/or important.

Time of Publication. Some contracts contain a provision in one of the first few clauses obliging the publisher to produce the book within a certain number of months after delivery. Though six to nine months is the normal gestation period from date of delivery to "bound books" (official publication date is always four to six weeks later), postponements do occur, either beyond or within the publisher's control. Reasons can range from lack of cash to war to strikes and to dilatory typesetters in South Korea (some publishers shop around the world for the cheapest bid). Publishers work within a yearly budget, a certain portion of which is allocated for producing books. Because costs for individual titles can only be estimated until production is under way, and as delivery of manuscripts from authors is erratic, some juggling always takes place on a publisher's production schedule. An unexpected manuscript, or perhaps a potential best-seller, may be delivered or contracted for, which can result in bumping one or more other low-priority books for later publication. Therefore, it is important to include a provision that states a specific amount of time within which the publisher has to produce the book. (Textbook publishers are more commonly self-indulgent with schedules.) Twelve to 18 months is a legitimate request.

If you cannot get this provision inserted, the best way to prod a procrastinating publisher is to remind them of your existence: Polite or aggrieved letters to your editor, followed up by phone calls, are more potent than most authors realize. If you are ignored, write to the editor's superior. One extremely silent and considerate author I knew had his low-priority book bumped for three successive years. It wouldn't have happened if he had kicked up some dust. Actually a contract implies, even if it does not explicitly state, that the publisher will fulfill its responsibilities within a *reasonable* amount of time. If an excessive delay seems to be stretching into an interminable one, an author can legally reclaim the rights to his book.

Examination of Accounts. (See rider #29.) Many contracts contain a clause permitting the author or her representative (an accountant) to examine the "books" once or twice a year for errors in computing the sales upon which the royalties are paid. Authors are sometimes shocked by low sales figures on a royalty statement, having concluded from certain indications—perhaps a number of excellent reviews in mass circulation magazines or newspapers—that the book is selling well (but note that these are not a surefire guarantee of sales). Textbook authors hear from friends and colleagues around the country that their book is being adopted at many colleges. This clause would permit an author's accountant to verify invoices to determine if mistakes in calculating the royalties have been made. The clause usually states that if the error is in excess of 5 percent to the author's disadvantage, the publisher will pay for the accounting. Inadvertent errors do occur, since the introduction of computerized accounting has often created as many mistakes as it has eliminated. Deliberate falsification is an occasional topic of conversation at cocktail parties, but the damage to a reputable publisher that might be found engaging in this would far outweigh the sums involved, so I would discount this possibility. High initial sales may sometimes be canceled out by unusually high returns, though the author may only see the final figure in the royalty statement, because returns are not always listed separately. Before taking any formal steps, call your editor for an explanation if you feel something is wrong with the figures.

Advertising Budget. Unless you are a "brand name" author, most publishers will reject a request for an advertising budget specifically allocated for your book. Instead, you will generally be told that it is obviously to the publisher's advantage to advertise your book, and when the time comes, and so on. This is one of those verbal assurances more practiced in the breach than in the observance. Yearly advertising budgets are theoretically apportioned among all the publisher's titles; in practice, 20 percent of the books commandeer 80 percent of the budget, so that many of the books get but a single ad or none at all (excluding general announcement ads, which usually include all the books for that season).

If you can clearly identify a specific and easily targeted audience, you can make a good case for insisting on a few ads and request that the assurance be put in writing, either in the contract or in a letter. A specific audience usually has several magazines or journals that cater to its interests: A book on wolves would appeal to readers of *Natural History*, a study of folk songs would appeal to readers of the *Journal of American Folklore*, and so on, ad infinitum.

In lieu of an ad, a flier or brochure sent to subscribers of particular magazines or to members of certain organizations may be more effective, especially since much more information can be packed into a flier than an ad. Books that are appropriate for specific college courses, whether they are trade books or textbooks, can often effectively increase their sales by offering free "examination" copies in a mailing piece, and it is a common form of promotion. So, rather than requesting a budget per se, you might have more luck with a request for several ads or a flier. It's worth a try.

Index. Most nonfiction books either do or should have an index. Your contract negotiation should include a discussion with your editor on whether an index is necessary or advisable, and if so, who should prepare it. Most houses give you the option of doing it yourself or having the publisher subcontract it to a freelance professional indexer. In the latter case the convention is for the publisher to lay out the fee (generally between $600 and $1,200) and have it deducted from future royalties. Hence, even if your book does not "earn out" its advances, you would not be required to ante up the cost of the index. If you do not elect to do it yourself, make sure that your contract spells out who pays and when. An elaborate index can cost as much as $1,800. Consider your dismay if your publisher deducts this amount from the advance due you upon publication or sends you a bill for it, payable upon receipt.

Electronic Rights. This right may be imbedded in another clause (in our sample contract it is contained in 8 B.(8) as one of the "Licensed Special Media"). It may also be identified as "information storage and retrieval systems," "electronic reproduction rights," or by some other, similar terminology. This right refers to the new techniques of converting books into computer software and storing them on diskettes, CDs, or other media for use on personal computers. Most houses are inclined to try to license these rights, although some are more capable of exploiting them than others. Microsoft Press, for example, which is owned by the large software company of the same name, is a publisher well prepared to produce books in both printed and computer form. Many of the larger houses, however, especially those with reference-book divisions, are hiring New Media Directors to oversee the exploitation of electronic rights (see the more extended discussion of electronic rights in Chapter 7).

Computers can provide not just the text of a book, but, using the CD format, a multimedia entertainment and information experience as well, including motion pictures, voice, and music. As I write this, *Jurassic Park* is on the verge of setting financial records not only at the box office and on the best-seller list, but with this right, and no doubt with several other "minor" rights— T-shirts and toys, just to name two. Still, the industry is in its infancy, and no one knows what it will look like when it grows up. It would be sensible for writers to put this right in a separate provision, and try to exorcise the publisher's broad phrasing, especially such wording as "all rights now or hereafter known or devised."

The A.A.R. recently issued a position paper on electronic

rights, in an attempt to define the current and potential half-dozen distinctive uses that are encompassed by the broad term *electronic*. For a 50/50 revenue share, it included the following clause, which is now accepted by several major houses and considered fair by both sides of the issue. Try to have it inserted into your own contract:

> Subject to Author's consent, publisher will have the right to license nondramatic reproduction of the verbatim text, without adaptation, of the Work or parts of the Work by electronic, mechanical or other form, the results of which serve as a substitute for the sale of the Work in book form (this grant of rights shall in no event be deemed to be a grant of audio-recording rights, which are reserved by the Author).

Subsidiary Rights. The particulars of subsidiary rights sales are too complex to explore in detail here (the publisher's role in and method of licensing these rights are explored in Chapter 7), but with a little imagination one can see that if the publisher has total control over the disposition of these rights, there are situations in which arrangements that are most advantageous to the publisher might not coincide with the author's best interests. Hence, every author should attempt to insert the following provision:

> The publisher shall submit to the author for his prior approval* (such approval not to be unreasonably withheld or delayed) the terms of any license for pre- or postpublication periodical rights, British, foreign translation, performance, and electronic rights. Copies of the contract shall be fur-

---

*In practice, most publishers are very reluctant to grant "approval," especially to an unagented author, and do so only for writers with very good track records or when participating in a lively auction with other houses also bidding for the same book. However, "consultation" ("we'll discuss it with you, but we have the final say") is both a reasonable and an achievable request, and I urge you to press for it where all subsidiary rights are concerned, save book club, for which it is not customarily given. Be prepared to listen to several standard but unconvincing arguments about why you should not have approval or even consultation.

nished by the publisher to the author upon request, and the author's share shall be paid within thirty days.

This paraphrase of an A.A.R.-recommended contract clause permits an author a chance to put in her two cents and perhaps modify, approve, or disapprove of an arrangement that is normally presented to her as a fait accompli. Many years ago, for example, a U.S. senator was chagrined to learn that a portion of his book—quite a sober and serious book, incidentally—was appearing in a magazine devoted primarily to illustrations of unclad females. The senator probably did not have this provision in his contract (he was able to sue and settle nonetheless). However, the value of this clause is that it permits you to evaluate the publisher's intention for a rights sale and decide whether the outside offer appears "reasonable" and is in your best interests. For instance, a client who had published a book before I met him told me that his publisher, a university press, was about to sell the paperback rights for a $500 advance, even though his book had received excellent reviews in a variety of newspapers and trade journals and had been chosen as a main selection for a major book club. His publisher apparently had a standing arrangement with a paperback reprinter to offer first crack at all the books, and since 99 percent of them had modest sales expectations, the normal advance that had always been offered was $500. Since many university presses are not particularly concerned with subsidiary rights advances, this one felt no obligation to attempt to secure a better offer. My client wrote a polite but firm letter and managed to make a better arrangement, but he could just as easily have found out about it months later, when it would have been too late to do anything about it.

The request for a 30-day "pass through" of the money is also generally resisted, but it ensures prompt payment to the author for her share of the rights sale, since she might normally have to wait six to nine months until the following royalty statement appeared. Any unearned advance, however, would be deducted from the author's share of this rights sale.

Anthology Permissions Budget. In addition to the anthology editor's advance, a publisher normally allocates a permissions budget, laying out the cost upon publication and deducting it from future royalties. Though the anthology editor—or author, to avoid confusion—may not be expected to know how much the total permissions costs are going to run, the editor will feel more comfortable with an educated guess, though he himself may provide a more accurate estimate than the author. Most journals and magazine articles run roughly $15 to $25 a page, whereas poems, short stories, songs, plays, and excerpts from novels or published books vary considerably in cost, depending on the specific publisher or copyright holder, as well as on the current reputation or prestige of the author of that selection. An outrageous request, say $1,000 for a short story (and sometimes even a pro-rata share of the royalties), can often be negotiated for a lower fee. If not, a substitute is probably the best solution. It is very important for the anthologist to make sure that the house is going to lay out the permissions costs and that this is stated clearly in the contract. An author I know received an unexpected letter from his publisher on publication date, reminding him that he should now mail out the $1,450 in permissions costs. Naturally, the author was flabbergasted; he had *assumed* this was the publisher's responsibility, and he had already spent his own advance.

Sometimes the author can press the publisher to pay a percentage of the permissions costs outright, perhaps up to 50 percent or more, especially if the anthology is obviously a unique and potentially promising one or if the author has a good track record or a distinguished reputation in his field. It's worth a try.

Negotiating an Advance for a Trade Book

Virtually every trade publisher pays an author an advance against royalties for a book, though there are some publishers that offer flat fees for books, an arrangement more common prior to 1950. The rise of book packagers (who prefer to be called "book producers") in the 1980s—there are now more than

160 of them—has kept the flat fee alive and well in an agreement known as a "Work for Hire." At a publisher's request, packagers can almost singlehandedly provide full-service publishing, from either concept or edited manuscript to bound books. With increasingly restricted budgets, publishers find it economical to have a smaller staff and to buy "product" from freelancers. Many packagers conceive of books or series, prepare an outline that is sold to a publisher, and then hire a writer—for a fee—to "flesh out the project" (this makes it sound like a simple mechanical task, perhaps in order to reduce the guilt feelings from failing to share royalties with the author). The packager can then provide the publisher with "camera-ready copy" or bound books.

Some few packagers do share royalties and other rights revenues with authors—the split is usually 50/50. Clearly this is what to press for. Most writers, however, with mortgage and college tuition payments due, when presented with an outline and an offer of a flat fee of $4,000 to $8,000—the typical range for a 45,000- to 65,000-word genre novel or nonfiction book—are hard pressed to refuse it. Under such circumstances one might ask for a share of any revenues from an unanticipated source, such as performance, reprint, foreign, serial, audio, and electronic rights.

Occasionally a book is commissioned by a publisher such as Time-Life (or perhaps by a national manufacturer) for a special market or for mail-order sales—for instance, a history of a company, a review book, workbook or study guide for the educational market, a puzzle or game book, or a small pamphlet for a very specific audience. Under these circumstances, a flat fee may be justified, especially for a book that will be given away rather than sold. But generally agents and authors frown on a flat fee arrangement. After all, if a book sells in excess of what it costs to produce, shouldn't the author have a share of the profits? Therefore, be wary of a flat fee offer. Even if one were to calculate the number of hours it would take to write a commissioned book, and charge a very generous hourly fee (or word rate), the chances are that it will take half again as much time to produce the final manuscript as the author imagined, and the rate might therefore not exceed the U.S. minimum hourly wage.

How does an author determine what to ask for or to accept as a fair advance? As a rule of thumb in publishing goes, estimate the potential royalties the book might pay in its first year, and then deduct 20 to 25 percent. In other words, if your book will tentatively list for $20, and the publisher expects to sell 5,000 copies in the first year, then it should be willing to pay up to $8,000 for an advance (you recall that even before an offer is made, the publisher has estimated a list price, a first printing quantity, and the first year's sales). Both publishers and agents tend to use this guideline in negotiating advances, though the book club and other rights potential (which may even be checked out before an offer is made) can jack up the figure considerably. One might therefore ask an editor for her tentative list price and first year's sales estimate and do some rapid mathematics before discussing the advance. The mean advance for trade books is roughly $10,000 to $20,000, a range to keep in mind if this is your maiden voyage. Make allowances for the fact that my experience is mainly with the top 100 nationally known publishers, since advances will run somewhat lower with smaller publishers, say, roughly $4,000 to $7,500.

These figures are predicated on the assumption that you earn a living, or part of one, in some other fashion or field, and that your book does not require extensive travel or extraordinary expenses. A writer with national magazine or newspaper credits, for example, would command a higher advance even for a first book, as would a previously published author with a good track record, or a celebrity, politician, jet-setter, magnate, and such. Most would have an agent, though, but there are some successful writers who are savvy about publishing and contracts and just do not believe in having an agent, but may employ a lawyer instead.

First novels are a stickier problem; not only are so few published every year (about 100) that it is difficult to talk about an average—and many of them are agented—but the odds are that the publisher is going to lose money even without paying an advance, especially if it's a literary novel. An over-the-transom first novel accepted for publication by a trade publisher is a rare event, considering the number that are submitted, and most authors are content to accept whatever token a publisher is willing to offer. For a literary novel I would consider $5,000 to $7,500 reasonable, and about the same for a genre or category novel, such as a mystery, science fiction novel, or a romance, if it is a paperback original (add another 50 percent or so for a hardcover original). These are low-end numbers; advances for fiction, even first novels, vary from four to six figures. A short-story collection—with some few exceptions—or a book of poems garners the smallest, if any, advance; say from $500 to $2,500.

Another way to deal with advances is just to ask for $2,500 more than an editor offers. He is usually working with a negotiable figure and will probably make an offer at the lower end of the spectrum, which you may be able to boost merely by *confidently* asking for it.

Many authors believe that the amount of an advance has a crucial relationship to the amount of effort the publisher will expend in promoting a book. Thus a small advance will inevitably result in a negligible effort. It just isn't so, or rather it is not true for books that have an advance of less than $20,000, which means most books. Almost every trade book requires a direct investment of $15,000 to $25,000, not counting the advance. Because of this, virtually every publisher will attempt to recoup its expense by performing the task of promoting and selling the book with at least a minimum of zeal. Of course, big advances place a greater pressure on the publisher to go all out for a book, but then, it wouldn't have given a big advance in the first place unless it believed the book would sell well, and had the intention to promote it heavily. This is kind of a Catch-22 in that the early decisions and expectations frequently become self-fulfilling prophecies. The exceptions, however, are frequent occurrences. Simon & Schuster paid $7 million for Ronald Reagan's autobiography (plus a book of speeches), but sales were disappointing, and the publisher undoubtedly lost several million. Random House also suffered huge losses with Donald Trump's *Surviving at the Top*, the sequel to his best-selling *The Art of the Deal*. No amount of publishing hoopla was able to recoup these large investments.

Finally, there are a few publishers that are just reluctant to pay advances—and even a few authors who feel they aren't really entitled to accept money unless the book sells well enough for them to "earn" it. "If you don't actually need the money," an editor may say, "since you don't intend to live off of it, why ask for it? You'll get it back anyway if and when the book sells. Why should we tie up our capital in loaning you interest-free money? Besides, we are already gambling (or showing our good faith) by spending ten thousand dollars to produce your book."

Well, the answer is twofold: Advances are a commonly accepted convention, and publishers are paying them to get an exclusive option on your book and its potential income. You will be tying up or have tied up your time and efforts to produce something from which they expect to gain, so the advance is compensation for these efforts, whether or not your book sells. One could compare it to buying the manufacturing rights for a newly patented invention. Of course, some publishers, particularly small ones, cannot afford a hefty or even average advance. They operate on a tight budget, and an author might just decide to forgo it. Even so, my own feeling is that if a publisher can afford to produce your book, it can afford at least a token advance for the author.

In any case, remember that if one publisher wants your book, probably another one will, too. If you feel that either the financial terms or the small print are grossly unfair or too unconventional, consider shopping elsewhere while you are "thinking it over." Most writers are unjustifiably timid about rocking the boat with their first contract and are inclined to go along with whatever is offered. Contracts *are* negotiable, and negotiations about specifics are only limited by how badly the publisher wants your book and by how badly you want that specific publisher to take it. Having said this, you can always console yourself—when the task is done, and you think you gave in too easily on the list of demands in front of you—with the thought that on the next one, either you will have an agent, or you will drive a harder bargain.

Other Divisions

Contracts with other divisions or types of publishers, such as mass market, college text, juvenile, and professional, differ in certain conventions, particularly with reference to advances and royalty rates. By and large, contracts are shorter and simpler and subsidiary rights play a minor role, but the basic elements of these contracts are indistinguishable from trade contracts.

Mass Market. Mass market publishers continue to increase their lists of originals, partly to offset the huge sums of money they have to pay in advances for best-sellers. The contract is basically the same as a trade contract, and while advances are also roughly competitive with trade books, the range is wider. For example, an advance for a literary novel can be as low as $1,000, whereas for a genre novel it can run as high as $5,000 to $15,000. The common royalty rate is 8 percent of list for the first 150,000 copies, 10 percent thereafter, though 6 percent to 8 percent (also after 150,000 copies) as well as a number of different permutations in this range is not out of line and equally common. In hard/soft arrangements, mass market royalties are generally slightly higher, such as to pay 10 percent on all copies.* An editor will not make an offer unless he or she can project minimum sales of 25,000 copies for the first year. Returns, incidentally, run much higher than for trade books, currently averaging more than 40 percent a year.

During the past 15 years book publishing has seen an implosion of major publishers through mergers and acquisitions, so that one parent house may have as many as a dozen imprints under its umbrella. For example, Random House now includes Knopf, Crown, Times Books, Pantheon, Schocken, and Clarkson Potter, as well as four mass market imprints—Ballantine, Del Rey, Fawcett, and Ivy—and yet another half-dozen hardcover imprints. Moreover, half of these imprints have their own trade

---

*I am indebted to The Authors Guild *Bulletin*'s "Annual Trade Book Contract Survey" for these and other advance and royalty statistics.

paperback lines, such as Vintage and Harmony. In such a complex stew of potential print formats (not to mention other media divisions, such as Audio and Electronic), it is important for an author to know whether she is authorizing a hard/soft deal—that is, the right to publish the mass market edition as well as the cloth edition and/or a trade paperback, and what other formats or media are being considered. The advantage is that the author will receive full royalties. She will not have to split paperback royalties as she normally would. The disadvantage is that if the book takes off and is quite successful in a cloth edition, the author may miss out on her half of a huge advance from a literary auction, which is often conducted by trade publishers for its clothbound titles. If the book has a strong potential for a long shelf life, such as a "how-to," the author may be better off in the long run to have the originating publisher issue the mass market or quality paperback edition. For a successful novel, an auction is generally the better gamble for the author. Some publishers are also interested in the bird-in-hand and generally decide it's in their own best interests to auction the book, with their own mass market division coming in as one of the bidders in order to recoup a portion of a large advance. The internal politics of publishing—each division is more committed to its own bottom line than to the whole corporation's—as well as a complex host of marketing factors and hunches go into each decision about whether to buy hard/soft or auction a book. It is not worthwhile to delve into this corporate whirlpool in this book, but if these arrangements are clear before signing the contract, or if you have a "right of approval" provision, you will at least have had a chance to voice your opinion.

For originals, the mass market publisher will sometimes also attempt to sell subsidiary rights and may try to license a trade publisher to issue a clothbound edition, postponing paperback publication until the cloth edition has been out for a year. In this instance, your split should range from 75/25 to 90/10 rather than the conventional 50/50. Royalties from export sales for mass market paperbacks are generally reduced by one-third to one-half.

Original Trade Paperbacks. With this format royalty rates and advances are still somewhat fluid. Quality paperbacks generally pay 6 percent of list for the first 15,000 or so copies, escalating to 7½ percent thereafter—or, just as commonly, a flat 7½ percent—though a request for an additional escalation to 10 percent after 25,000, 50,000, or even 100,000 is worth trying for. Advances are generally somewhat lower than for clothbound trade books; say, in the $6,000 to $10,000 range.

Juveniles. Again, the contracts are virtually the same as trade contracts, but some conventions change. Advances are generally lower, averaging $3,000 to $4,000 for a picture book text and $5,000 to $7,000 for a novel (the illustrator of a picture book generally gets 50 percent of the royalties and an advance equal to the author's). The common royalty rate is 10 percent of list for the first 20,000 copies; escalations to 12½ percent and then 15 percent after say, 35,000 and then 50,000 copies are much less common than they used to be. Still, you might as well try for them even though you should not expect or insist upon them.

Rising production costs and shrinking markets are now beginning to be reflected in royalty rates; some publishers may offer lower royalties, such as 8 percent, for the first printing. The "library edition" occasionally pays royalties based on *net* receipts. Try to delete this provision, since more than 80 percent of juvenile sales are to libraries. Royalty rates for young adult (YA) books are often set as for regular trade book royalties, and those rates should be requested (10 percent to 5,000, 12½ percent to 10,000, 15 percent thereafter). Reduction of royalties for subsequent small printings is conventional but should be resisted; no more than a 25 percent reduction of royalties (if semi-annual sales do not exceed 500 copies) should be accepted, since juveniles generally sell in smaller quantities over a longer period of time. All of these numbers pertain to *trade* children's books, as opposed to *mass market* books, such as Western Publishing's Golden Books or the mass printings of Muppets, Disney, and Ninja Turtle titles. Here, royalties can be as low as 2½ percent to 5 percent of list, but high-volume sales expectations—100,000- to 250,000-copy first printings—presumably make up for lower royalty rates.

Because the shelf life for a juvenile averages 5 to 20 years, in contrast to the six-months to one-year shelf life of most trade books, you might have an annuity if your juvenile is successful.

College Textbooks. Subsidiary rights for textbooks are negligible, and a 50/50 split is taken for granted. The major difference is in royalty rates, which are usually paid on the *net* receipts, the amount the publisher receives from the college bookstore. The usual textbook discount to the bookstore is 20 percent, so the royalty rate is based on 80 percent of the list price. However, some publishers have increased their discounts to 25 to 33 percent, and many, if not most, text houses now employ "net pricing." They let the bookstore decide what markup to use (although the 25 percent to 33 percent range is normal), and so what list price to charge. The increase stems partly as a result of legitimate gripes from college bookstore owners and managers, whose operating costs hover at 26 to 27 percent—that is, the bookstores often lose money selling textbooks. This lower discount, known as a "short discount" (as opposed to the "long discount" for trade books, which averages 47 percent), accounts for the absence of textbooks in regular bookstores. No bookstore owner feels she can afford to stock them, even though some of them would appeal to the general public.

The royalty rates and advances are more flexible than for trade books and are definitely negotiable. Because of the sparsity of agents in this field, the naïveté of academics about contracts, and the general feeling among them that publications are valuable primarily as a means of securing promotion or tenure—rather than as an important income-producing avocation—many authors accept whatever terms a textbook editor offers. Don't.

A clothbound textbook should command a 15-percent-of-net royalty, but many publishers will start at 10 percent and escalate in two stages to 15 percent. An author should initially ask for 15 percent of net escalating to 18 percent after the sale of 15,000 to 25,000 copies. This is particularly warranted for a basic text, that is, a book appropriate as the sole text for a standard undergraduate course. The author should negotiate in the 12-to-18-percent range and certainly accept no less than an escalation to 15 percent. Escalations can also be linked to sales in any given year: for instance, 15 percent of net receipts to 10,000 copies, 17½ percent thereafter for additional sales in that particular year, or 17½ percent in any given year that the book sells more than 10,000 copies. Rates for paperback text originals run a bit lower, in the 10-percent-escalating-to-15-percent range, as they do for anthologies.

Advances vary, and textbook editors are more inclined to use the "what do you need it for" spiel, even though advances are as much a convention in texts as they are in trade. Again, a fair advance depends on the potential market for the book, so that a hefty basic textbook for an undergraduate course may be worthy of a $25,000 to $50,000 advance, whereas a supplementary book, a graduate-level text, or an upper-division anthology may warrant no more than a $3,000 to $7,500 advance. Advances in the six figures for basic texts by academic superstars are no longer rare.

Most textbooks have their peak sales in the first or second year, primarily because of secondhand book sales, a flourishing business for the half-dozen major used textbook wholesalers, who now own almost half the large college bookstores in the United States. The profit margin on a used text far exceeds the standard 20 to 33 percent made on a new one, so these chains are very aggressive in buying and selling secondhand texts. A student might receive only $10 for a book for which he paid $40 four months previously; the bookstore will then resell it at $35. Since basic hardcover undergraduate texts average $40 to $50, it is understandable that most students will recycle rather than squirrel them away. This development has become a giant headache for text publishers, who find that their biggest customers are also their biggest competitors. Some few texts go on to become legendary perennials, such as Samuelson's *Economics*, which was first published in 1948 and is now in its fourteenth edition. Several other similarly famous living fossils, such as Fess's *Principles of Accounting* and Jansen's *History of Art*, have earned their authors millions of dollars over a 25- to 40-year period.

El-Hi Textbooks. These contracts are similar to—if more elaborate than—those of college text publishers, and the terms and clauses are usually less flexible, that is, there is less room for negotiation. Perhaps the reason is that there haven't been, nor do there seem to be, any agents operating in this genre. Advances, especially considering the huge sales potential, range from token to minimal. A high advance would generally not exceed $5,000.

Royalties, paid on net receipts, are equally modest, but the potential volume of sales can more than make up for this disparity. Elementary text royalties range from 4 to 6 percent, and can descend to as low as 1 to 2 percent for basal reader or math series (though sales here for a successful series can reach astronomical proportions). Some publishers now try to insist on a flat fee for the first edition; try to resist this stipulation or to limit it to the first (or the first and second) printing. Junior-high text royalties are now in the 2-to-5-percent range, as are those for high school texts. Incidentally, royalty escalations for el-hi contracts are not conventional, but that doesn't mean you shouldn't ask for them after the sale of, say, 50,000 copies. The royalties are usually split two, three, or four ways, since multiple authorship is much more common than not.

The revision clause is important here (and generally too restrictive in el-hi contracts). For a second edition you should attempt to write in a higher escalation, an additional advance, and try to make sure that you have the right to "approve" both the writing and financial arrangements in case you cannot or will not prepare it yourself. After all, a revision means that your book was successful and made a nice profit for the publisher. You should therefore have some more clout with the second edition, but you will have to negotiate it into the initial contract.

One important issue that is particularly relevant in the el-hi field is that books are often very heavily edited: Publishers can and will rework and rewrite manuscripts for readability, political correctness, and to fit their perceptions of the needs of the market. If this possibility unnerves you, consider requesting a provision such as: "Publisher agrees to submit to the Author(s), for his prior approval, which shall not be unreasonably withheld, the text of any substantive revisions." Or, as a fallback position, "to consult with the Author(s) with regard to any substantive revisions of the text."

Professional, Technical, and Scientific Books. As in college texts, subsidiary rights are negligible, except possibly for book club rights. More than 100 small to medium-size book clubs cater to professional and special interest groups, from lawyers to coin collectors, and the 50/50 share of revenue may be surprisingly high, considering that these "markets" have a much smaller base. Royalty rates are also based on net receipts, ranging from 8 to 18 percent, with or without escalators, and bookstore discounts generally range from 30 to 35 percent. More than 50 percent of the sales are from mail order, libraries, or overseas markets, and a reduction in royalty rates for these sales is common. Advances are generally low, ranging from nothing to $10,000, but they are nevertheless negotiable.

A Word to Translators

Translators have traditionally occupied the bottom rung of the financial ladder in publishing, although rates in recent years are improving. It is still common for translators to be paid a flat fee for books; the current rate for literary works ranges from a modest $45 per 1,000 words, up to $65, which is scarcely a living wage even for rapid and proficient translators. Technical works, however, may command as much as $75 per 1,000 words, and upward to $150 for legal, scientific, and banking books.

Some translators are now asking for—and getting—a "royalty override," that is, a small royalty, usually 1 percent of the list price for trade books. In this case the flat fee can be construed as an advance against royalties or, preferably, the royalty is paid in addition to the flat fee. Furthermore some translators are asking for—and receiving—a share of the subsidiary rights, especially book-club, paperback reprint, and sometimes British rights. Here you may want to ask for 10 percent of the net receipts. If *you* approach the publisher with a project, you are in a much stronger position and can negotiate upward from these figures; moreover, if the work is in the public domain (i.e., there is no royalty to be paid to an author), there is no reason for you not to ask for and get conventional author's royalties. Royalties and fees for translators are now so fluid that it is difficult to state the conventions; when in doubt, ask for more than you expect, since it's a lot easier to work downward than upward.

Also significant is the issue of billing, which you will want spelled out in your letter of agreement: Is your name to go on the jacket and/or the title pages, in the press release, and in advertising in which the author's name appears? (I would say yes to all of these.) And is the translation to be copyrighted in your name? (Yes again.) Reviewers and publishers have traditionally been notoriously deficient in giving adequate credit to translators—except perhaps for poetry and drama—but in recent years they have gradually been redressing this omission. Translators are well advised to write to The Translation Center* for a general description of its aims and services. This office was founded in 1972 with a grant from the N.E.A., and operates as a nonprofit clearinghouse between translators and publishers. Twice a year the center publishes a book-length magazine that contains translations of poetry and fiction. Prizes, awards, and fellowship competitions are listed in the magazine. You may call them up for free informal advice on publisher/author relations as well as on fees, royalties, letters of agreement, and other matters that arise in working with book or magazine publishers.

---

*The Translation Center, Columbia University, 412 Dodge Hall, New York, NY 10027.

The Last Word

Obviously there is no last word on contracts and negotiations. We have only skimmed the surface here, but many editors, agents, and publishers will disagree with some of my suggestions, guidelines, and interpretations. Let me emphasize again that virtually all clauses are negotiable and that I have addressed myself primarily to unagented authors who do not yet have a strong enough track record to make greater demands. An agent or professional writer will increase the ante and may insist on more deletions, insertions, and modification than have been discussed or suggested here.

Let me repeat also that a telephone call or a discussion in a restaurant is not the way to cement terms for a contract: There are too many details to consider, and it is too disconcerting a setting for a ruffled author in which to represent himself adequately or rationally. Get a blank contract, study it, make notes, and write your editor a letter.

The writer who has the inclination to know more about contracts and negotiations will find several additional references in the Selected Bibliography, but the best piece of advice I have to offer, for a writer who has published a book, is to join one of the several excellent writers organizations: The Authors Guild, the National Writers Union, Poets and Writers, Inc., or the ASJA. Members have access not only to a number of specific publications about contracts, but also to regular reports about publishing, such as those in The Authors Guild quarterly *Bulletin*, which is a source of up-to-date information on the publishing industry, as well as on many topics in this book. In different ways, these organizations lobby publishers (and Congress) to improve the writer's position by slowly but surely establishing industry "standards," by sharing with writers information about policy at specific houses or customary publishing practices, and by supporting or initiating legislation favorable to writers on matters concerning freedom of speech, copyright, libel, and so forth. Publishing is no longer the province of the Maxwell Perkinses or T. S. Eliots of yore, so writers are more than ever in need of professional organizations. I do not mean to disparage either the commitments or virtues of my colleagues, but merely to stress that publishing is big business, and that most of the key financial decisions have been taken over by executives who generally pay more attention to the bottom line than to the well-turned phrase.

4

How to Prepare a Final Manuscript

The tools I need for my work are paper, tobacco, food, and a little whiskey.
—WILLIAM FAULKNER

The ashtray is filled with cigarette butts, the eighth cup of coffee is sour in your mouth, your back is killing you from bending over the word processor for seven hours, but you feel like a tiger (or tigress); you've just finished your book. Now you are ready to think about sending it off to a publisher or an agent. Maybe you have a contract or a "nibble" from an editor who—because of your previously sent proposal—has asked to see the final version of the manuscript. Or maybe you just sat down and wrote the book, deciding to worry about publication when it was finished.

The revised version was prepared after weeks or months of reading chapters to your patient spouse or after getting feedback from friends or colleagues. The manuscript is a mess: Pages are cut in half and pasted together, coffee stains decorate several chapters, scribbles you can barely decipher fill the margins, and the page numbers were fouled up somewhere around chapter three. It's time for the final typing, and the preparation of a professional-looking manuscript.

The Mechanical Basics

First things first: If you don't already own one, I strongly urge you to get a computer or a word processor. A perfectly adequate dedicated word processor—which can store your book on disks—can be bought for about $400, printer included. A satisfactory computer and printer, on the other hand, will cost about $1,000. Although most publishers have no difficulty in translating Macintosh disks to MS-DOS format, it's probably still better to use a computer compatible with MS-DOS to begin with, in case your publisher wants to set type from your disks. If you buy a dot matrix printer—fancy laser printers are nice, but they cost about three times as much as a dot matrix—it should be a 24-pin model; some less-expensive models produce "draft" quality that publishers and editors may refuse to read. Better still, shop around for used equipment, which can be purchased for about 30 percent less than new models. Even cheaper machines can be found, but equipment that is more than a few years old may be obsolete, and it can be difficult to locate parts to repair them with, or software to run on them.

Most contracts demand two copies of a neatly typed manuscript, and you'll give your editor a pleasant surprise if you actually submit two copies. Most authors don't, but it's useful for the editor to have; she'll use the extra copy for design and costing. Of course, if you don't give her two copies, she'll just make a photocopy for the purpose. Strictly speaking, she could charge you for the copy, although this has never happened in my experience.

If you're using a pin-feed printer, tear off the edges and separate the sheets before submitting the manuscript. Editors do not appreciate being given the task of tearing the perforations on a 300-page manuscript.

You probably already know that the manuscript should be typed (or, to use the computer term, *printed*) on one side of the paper only, that it should be double-spaced with margins of 1½ inches all around, and that it should be all printed on the same printer in the same typeface all the way through. But let's reaffirm those principles anyway. Remember that bibliography, quotations, notes, and captions should also be double-spaced, and that you should leave about a third of the page blank at the beginning of the introduction, each chapter, and any appendixes. Number the manuscript consecutively start to finish (starting with 1 for the title page). Starting over at "1" for each chapter is not acceptable.

Almost anyone who has used a computer has been tempted to add type flourishes like italics and boldface throughout a manuscript, or to push the button that causes the margins to be justified on the right. Resist these temptations. The design of the book is a complex matter best left to the experts—the book designers employed by the publisher. It is enough for the author to respect the usual style conventions (see the following section) and let the designers and copyeditors do their work.

Most publishers now will ask that a floppy disk—which, by the way, must be identical to the hard copy manuscript of the book—be submitted along with the hard copy. This is useful for the publisher because the disk can be used for setting type, saving many keystrokes. It costs the author almost nothing. A floppy disk costs a few cents, and making a copy of the disk on which you've saved your manuscript (you have, of course, made several floppy disk copies of the manuscript, and stored them in different places) takes only a minute. Although it saves the publisher money, and gives nothing to the author, still only the most petulant of authors would refuse to send one.

But now there is a new development. Some publishers are asking authors to insert "type codes" in their disks. These are the computer codes, typed in one at a time on the disk, that indicate where italics, boldface, font size, indentation, and such are supposed to go. This can take hours of your time, which you may not want to give away for free. A careful discussion of such requirements before the contract is signed is therefore important. Understand, however, that a publisher can have an 80,000-word manuscript keyboarded, with type codes inserted,

for as little as $1,000 by exporting the labor to foreign countries.
So when you discuss compensation for your keyboarding work,
there isn't a lot of money to be shared between you and the publisher.

Reference Shelf

Many publishers, particularly the bigger houses, print their
own style guide, which they will send you along with a contract.
Obviously, unless you have a contract before you prepare your
final revision, it won't help you. Most writers have a small collection of reference books—you can't get by without at least a
good dictionary. I recommend adding a thesaurus and a handbook for the mechanics of grammar and usage. Many good ones
are available; you may still have a copy of one from your high
school or college days. My favorite is Strunk and White's *The Elements of Style* (third edition, New York: Macmillan Publishing
Co., 1979), a classic because of its amusingly pithy tone and concise rules. But it's a bit short; you should have something more
substantial.

For complete coverage, and to learn all the ground rules in
manuscript preparation—from style to book production and
printing—you might consider buying one of the standard style
manuals. Three well-known and highly respected manuals are:

The Chicago Manual of Style, 14th edition. Chicago: University of Chicago Press, 1993.

*U.S. Government Printing Office Manual of Style and Us-
age*. Washington, D.C.: U.S. Government Printing Office,
1984.

Thomas Warren, *Words Into Type*, 4th edition. Englewood
Cliffs, N.J.: Prentice Hall, 1994.

In any case, you are probably preparing the manuscript without the publisher's style guide, but since most of them adopt
some slight variation of a standard stylebook practice, you are

on safe ground if you follow any reasonable format. The copyeditor may ask you to change your footnote style or placement, for instance, to conform to house standards, but if the conversion is only a few hours' work, the editor will probably have it done for you.

The Basic Arrangement

A manuscript is divided into three parts: the front matter (sometimes called preliminaries), the text proper, and the back matter (sometimes called end matter).

Front Matter. The front matter will vary considerably, depending on the type of book, but can consist of any or all of the following:

Half title (the title of the book without the author's name)

Card page (the list of books by the same author)

Title page (with your name and address 3 inches below the title)

Copyright page

Dedication

Epigraph

Table of contents

List of illustrations

List of tables

List of abbreviations

Preface or foreword

Acknowledgments

Introduction

All of this front matter (except the introduction) should be numbered in lowercase roman numerals in the upper right-hand corner.

Preface, foreword, and *introduction* are terms sometimes mistakenly used interchangeably. The preface is the author's account of the scope and purpose of the book, how it came to be written, and often includes the acknowledgments unless they are extensive. The foreword, frequently written by someone other than the author, is a kind of send-off for the book, suggesting the contents in a general way (sometimes relating it to other books in the field) and, ideally, stimulating the reader to proceed further. The introduction is concerned specifically with the contents of the book. The preface and/or foreword may precede the contents page and the introduction follow, but this varies depending on the book and house style. Most of these minor decisions on positioning take place "in house" so let's not quibble about them.

Text. Begin numbering your text with Arabic numerals on the first page of the introduction, numbering the pages consecutively in the upper right-hand corner, from beginning to end, *not* chapter by chapter. Chapter numbers should be placed in the upper center of the page in uppercase roman numerals. It's a good idea to type your last name, title (abbreviated to one or two words), and chapter number in the far upper left margin on *every page* of the text. (This is a process made considerably easier by using the "header" function of any good word processing program. It simplifies retrieval of pages that have mysteriously migrated into some other editor's office.) Chapter titles are typed on the first page of each new chapter, about one-third down the page; use upper- *and* lowercase—the designer will decide on the style for these and other titles, headings, and subheadings.

If you are writing nonfiction, you will probably have subheadings in each chapter. Subheads should not be underlined (ditto for chapter titles) and should be typed with "initial capitals" only, meaning that the first letter of each word is capitalized except for prepositions, articles, and coordinate conjunctions (do not number or alphabetize these subheads). If you have major and minor subheads in a chapter ("A" level and "B" level), center the major subhead on the page, and begin the minor subhead flush with the margin. If it begins a paragraph, put a period after it and skip two spaces. Skip five or six lines if your subhead begins a new section.

If you cross-reference to other pages in the text, type one, two, or three dashes (space for the final printed page numbers) and write the proper manuscript page number in the margin, *in pencil* (as with all other handwritten notations). Try to avoid cross-references as much as possible, particularly of the "as I mentioned before" variety; they are usually unnecessary if your reader is reading carefully (let's be optimistic) and they increase typesetting costs considerably.

Back Matter. After the text proper you may have one or more appendices, footnotes by chapter (we'll get to notes later), a bibliography, a glossary of terms, and an index of titles or authors or both (the subject index is prepared after the manuscript goes into proof). The back matter is listed with page numbers on the contents page.

Appendices are less popular than they used to be and should be used only if necessary—not to pad the book with odds and ends of research that do not fit into the text. Documents, laws, charts, tables, or maps that are either too extensive or do not illuminate the text usually belong in an appendix.

The reference notes—footnotes numbered in the text on a chapter-by-chapter basis—are now usually printed with the back matter, though they can be placed at the end of each chapter. When you submit your manuscript, type the footnotes for each chapter on separate pages, numbering them consecutively (by chapter), and place them at the end of the text proper or after the appendix, if you have one (we'll get to the complete story on footnotes later).

The bibliography will contain at least a listing of your footnote sources, this time alphabetically either by title or author. It may be broken down into subject divisions as well. If you wish to add further suggested readings or books on the subject not specifically documented in the text, it's better to discuss this with your editor before you go to the trouble of preparing it. Follow a consistent style—author, title, publisher, and publication date—and double space throughout. An editor will be (justifiably) irritated by a single-spaced bibliography, or one that is inconsistent within itself. Editing such a document is almost impossible without completely retyping it.

Glossaries are helpful in technical books or those with many foreign words in them. Words are arranged in alphabetical order, each on a separate line and followed by its definition.

More than 90 percent of the trade books published do not require more complex front or end matter than has already been mentioned. If your book falls into the minority category, it's time for you to buy one of the major style manuals.

Extracts. Any quotation that is set off from the text is called an extract. A short quotation of up to two lines of poetry and up to ten lines of prose can remain incorporated into the text. Merely set off the prose and poetry with quotation marks; if you are quoting two lines of verse, separate them with a slash. Larger quotations are indented on both sides and triple-spaced from the preceding and following text. If you wish to delete part of a quotation, use three ellipsis dots (periods) in the middle of a sentence, or four at the end. Do not use quotation marks to begin or end an indented extract; if they appear in the quoted material, use a 'single' quotation mark. With poetry, duplicate the appearance of the original as closely as possible. Then make sure you triple-check your version against the original (ditto when you receive proofs). If you are finicky about it, and you should be, don't take your quotation of poetry, for instance, from an anthology, but go to the collected works or some similar scholarly, original, or fastidious source. If you make any changes in the original—adding a comment or italicizing—either point it out in the preceding text, in brackets within the quote, in parentheses after the quotation, or in a footnote.

Footnotes. There are basically two kinds of footnotes: a discursive reference to something in the text, or a citation for a source. Conventionally, the former is placed at the bottom of the page, and the latter at the end of the chapter or the end of the book. The various styles and complexities of footnotes are legion, and you ought to consult a style guide if you make substantial use of them in your text. As the University of Chicago's *Manual of Style* (widely used in publishing) points out: "No one manual can hope to protect editor and author from every thorn encountered in the thicket of scholarly documentation." Amen. I personally find superfluous footnotes annoying; most readers do. Try as much as possible to incorporate those discursive references into the text, or else drop them completely. The discursive reference is indicated by an asterisk and a second one on the same page by a dagger. (Some word processing programs can produce daggers. Just use two asterisks if yours can't.) There are two additional symbols, but if you put three or four symbols on the page your reader may stop reading right there, so I will not tempt you by listing them. The more powerful word processing programs now commonly in use can put footnotes neatly at the bottom of the page. If yours doesn't, put the note on a separate page marked "23a" (or whatever) in the upper right-hand corner, and title the page "Footnote for page 23"; place the page directly after page 23.

Numbered footnotes, usually citations for sources, are placed either at the bottom of the page or on a separate page (or pages), preferably at the end of the manuscript. Use a new set of numberings for each chapter's footnotes, titling the first page "Footnotes to Chapter 1," etc. The number in the text itself is placed a half space above the line on which it appears and outside the period, though it is sometimes more sensible to put the note in the middle of the sentence—common sense will usually serve you here. Avoid footnoting either chapter titles or subheads. If cited books, articles, and poems are to be included in a bibliography, then an abbreviated version in the footnote will suffice (e.g., A. B. Keith, *Indian Logic*, p. 24). This would appear in your bibliography as "Keith, Arthur Berriedale. *Indian Logic and Antomism.* Oxford: Oxford University Press, 1921." I won't go into the matter of *ibid.* and *op. cit.* except to repeat that substantial footnoting is best left to scholarly and technical books, or textbooks. Of most importance for your manuscript is *consistency;* decide in advance which style of footnoting you will use, and stick to it throughout the manuscript. Use the fullest possible documentation in footnotes, so that whatever style the house employs, you may only have to delete matter later rather than add it—a much more time-consuming task. The same advice regarding consistency holds true for spelling, punctuation, and capitalization.

Tables and Illustrations. Tables differ from illustrations: They are typeset rather than reproduced from artwork. Illustrations include many different kinds of material: charts, graphs, maps, photos, paintings, and line drawings. Let's examine them separately, since they are listed and arranged separately in your manuscript. Only one copy of these is necessary for the publisher.

Tables are typed or pasted on the same size paper as your manuscript. Regardless of size, each one should be pasted on a separate page and numbered consecutively throughout the book: for example, Table 3, not chapter by chapter, if you have less than, say, six. For more than six tables, I recommend incorporating chapter references, (e.g., Table 6.1, 6.2, 6.3, and so on). Always refer to your table by number in the text. At the top of the page, directly beneath the table number, goes the title or caption, which should be extremely brief:

> *Not:* Amount of money earned per year by freelance writers
> on a state-by-state basis.
> *But:* Yearly Freelance Writer Income
> (By state)

Just facts, no description or comments. Tables should be placed in a separate envelope, along with a numbered listing of them. (Duplicate the copy from your front matter.)

The best method of indicating the placement of your table or illustration to the designer and copyeditor is to type or draw two horizontal lines across the page and place the instructions within it.

Table 6.2 about here

Since the margins will soon be filled with copyeditor's or designer's notes, your own instructions may be confusing or overlooked there. Avoid the following: "As we see in Table 6.2 . . ." It implies the appearance of your table or illustration directly following the colon. In all likelihood, only short extracts or formulae will follow directly after the colon. Artwork, because of layout and page makeup requirements, rarely appears exactly where you want it to. This is the reason for referring to your table or illustration by number in the text.

A complete one-page table on 8½" × 11" typing paper will just about reduce to the average book page size (approximately 6" × 9"). The making of tables is a story in itself, for which I refer you to one of the standard style manuals.

If you have more than one kind of illustration, such as charts, maps, and plates (photos or engravings), then your list of illustrations for the front matter should be broken down by category and a copy of this list enclosed in the separate envelope in which you place the illustrations. They should be numbered in the sequence in which they appear in the manuscript (keeping in mind that more than six should be numbered by chapter, e.g., Map 6.1, 6.2, and 6.3), although they may go unnumbered in the book—as movie stills frequently are, for instance. At the top of the page, the caption or title of the illustration is typed in:

Map 10. The Battle of Waterloo

Underneath the illustration, you may type in the legend, the explanation, usually in the form of a sentence or two, which illustrates the point of what you are reproducing. In print, caption and legend may be run on together, or only one or the other used. This decision and other related problems, such as placement, manner of reproduction, and the size of final illustrations should be, are all determined in conference with your editor.

Keep a separate list of photos or original artwork (what? another list!), numbering them consecutively. The back of each piece of artwork should identify it by number and caption, but never write on the back of a photograph—this can mar the glossy finish on the front, or allow ink to bleed through the paper. It's best to label photos and other artwork with one of those yellow Post-it stickers, preferably taped down to make sure it doesn't fall off. All artwork from which the publisher will reproduce should be protected by cardboard when you send it, and not folded, spindled, or mutilated—do not hold them together with paper clips, pins, staples, or whatever, for obvious reasons. Use rubber bands.

Whether or not you secure permission for an illustration, a "credit line" (statement of the source) is either necessary or appropriate. There are a variety of possibilities as to where they will appear in the book. For your manuscript it is sufficient to identify the source on the list provided with the separate envelope of illustrations. Just as for tables, indicate with two horizontal lines and a note therein where you think the illustrations should be placed.

Permissions and Copyright

The purpose of copyright is to grant the publisher or the author the exclusive right to control the publication of the author's work for a specific period of time. Congress passed a major revision of the law in 1978—they'd been working on it for more than 20 years. As you can imagine, the provisions of the law are lengthy and extremely complex, and many of them concern such matters as jukeboxes, cable television, record royalties, and other issues that have little to do with authors.* We will confine our discussion to several features that are pertinent to writers. It should not be necessary to add a disclaimer, but we will any-

---

*Circular 1, *Copyright Basics*, a 12-page pamphlet published in 1992 by the Copyright Office, is thorough and lucid on matters concerning writers. Circular 4 on copyright fees and Circular Rlc on registration procedures are also useful. Circular R2b contains bibliographies on the subject of copyright. All are available free of charge from the Library of Congress, Washington, DC 20559; you can also call to request them (202-707-8180).

way: What follows is not a complete discussion of copyright law, nor even a primer on the law for all authors, and it certainly does not constitute legal advice. It is rather a brief discussion that offers some practical guidelines for working writers.

Copyright protection is now extended to 50 years after the author's death, which conforms with international copyright provisions.* Previously, copyright had been for a period of 28 years after the date of publication, renewable for another 28 years, but in 1962 Congress extended protection to works whose copyrights would otherwise have expired in that year while they worked on renewing the law. Eventually, the new bill extended protection to 75 years, provided the copyright was renewed. A provision passed in 1992, however, makes this renewal optional. The term of copyright in works published or copyrighted between January 1, 1964, and December 31, 1977, is now 75 years whether or not a renewal filing has been made. There are some advantages, nevertheless, in renewing, especially in cases in which the original copyright holder is deceased, but the practical effect for writers is that a work published in, say, 1966 will not be in the public domain until 2041—whether the copyright was renewed in 1994 or not. Unpublished manuscripts, including letters, diaries, and other documents, also are protected. Recent court decisions have strengthened the protection surrounding unpublished works and writers should be especially wary of quoting even small extracts from them without gaining permission.

Currently (that is, as of 1994), you may quote any kind of material published prior to 1919 (or from any U.S. Government Printing Office publication†) without securing permission. After 1919, the doctrine of "fair use" determines how much material you may quote without securing permission. Some books published between 1919 and 1964 may not have had their copyrights renewed, and are therefore public domain, but don't assume that

---

*In fact, copyright terms in the European Community will probably be extended to 70 years after the author's death.

†Only a few works produced under government grants may be copyrighted and will contain such a notice.

they are—quote from them freely only if you have initiated a copyright search to determine their status. Some publishers will tell you that you can quote up to 500 words from a full-length book without permission, but this is just a rule of thumb, and not a legal principle. In fact, depending on which 500 words you quote and how you intend to use them, you may well need permission. "Fair use," is, in part, a commonsense principle: You can use material without paying for it only if it's fair to the copyright owner to do so. Quoting 500 words of a novel in a book review would, under this theory, undoubtedly be fair use. On the other hand, if General Motors used the same 500 words of the same novel in an advertisement for a Cadillac, this would not be fair use. Nor would it be fair use if you used 500 words of a book in a way that would help your book compete with the one you are quoting.

The number of words that constitutes fair use also depends on the circumstances. If you quote even two short lines from a T. S. Eliot poem, you will need permission to do so from Harcourt, Eliot's publisher—even if you just want to use it as an epigraph. On the other hand, there may be circumstances under which quotes as long as several thousand words could be considered fair use—quoting a published scientific study, for example, in another scientific study designed to prove or disprove the original study's conclusions.

The new copyright law specifies that unpublished work may also be quoted under fair use doctrine, and lists four factors that should be considered in determining fair use for both unpublished and published material:

1. the purpose and character of the new use, including whether such use is of a commercial nature or for nonprofit educational purposes;
2. the nature of the copyrighted work;
3. the amount and substantiality of the portion used in relation to the copyrighted work as a whole; and
4. the effect of the use on the potential market for, or value of, the copyrighted work.

If in doubt, it is usually best to write for permission. Remember, you have promised the publisher that nothing in your book violates copyright laws. This warranty is legally enforceable, and you can be held responsible if you fail to live up to it. Also, remember that, human nature being what it is (and lawyers being what they are), a permission costs much less to secure before a book has been published than after the book has come out and someone notices that you've violated his or her copyright. Every publishing house has its own policy and guidelines on these issues; consult your editor.

For photos,* songs, more than a line of verse, maps, and tables, you are obliged to write for permission. Write to the *original* publisher or the copyright holder who is listed on the copyright page of the book; do not write to the paperback publisher that is reprinting the book. If you address your letter to the "Rights and Permissions Department" of the original publisher, they will forward it to the author, his estate, or his agent if the publisher no longer controls permissions. Be explicit about the material you wish to quote: title, passage, page number(s), and number of words. You probably won't have to pay for any incidental quotations or extracts, but you need to identify the source of the quotation on the copyright page, having asked the copyright holders for their preferred wording.

Be sure to secure permission when quoting popular songs; music publishers are notoriously possessive about their rights to song lyrics, and quoting popular songs without permission can be disastrous. Getting permission to use them can be very expensive, and when you hear the fee, you may want to consider whether that lyric from Paul McCartney's song is really essential to the development of your character, or whether some other device might serve the purpose just as well.

If you are preparing an anthology or any kind of work that draws heavily on copyrighted material, whether it is written or illustrative matter, permissions fees will generally have to be

---

*Some writers and publishers now consider a modest number of movie stills and film-clip blowups as being covered by the doctrine of fair use.

paid. Your editor will discuss with you the extent of the rights you should secure—that is, both the territory requested and the manner of publication (paperback, textbook, clothbound, etc.), because the amount of the fee will depend on these variables. Your contract will state a permissions budget, which is usually structured as additional advance against royalties. In other words, the publisher advances you money to pay for the permissions, but ultimately you pay for them out of future royalties. This is good motivation to try hard to obtain the lowest possible permissions fees. The compiler of the anthology should begin writing for permission as soon as a contract is signed. Sometimes a copyright holder is difficult to track down, and many are tardy in responding to requests, which may require follow-up letters. The original copies of the letters or forms that grant permission should be turned in to the publisher with the final manuscript; authors should always photocopy a set for their own files. It is useful to identify the permission letters by writing the manuscript page number where the excerpt appears at the top of the letter.

Preparing an Anthology

Not every manuscript consists primarily of original typewritten pages. The anthology or collection of previously published material is common in trade, textbook, and el-hi publishing. Sometimes referred to as a cut-and-paste job, an anthology only *looks* like an easy way to make a book. In practice, it presents considerable permissions problems; and, if not assembled accurately and carefully, it can become far more difficult to copyedit and produce than the average manuscript.

In serving as the editor of other writers' materials, you assume the obligation to respect their messages and their rights. In addition, you face the task of gathering material from many disparate sources and making certain that it appears in clear, legible form in your finished manuscript. Permissions problems aside, then, the primary objective in putting together an anthology is to avoid the kinds of typographical errors that will invariably be introduced if you retype the material. Whenever possible use original tear sheets from your sources. If none can be obtained, then you must rely on photocopying or photography.

Let us assume that your anthology will contain articles selected from readily available mass magazines and journals or books. Purchase enough copies so that you will have two complete versions of each chapter or article. You need two copies, obviously, because in pasting up you lose the reverse page. Make photocopies or disassemble the magazines or journals and cut up the pages, then assemble the individual articles. Cut away all the advertising or extraneous matter; if an article appears two or three columns to the page, carefully separate these and keep them in sequence. Paste the resulting pages or columns on $8\frac{1}{2}'' \times 11''$ bond sheets, leaving ample margins at top and bottom; number these sheets lightly in pencil, per article, as you create them. If you don't have rubber cement, use "magic" cellophane tape that can be written on with a pencil. Never use regular cellophane tape or staples.

If you're working with materials that are still in copyright but 10 or 20 years old, or if you're taking selections from bound books, tear sheets may not be appropriate. Instead, you have to utilize the copier. For books that cannot be removed from the library you will have to use the coin machine there, but you can probably save some money (and certainly some time and effort) by taking the books to a copy center if you can check them out. Make sure you get $8\frac{1}{2}'' \times 11''$ copies. Inspect each of these carefully, and be realistic: If you can't make out every character or symbol, the copyeditor can't either, and the typesetter will refuse to look at such material. Try again, or try a different machine. Be especially careful when photocopying sections from large, thick books; in such reproduction, the inside edges tend to blur and fade out. If you're taking materials from rare or oversized books, you may have to find someone who can use a 35mm camera and ask him or her to photograph the pages you need. The resulting prints should be examined carefully for size and legibility. One more thing: Go through the pile of photocopied pages and make sure there are none missing—don't leave it to your editor or copyeditor to notice it for you.

When you've assembled the articles in series according to your proposed table of contents, go over each article carefully and edit it. That's your job; you're functioning not as author but as editor of other people's writings. You can't change what they say, but you can, if you wish, shorten the selections—if you do, mention this and include a copy when you write for permission. Use dots (ellipses) to indicate cuts of a sentence or less (four for a complete sentence, three for part of a sentence) and line breaks for deletions longer than a paragraph. You should also assume the responsibility of doing some mechanical editing. Cut off or cross out anything—advertisements, running heads, page numbers, display type—that appears in the original but should not appear in the anthology you're creating. If the articles you've chosen are taken from 20 different sources, chances are that the original authors will be listed in 20 different ways. In your book, you don't want a headnote that gives the complete details of Margaret Mead's academic career, followed by an article that says only "by Barry Commoner." If you want headnotes for both, you've got to provide one for Commoner. Far better to eliminate such biographical matter, or present it briefly at the front of the book on a "Contributors" page. Incidentally, it would be your responsibility to create and type up such material, not the copyeditor's. Similarly, in the front matter of your manuscript you should give the complete data concerning your acknowledgments and permissions.

Unless you and your editor have discussed the necessity of doing so, avoid making stylistic changes in the individual articles—changing British spelling and punctuation to American, for example. If your articles have footnotes in the originals, these will probably vary considerably in format. One may list city, publisher, and date in a bibliographic reference; another may list only city and date. Discuss with your editor whether to regularize these or to let the discrepancies stand. And speaking of notes, remember that if you cut material that includes footnotes, you must go through the remainder of the articles and adjust both the numbers that appear in the text and their corresponding numbers at the foot of the page or end of the article. If, in your anthology, you annotate the material yourself, type up your notes on separate pages and interleave them with the mounted tear sheets, or place them at the end of each selection.

In a few rare instances you may be unable to produce a good, legible copy of a page or pages. Do not take the necessary retyping job casually. Even at the hands of the best typist the copy may shift slightly in a hundred minute ways. Any newly typed copy of previously published material should be proofread carefully, character for character, line for line, before you incorporate it in the main manuscript. When ready for submission in its finished form, the manuscript will, of course, contain some original, typewritten pages—the front matter, possibly your own introductions or headnotes for the individual pieces. Treat these in the manner described earlier in this chapter.

So far you've created only one copy of the anthology, yet you are going to need three: an original and a copy to forward to the publisher, and an editor's or author's copy for yourself. Back to the photocopying machine. Now the wisdom of avoiding staples becomes apparent. Pages containing them cannot be loaded into an automatic copier and must be fed into the machine by hand, a page at a time. When you get them back, or if you make the extra copies yourself, it's time for more scrutiny. Look at all the pages of your new copies. A photocopy of photocopied material can often be so light as to be illegible, though some machines have a "dark" button which improves its reproduction. If copies are too light or illegible, you must track down more tear sheets or better photocopies and repeat the process just described for each of your additional manuscripts. Remember, if what you send to the publisher can't be read, it won't get worked on; similarly, if the copy you keep for yourself is illegible in places, you will have a hard time working with your editor and copyeditor when they send you their queries.

One last *caveat:* If the articles you select for your anthology contain *photographic* illustrations, do not bother to paste these into your manuscript except for reference. They may look great to you, but they are of no use at all to the publisher. If you want them to appear in your finished book, you will have to correspond with the original publisher or magazine and obtain glossy prints of the photographs you want to appear in your book. If there are black-and-white line drawings or diagrams in the original and you provide tear sheets, they will satisfy your editor; if the drawings you submit are photocopies, they cannot be used for producing the book. Either they must be redrawn, or, as with the photographs, you should contact the original publisher and inquire about obtaining photostats of the drawings. If your anthology is to include a large number of either drawings or photographs, bring this to your editor's attention while you're still in the selection and planning stages. He or she can provide suggestions that may save you considerable labor, expense, or both.

Doing a Revision

Let's jump ahead for a moment and assume you've already published a book. It's nonfiction, and it's sold well because it contains the latest information on the subject. But in two or three years new developments in the field begin to make what you've written seem a bit dated. Sales have tapered off, too, while newer competing books on the same subject have begun to appear. It's still a promising market, so your editor suggests you revise the book. The kind of manuscript you're expected to produce will be similar to an anthology manuscript. It will contain new typewritten material interleaved with printed tear sheets from the first edition. The main technical problem in preparing a manuscript of this sort is knowing how and when to change anything in the old typeset material. And when not to.

The lines and paragraphs in a book are reusable. The publisher's strategy in proposing a second edition depends in part on his workers photographing this type and moving it around within the revised book. While you're negotiating the revision, find out if the company intends to reset the type of the entire book. This is rare, but it might be done for a book with very little text but a great many illustrations—a children's book, for example. If the type is to be reset, you will have considerable freedom in rewriting and making changes. In most instances, however, the company expects you to rewrite and revise only certain agreed-upon passages or subjects, leaving considerable blocks of type, or even entire chapters, untouched.

Assembling the Manuscript for Revision. You must convert the book pages back into manuscript form, with type on only one side of the page. To do this, obtain two copies of the latest printing of the book. If in doubt about the number of that printing, consult your editor. When you have the right books, use a razor-bladed knife to remove their covers. Cut or carefully tear the pages out of their bindings in order to produce two stacks of identical pages.

Paste or tape these pages on individual sheets of 14- or 20-pound 8½″ × 11″ bond paper, following the pagination of the book. Paste down page 1 from the first stack, page 2 from the second stack, and so on. If the pages of your book are 8½″ × 11″ to begin with, don't bother taping them to blank sheets. Simply use a pencil to cross out alternate sides until you have a complete set of pages in sequence on one side only. If your book pages are larger than 8½″ × 11″, you must cut columns of type from each page and mount these in proper sequence, one to a sheet.

Special planning must go into the process just described if your book contains numerous tables or illustrations. Remember that when you created the manuscript for the first edition, you had to make stacks of different elements that were going into the books—figures, graphs, photographs, maps, tables—and indicate approximately where you wanted them to appear in the text. Now you're reversing that process. And you may find that the numbers you gave to your photographs the first time around were used for in-house reference only, and dropped from the actual book. This is a common practice for nontechnical works. Before you begin to cut and tape, look through both copies of the books you obtained, and make certain everything has a number. If it doesn't, whatever it is, give it one—in both copies.

If your book has a lot of photographs, and they appear on glossy paper, bunched up at intervals throughout the work, they're in *signature* form, and relatively easy to locate. Diagrams or drawings may appear virtually anywhere. In either case, if they lack numbers assign them numbers by chapter: Figure 3.1, 3.2, and so on. As you go through your disassembled pages and encounter these figures or tables or other elements, tape them to sheets of white paper and make separate stacks of them off to one side. When complete, these should be placed at the end of the manuscript; they are an integral part of it, but they do not carry manuscript page numbers. (Such a series of taped-up, printed photographs, for example, will be for reference only, but it will prove invaluable to anyone working with the actual negatives.) Each time you extract a table or drawing, there will be a "hole" or sometimes even an entire blank page in the typeset material you're remounting. Don't skip over these. Where such holes appear, write "Figure 5.18 about here," with a line above and below it, just as you did when you were putting together the first-edition manuscript.

In preparing a revision, the object is not to lose or misplace anything you might want to keep. Take the renumbering business seriously. The ease with which you will shortly be adding new tables or taking out old diagrams depends on how accurately you can identify and alter such series of elements. Incidentally, when you're making separate stacks of artwork, remember that the captions go with the figures; they move together. When you've attended to all such matters, and you're satisfied that the two books have been converted to a single, coherent manuscript, the next step is to make a photocopy of what you've just assembled.

Take into account the various kinds of copiers available in your vicinity and select the one that will produce the best, clearest copies. During your first visit you'll need to make only one copy of the pasted-up material. When you get home, put that stack of original pages away for safekeeping. Do not write or mark on it, since you may discover a need for more clear copies of certain pages or passages later on.

Revising the Manuscript. If you've kept a corrections file for your book's latest printing, transfer to your photocopied set of pages all the notations you've been saving that ask for appropriate and necessary changes. The process is very similar to that of correcting or changing proofs, and you are expected to use the same proofreader's symbols. (This process is explained more fully in Chapter 6.) Whatever you write on these pages, be sure to respect a margin of at least a half-inch on all sides of the 8½″ × 11″ sheet. You do not want anything to appear faded or illegible when you photocopy these pages again after finishing with the revision.

Similarly, if you have been keeping a revision file, get it out and review its marked copy and its notes and enclosures before you turn to your word processor. Rewriting and revision are creative processes and not within the province of this book. Here your own writing habits will guide you, along with whatever understanding you have developed with your editor about what is to be rewritten or changed.

When you identify a passage that should be deleted entirely, simply draw a line around it (i.e., enclose it within a box) and an *X* through it. Draw an arrow from the last line of text you want to keep to the point where the text resumes. Continue the line of the arrow to the next page, if necessary. If you decide to rewrite a line or two, do it in the margin; the same goes for changing words or phrases.

Minimizing Changes. You have a right to mark typographical, grammatical, and factual errors, or anything else that will clarify a scrambled or obscure passage. You do not have a right to change anything that catches your fancy. It might be tempting to rewrite or reword something you have decided doesn't suit you, even though you and your editor agreed to it in the first edition. Don't do it. Such requests will be overruled if they do not fall within the agreed-upon limits and needs of the revision.

Adding New Material. If you want to add three new paragraphs totaling 100 words at a point in the middle of what is now book page 10, simply type these out on a separate sheet, label it 10A, and write "Insert 10A goes here" with an appropriate caret (∧) at that point on page 10. Additional pages become 10B,

10C, and so on. At the bottom of the last page in any such series, write "Go to page 11" or whatever page you decide should follow page 10 (11 may have been removed already).

When you're satisfied with the revision of the text proper, go through the manuscript a few more times to check and readjust all numerical sequences—such as those of footnotes, figures, or picture captions—that may have been interrupted by the changes just made. You may have new permissions to obtain (and thus new credit lines on the acknowledgments page), new diagrams to prepare, new definitions for the glossary or out-of-date titles to be removed from the bibliography. You may also have to provide a new preface to the second edition. Treat all such material as inserts, and don't renumber the entire manuscript. The original page numbers—as much as you have been able to preserve of them—will be useful guides to the production workers whose task it will be to salvage as much type from your original book as possible. When everything is finally the way you want it, put your last name and the book's short title on each page. Having a rubber stamp with your name on it would be helpful at this point.

On your second trip to the copying machine, make the two copies to send to the publisher. It's all right if the images of the existing type look a bit faded this time, since type will not be set directly from those pages. Everything else, though, should be clear and legible, especially your marginal changes.

Some Additional Tips

If your manuscript contains uncommon foreign words (particularly those written in other than the Latin alphabet), mathematical symbols, unusual names, unorthodox spellings, chemical symbols, and such, then prepare a separate sheet of them to which you draw specific attention. The same is true if you purposely "mispell," misname, misquote, or have an unconventional preference in usage. Be consistent throughout the manuscript if you use certain words or names the spelling of which is open to question (e.g., Shakespeare, Shakspeare, Shakespere). Foreign words are always italicized by underscoring, except for those in common use.

Try to avoid word breaks on the right-hand margin (for the typesetter's sake), especially of foreign words or technical terms. When called for, use two hyphens for a dash, one for hyphenating words. Avoid capitalization of complete words (in titles, captions, or anywhere else); the book designer will make these decisions.

Any diacritical marks not on your computer should be written in ink, carefully and clearly; do not use the single quotation mark (') for a *grave* or *aigu* accent, for instance.

And do not forget to write "The End" three spaces below the last line of the last chapter.

You're Not Finished Yet

When you're come this far with your manuscript, put it down for a few days and forget it. Then, before you send it off, give it another close reading. You are bound to find a few errors, a phrase to add, some punctuation to change or a missing sentence. It wouldn't hurt to compare the rough draft with this final version, page by page, to make sure you haven't left something out in transcribing.

Avoid using the margins for final corrections for reasons already mentioned. Be especially careful and clear with these corrections; do not change or erase a letter, cross out the whole word and print or type the corrected word above it. To add an additional word or short phrase, indicate by a caret (∧) where it should appear, and print or type it directly above the caret and between the lines. If you have to change or insert a paragraph, retype the page. If an additional page is necessary, title it "25A," insert a caret where the new material is to be placed, and in pencil in the margin write "insert 25A." Be sure you indicate whether it is a new paragraph or to be run in. If there's more than one page of new matter, write "25A follows" on the bottom of page 25, number the new pages 25A, 25B, etc., and on the bottom of the last page write "26 follows." If you drop a complete page, say page 26, print "27 follows" at the bottom of page 25. If you add or delete more than a few pages, you should renumber the entire manuscript.

If the manuscript is messy and rife with changes, corrections, and cut and pasted pages, you are going to have one disgruntled editor on your hands (if you have a contract) or you may turn off a prospective publisher or agent. You might even have the cost of retyping the manuscript charged to your royalty account, or get a bill for 10 percent extra on composition costs (which you may be requested to pay on receipt). Be as neat as possible.

Sending the Manuscript

After all the effort you've put in, you will want to exercise some care in wrapping and sending the manuscript. Typing-paper boxes are excellent containers for mailing (paste a label on the box with your name, address and book title), provided you wrap and tie them well. Don't use staples or other bindings on the manuscript; keep it flat without pages of chapters fastened. Any artwork should be placed between cardboard in the separate envelopes previously mentioned, and secured with rubber bands.

If this is your final contract copy—the original printout—send it by Express Mail; send the floppy disks or a second copy under separate cover. If it is a first submission to an editor or agent, I recommend a good quality photocopy which you can save some money on by marking it Fourth Class, Book Rate. Federal Express, United Parcel Service, and other package deliverers will guarantee next-day delivery, but at a higher price. Any submission should be addressed to a particular person in the company, or at least to the appropriate department or division (see my previous suggestions in Chapter 1).

Now, mix yourself a martini, pour yourself a glass of sherry, or crack open a bottle of champagne—you've earned it.

5

How a Manuscript Is Processed by a Publisher

> A book must be done according to the writer's conception of it as nearly perfect as possible, and the publishing problems begin then. That is, the publisher must not try to get a writer to fit the book to the conditions of the trade. It must be the other way around.
>
> —MAXWELL PERKINS

You have delivered the goods. And you followed, as closely as possible, the guidelines for manuscript preparation described in the preceding chapter. Take that well-deserved rest while you can, for there is additional work to be done, on your part as well as on the part of many others, before your manuscript becomes a book. Familiarizing yourself with what goes on inside a typical publishing house will make your contribution easier, speed the book's progress, and help to reduce any anxiety you may experience during the ensuing months.

Why should you care about the publisher's responsibility in the agreement you have made? Publishers, like nearly everyone else, work with possible combinations of time and money, and you have a vital interest in helping your publisher strike the right combination. Editing and producing your work economically means a lower cost for the finished book; getting it out on time, in the right season, at a competitive price, can boost sales. Greater sales mean more money for both you and the publisher;

they can also mean wider distribution and greater acknowledgment of your status as an author.

The opportunity to cooperate with various members of the publishing house, then, is one of those offers you really cannot afford to refuse. In addition to these short-term reasons, there are some long-term considerations to be kept in mind.

No one wants or expects to be a one-book author. What you learn about the publishing process while your first book is coming out may give you a critical edge when the time comes to determine if your second book, assuming you write one, will get a contract. Publishing is currently undergoing considerable changes in its technology; in addition, job turnover among its editors and production specialists is often high. During such transitional times, the successful author is the one who knows, literally, at all times during the life of any of his or her books, what's going on.

Why Does It Take So Long?

An old saw in the publishing business states that "it takes about as long to make a book as it does to make a baby." True enough, but not inherently so. Bookmaking is a succession of tasks, many of which can be performed simultaneously, some of which can be speeded up considerably, depending on the available labor and money the publisher is willing to devote to the project.

In fact, mass market paperback houses, geared up for the imminent release of important information (such as President Clinton's 1993 health-care-reform proposals) or seeking to capitalize on the timeliness of events (such as the Gulf War) have managed to put books on the newsstands within weeks or even days after the events described occurred.

Seasonal needs can dictate a book's schedule, too, causing copyeditors and printers to work overtime, for example, to get an expensive new cookbook out in time for the Christmas buying season or a textbook ready well in advance of the fall semester. At the other end of the spectrum, certain specialized art books, technical works, dictionaries, and encyclopedias may be years or even decades in the making.

In between comes the "average" book—the novel, the freshman reader, the collection of critical essays, the illustrated children's story. Depending on their length, complexity, and the house priority assigned to them, all will require from 6 to 12 or even 15 months before the finished volumes reach the bookstore. There are three main reasons for this, and they are often overlooked by the novice or even the experienced author: other books, subcontracting, and house priorities.

The House Workload. A publishing house—its employees, facilities, and associated suppliers—is not infinitely elastic. Typically, the staff is working to produce not only your book but 10, 20, or 100 additional books as well. In the course of a single day, many of these books compete with your book for the attention of the editorial and production staff. Invariably delays, changed priorities, distractions, and communication failures plague this process. This state of affairs is industrywide and does not seem to be affected by the size of the publishing operation.

In the smaller houses, which publish anywhere from 5 to 20 titles a year, as few as two or three persons, each wearing a variety of bookmaking "hats," may handle the entire production workload. Mid- to large-sized companies employ considerably more persons, many of whose functions are very specialized, to perform the tasks necessary to get your book out; but the greater number of titles issued annually by the larger firms offsets such increases in staffing. Neither extreme is inherently better or faster than the other, since all publishers, large or small, produce books in essentially the same way.

Going Outside. Another old saying holds that all one needs to become a publisher is an office, a secretary with a typewriter, and a supply of Maalox. This is because a considerable amount of the effort put forth to publish a book is not expended on the premises of the publishing house. Virtually every task or function to be described in this chapter can be subcontracted to another individual or firm. This extensive brokerage of assignments gives considerable flexibility to the publishing operation. During periods of slack time, the house is not encumbered with a large payroll; yet when the occasion demands it the supervisors are able to call on a large, diversified work force of specialized professionals. Heavy reliance on outside editorial and production help is not without its hazards, however; it can dissipate control and contribute to the unevenness of the final product. Moreover, the success of this concatenation of tasks is sometimes dependent on the availability and schedules of the outside subcontractors. If a typesetter, for example, misestimates the time necessary to set a particular book, or if a freelance indexer fails to produce an index when it is needed, the house staff may be unable to make up the lost time. The book may lose its turn at the printer's—or, worse, miss its optimal marketing time. In house and out, workers strive to reduce the intervals and avoid delays, but this in turn can require more time for consultation and paperwork. If all the tasks *could* be performed under one roof, the book would come out sooner, but that is hardly, if ever, the case.

The House Priorities. Books are scheduled so that they will be available for distribution and sales during a selling season or list. Once your editor is relatively sure of when you will deliver the final manuscript, it will be designated to appear on one of these lists. Some trade publishers sell their books on the traditional two-list system. "Spring" runs roughly from February to July and culminates with the kinds of books that are expected to appeal to summer vacation readers. "Fall," which runs approximately from August to January, is geared to the all-important Christmas buying season. Other publishers work with three four-month-long seasons (these run roughly January to April, May to August, and September to December, although it varies from house to house), reflecting the fact that books are now published every month of the year.

For textbooks, the time spans are more narrow, since the publisher must schedule books to appear during the major "adoption" periods. While textbooks can be finished anytime from August to early March, the majority are ready between September and mid-November. First editions must be sent to the teachers, professors, and textbook selection committees in ample time before they make their decisions (in the spring for the following fall semester). Revised editions of textbooks are often published particularly early, in the hope that they can be used in the spring semester.

A medium-sized publishing house, planning to issue a total of 40 titles for its spring and fall lists, still expects only a fraction of those titles—from three to ten—to do well financially and to bring in most of the year's revenue. These especially promising titles, then, will be given higher priority than the other books proposed for the lists. Should delays from any quarter threaten these priority titles, time and effort will be diverted from works of lesser importance to ensure that the important titles will appear on time. The lower priority works get "bumped" on the monthly production schedule for periods ranging anywhere from two to four weeks to six months or even more. Alternatively, a new and unexpected manuscript may suddenly be delivered, and the publisher may decide that this potential best-seller *must* come out during the following season; other books suffer accordingly. Aside from hoping that your book will be considered a potential best-seller, too, there is little you can do about such in-house juggling of priorities.

Taking these three factors into account—the house workload, the widespread practice of subcontracting, and the differences in priorities—it is clear that, even though the actual hours of editorial and production time devoted to your book may add up to only a few weeks or months, the average book still has a gestation period somewhere between that of a human and an elephant.

Editing

Publishing houses come in various sizes and shapes. While their daily work remains essentially the same, titles and procedures may vary from one company to the next. Your manuscript may land in a large publishing house having a number of specialized departments, each with its own way of doing things and cast of official-sounding titles. In another house of equal size, all the work may be carried out by seemingly nameless assistants who work almost exclusively for the book's acquiring editor. Or, your book may be turned out by some courageous soul operating out of his basement or garage who does almost everything himself.

The assumption for this chapter and the next will be that you have delivered a manuscript to a medium-sized trade house issuing, say, 80 to 100 titles a year. (If you have also been asked to deliver your diskettes, we will take that into account.) The practices and procedures described in this chapter and the next are typical, but keep in mind that every publishing house does things a little differently; you should always follow the publisher's specific instructions whenever they vary from anything stated herein.

This medium-sized house has departments, and within those departments there are individuals wearing more than one hat. Chief among such multitalented individuals, for your purposes, is your editor, who has a number of functions to fulfill before transmitting your manuscript to the copyediting and production departments. We will take a closer look at the editor's responsibilities and at the kinds of discussions he or she might have with other staff members and department heads.

Substantive Editing. The making of books, regrettably, does not always go like clockwork. No matter how knowledgeable the author or how optimistic the acquiring editor, a newly arrived manuscript can sometimes turn out to have things wrong with it—not minor things, such as a missing footnote or an uncleared permission, but something major. The third chapter simply makes no sense, or the last quarter of the work is written in embarrassingly purplish prose, to give but two examples. Such calamities, having to do with the substance or meaning of the work, are the province of the book's acquiring editor. If your manuscript is destined for the trade market, he is probably the person who offered you the contract. He may have been in touch with you all along as you worked on earlier drafts. He may even have gone over them with you, page by page, making suggestions for improvements, offering more honest and more specific criticisms than you are likely to get from well-meaning colleagues or friends. In other words, there is a good chance that he has already devoted considerable effort to make certain the manuscript arrives in good shape. But he often still double-checks it to be sure your complete final manuscript *is* in good shape.

Biographies and novels have been written about great editors: They are a rare breed. Perhaps Maxwell Perkins is best known, but there are other editors, less celebrated, whose achievements have been as great. Precisely what they do for an author and her manuscript is sometimes difficult to say, since their responsibilities are so broadly defined. In his posthumously published *Words & Faces*, Hiram Haydn, one of the preeminent American book editors of the postwar period, described it in this way:

> Editorial work includes the study of the text of a given manuscript; the attempt to grasp, with imaginative precision, the writer's overall "intent" (including, sometimes, themes or counterpoint of which he is not consciously aware), and to establish where he has fallen short; and finally, the give-and-take of the process of revision. . . . The editor must walk a thin line between remaining firm on changes he considers crucial and "taking over" the book. . . . It is his function to act as catalyst and as sounding board. It is not his book; he is the reader and consultant, not the writer.

The foregoing is an ideal description of what every editor would like to be able to do. In reality, and like nearly everything else in publishing these days, editors have felt the effects of the bottom-line mentality dictated by the corporations now controlling publishing houses, and many of them are running as fast as they can simply in order to stay in one place. The fact that top editors spend most of their time chasing down new projects, especially the potential best-sellers by brand-name authors that all publishers want to acquire, has been mentioned repeatedly in various magazine articles over the past 15 years (all with titles like "The Decline of Editing").

What this means is that the bigger the company, the greater the chance that the person who signed up your book won't do any line-by-line editorial work on it. The acquiring editor who took you out to lunch after signing up your book may turn the manuscript over to a line editor—a junior editor in the company, her assistant, or an outside freelancer—or may even assume that the freelance copyeditor the company hires later will take care of that work as well. That the book make sense is still the acquiring editor's responsibility; but especially if the manuscript is messy or complex, making it make sense is often delegated to someone else.

Readers' Reports. If your work is a textbook, having outside experts review it critically will be an integral part of the process. At most college textbook houses, readers' reports from scholars qualified in the same field are solicited at least three times: before an author is offered a contract; when a first draft is ready; and after the final draft, which has been revised partially along the lines suggested by earlier readers' reports, comes in but before the manuscript is officially deemed acceptable. The acquiring editor (or the developmental editor, who does much of the substantive editing on a textbook) has a long list of scholars in all fields available to do this work. If, for instance, your work is a sociological study of prison conditions and recidivism, it will be sent for critical readings by sociologists with reputations and published works in similar areas.

For an honorarium of from $100 to $300 apiece, the readers will look through a copy of your manuscript and return it with comments about its strengths and weaknesses. For larger sums, and as requested, they will undertake more thorough readings and return more extensive, detailed reports. With these at hand, the acquiring or developmental editor can work through the troublesome sections of your manuscript, pointing out those changes or revisions that seem advisable.

The process of soliciting, evaluating, and implementing changes recommended by outside readers can be extremely time-consuming. In the textbook world it is a commonplace. University presses send all nonfiction out for review (their fees are generally low, and they may offer free books instead). Trade publishers reserve the option for their more serious medical and scientific works. For reference works, such as dictionaries or medical books, several pages are sometimes needed to list all the experts, consultants, and advisers who at one time or another gave their opinions about the substance of the work. If serious, qualified readers believe there is something wrong with your manuscript, your editor will let you know what should be done. Never mind where her expertise is coming from—the identity of outside readers is usually not disclosed. Instead, remember the clause in your contract obligating you to deliver an *acceptable* manuscript. Weigh your editor's arguments, work with her, and try to satisfy both her and yourself that the work forms a meaningful and coherent whole.

Contracts, Rights, and Permissions. Months earlier, in order to convince higher management of the rightness of offering you a contract, your acquiring editor prepared a written evaluation of your book proposal. In that report, his designation of the marketing area—trade juvenile, for example—and the rights to be obtained—perhaps U.S. and Canadian but not British—governed the subsequent agreements you made with other publishers or authors for permission to reprint copyrighted material. This requirement of manuscript preparation, discussed in greater detail in the preceding chapters, now becomes crucial. In some houses the acquiring editor or an assistant will check every permissions document; in other houses, the responsibility may fall to a copyeditor. Most large houses have a contract department (not to be confused with the rights-and-permissions department) that specializes in poring over the fine print of such documents.

If you have included five maps of Outer Mongolia that appeared two years ago in the *New York Times*, and you carefully obtained permission agreements from the *Times* corresponding to the marketing area or areas stipulated in your contract, you have no problem. Someone in the house will routinely check the form from the *Times*—and, as previously mentioned, that individual and your editor will insist that you submit the *originals* of such forms, while advising you to keep photocopies for your own reference.

If you have failed to clear the necessary permissions to use copyrighted material of any sort, or if you secured what you thought were the correct agreements but they turn out to be for the incorrect rights (either too restrictive or too broad), you will be asked to obtain the correct, appropriate agreements. Since the contract usually states that permissions fees are to be paid by the author, the company's reasons for reviewing the forms so closely are strictly legal, not financial. It is your money that is being spent, not the firm's. Therefore you have a personal interest in helping to clear up any discrepancies—especially since if authors err in this respect, it is usually by obtaining rights that are too broad rather than too narrow. You may have agreed to pay $100 for world rights to reproduce half a page of another writer's work; but, since your book is to be sold in the United States only, if the discrepancy is pointed out by someone in the house, you could probably renegotiate and save yourself half the original fee.

The state of your permissions file may have still another effect on your immediate finances. Many houses will not officially deem your manuscript contractually "complete and satisfactory" until these documents are in order, and may withhold payment of the final portion of your advance until you obtain the correct agreements. If necessary, and if your acquiring editor agrees, you can resolve this problem while the manuscript is being copyedited and designed. However, your manuscript generally will not be sent out for typesetting until you have turned in all of your permissions agreements. The reason is obvious: The company loses money if material set in type must later be deleted from the galley or page proofs because it is discovered that proper permission to reprint copyrighted material simply cannot be obtained or proved to be exorbitantly expensive.

Legal Review. The United States has more lawyers per capita than most Western democracies, and legal matters play a prominent role in modern American society. Newspapers and magazines are chock-full with dispatches from celebrated trials and stories of lawsuits and threats of lawsuits. Nonfiction accounts of some of these trials are a staple on many publishers' lists. Novels, plays, TV shows, and films centering on dramatic courtroom action have been particularly popular recently.

It should thus come as no surprise that book publishers—like all media companies—and authors are themselves frequently the target of legal action. Libel and plagiarism suits are the most common, but publishers have also been sued for using a photograph on a book jacket without model releases for all those shown. Therefore, for their protection and yours—since, when there is a lawsuit, the author is usually a codefendant—publishing houses now pay close attention to legal issues. Larger houses often have a legal department in-house, whereas medium-sized and smaller houses keep counsel on retainer.

While much of the work publishing lawyers perform is far removed from the content of your book, it is important for you to know that many nonfiction manuscripts are subject to legal review during the editorial process. Biographies of living figures (or even those recently deceased), works examining scandals or cover-ups in government or the business world, and, of course, books about celebrated crimes and trials are all routinely reviewed for potentially libelous statements. Even if you haven't written such a manuscript, your work may still be vetted by the publishers' lawyers.

If, for whatever reason, the publisher determines that your manuscript needs a legal review, the lawyer assigned to the project will read a duplicate of the final, edited manuscript around the time it is transmitted. This lawyer will then write your editor a memo about any potentially troublesome passages. You may then be asked to produce your notes, tapes, transcripts, or other forms of research to substantiate what you have written. If satisfied, the lawyer will let your statement stand; if not, you may be asked to rework the passage in question or approve an alternative the lawyer and your editor suggest. This process is usually completed by the time the copyedited manuscript is ready to be typeset.

Paperwork. The acquiring editor or his assistant must fill out several forms for your book, and other departments may also need to do so as well (large publishers, with the job specialization of many departments, generally have more forms than smaller houses). Some of these forms circulate only within the house—for example, to obtain the International Standard Book Number, to initiate the design of the book's cover or jacket, or to provide information on the word-processing equipment you have used. Other forms will travel outside the house: to obtain Library of Congress Cataloguing-in-Publication data for your book, for instance, or to ensure that it's listed in *Books in Print*. At this time, if you have not filled out an author's questionnaire, your editor or the publicity department will send you one. Even after submitting it, you may be queried by members of the editorial or promotional staff for additional information. And you may be asked to provide one department with information you have already given to another department. Whatever they want to know, try to provide it for them as quickly as possible.

Transmittal. As the substantive editing, checking of permissions, and filing of in-house forms nears completion, the acquiring editor arranges to transmit your manuscript—the original and several photocopies, as well as your diskettes (if any) and a transmittal form—to the managing editor's department (called editing, copyediting, or editorial production) and the production department.

Transmittal, which is often referred to as "putting a book into production," is a key time to compare the somewhat theoretical projections made earlier against the realities of the manuscript at hand. The substantive editing may have enlarged, reduced, or otherwise modified the manuscript. The market may have changed, so that publishing in paperback rather than hardcover or adding a photo section or, for a textbook, printing in two colors should be considered. The other departments involved see a complete manuscript (perhaps for the first time) and thus have a chance to check the status of the project as it concerns their area of expertise, to raise questions, and to make recommendations.

At the very least, your editor will be looking at the estimates and recommendations contained in his or her original evaluation of your proposal. That report treated not only marketing areas and rights but also proposed list price, trim size (the width and height of the book page), binding format and style, print run (number of copies of the first printing), projected publication date, estimated costs, probable profit margin, and so on. If the book's physical specifications ("specs") have changed substantially, or if the black-and-white line drawings originally envisioned will not do and a dozen full-color photographs are absolutely essential to illustrate your points and to compete with existing books, the acquiring editor will ask the production department to prepare a revised estimate.

Your editor will also be talking with other key personnel about facets of your book. He will discuss with the managing editor the kind of copyediting the manuscript requires, make suggestions concerning the design of the book's jacket or cover with the art director, and review ideas for a different title or subtitle that have come from the marketing staff. If your book contains photographs or other illustrations, your editor will ask the sales department whether they need advance photocopies to help them sell it.

Each publishing house goes about addressing the issues that arise around the time of transmittal in a different way. College textbook houses and some trade houses have formal transmittal or launch meetings, where department heads and key personnel convene to review the entire status of the project. At other publishers, the issues are examined on a more informal basis (e.g., through a series of one-on-one conversations between your editor and the others concerned, or at an informal get-together in, say, the publicity manager's office); there may be meetings later to discuss some of these questions.

However it happens, out of these discussions come the various agreements, assurances, modifications, and counterproposals that will enable the acquiring editor, as management's representative, to develop a tentative notion of when bound books will be available and approximately how much they will cost. This editor may not make such estimates, however. It will be left up to the managing editor and the production supervisor to draw up the proposed schedule, showing the sequence of tasks and the dates by which they are to be accomplished. Now that decisions regarding the book's final specs have been made, the production supervisor will also work on a more accurate preliminary cost estimate for the entire project.

As all of this has been going on, the original copy of the manuscript has entered the copyediting phase and one duplicate copy is being looked at for preliminary design. Before we discuss those processes, however, it would be wise to take a closer look at the techniques of estimating costs and of scheduling editorial and production time.

Planning to Publish

An earlier chapter in this book described the nature and purpose of the cost estimate. This form, usually prepared by someone from the production department, enables the acquiring editor to make further calculations involving price, profit, and the feasibility of issuing a contract. If the manuscript delivered is not much different from the manuscript proposed, the original or preliminary cost estimate drawn up when the contract is signed may be sufficient to see the work through all but the final stages of book production. Two or three months prior to the bound-book date, however, a final, more accurate cost estimate is made; this enables management to review actual expenses and to assign the book a final price. For the moment, let us consider the manner in which the production supervisor evaluates the manuscript in order to prepare a cost estimate.

Breakdown and Page Estimate. In order to project material and manufacturing costs, the production supervisor must have ways of assessing and measuring the manuscript mechanically. For very brief works (such as a 32-page juvenile picture book), he or she may, of course, count pages or even words. For longer original works in which the company intends to invest considerable sums of money, the supervisor's measuring must be more accurate. Therefore, the production supervisor will have a breakdown, or character count, of the entire manuscript prepared (this may be done by an assistant in the production department, a designer, or by a typesetter). This involves making a careful estimate of the total number of typewritten letters, punctuation marks, and spaces in the different parts of the typescript: front matter, text, back matter, footnotes, and so on. Also included are estimates for space that will be needed in the finished book for "display type" (chapter openings, subheadings), artwork, photographs, tables, and "white space." While these estimates can be made on the basis of the acquiring editor's or production supervisor's "feel" for what the book should be like, by this time they are usually made on the basis of actual design specifications. With these figures, the supervisor can "cast off" the manuscript—estimate the total number of pages the finished book will contain. He or she may have instructions to "pad out" a short manuscript or to fit an overly long one within a fixed number of pages.

Whatever the guidelines, the ease with which a reliable forecast of page length is arrived at depends partly on the orderliness and internal coherence of your manuscript. If it is typed on different typewriters, set at various line lengths (or printed in different formats); if the number of lines per page varies considerably; if you have written in numerous corrections, pasted on strips of new copy, or made extensive deletions; or if your acquiring editor or his or her designate has done heavy editing—the manuscript may be very difficult to cast off. It will also be harder to copyedit an already heavily marked-up manuscript, and it is obviously more difficult to typeset a messy one accurately. In addition, the typesetter may decide an especially sloppy manuscript is "penalty copy" and charge a proportionately higher rate to set it. For all these reasons, before work on your book can progress, it's possible that the entire manuscript may be sent out for retyping (usually at your expense) or that you may be asked to input all the last-minute line editing and return a clean printout and updated diskettes.

Scheduling. In the words of John P. Dessauer, in his *Book Publishing*, "it is a lot easier to prepare a schedule than to keep one." Nevertheless, the challenge of preparing and enforcing your book's schedule must be accepted by someone in the publishing house. At some houses, it is the managing editor who takes primary responsibility for planning a schedule and seeing that it's adhered to as much as possible; at other houses, the production supervisor has that responsibility; at still others, the two share the task or a third person is in charge. For our purposes here, we'll call whoever must face this challenge the scheduling director. Of course, this person is assisted by the acquiring editor and by representatives from all the various departments involved in working on the manuscript.

If your work carries a normal priority and does not require an accelerated production schedule in order to reap maximum sales, the scheduling director will work out a series of projected dates, from manuscript to bound books, by which certain essential tasks must be completed. For example, what follows is a proposed publication schedule for an average book issued by a well-known New York trade house:

Weeks necessary	Activity
6–8	Transmittal, copyediting, author review; designer prepares layouts simultaneously
1	Copyedited ms. marked up by designer; production sends to typesetter
3	Typesetting
3	Proofreading and revising of galleys or first-pass proofs
2	Typesetting the corrections and making up page proofs

2	Proofreading page proofs; duplicate set sent to indexer to prepare index, if any
1½	Typesetting corrections and preparing final reproduction proofs
1½	Checking and correcting reproduction proofs
6–8	Camerawork, blues, printing, binding
1	Shipment to warehouse from bindery (bound-book date)
2–4	Shipment to bookstores
29–35	

The bound-book date is the date that the publisher sees sample finished books from the bindery and approves their release to the warehouse. In trade houses, a publication date follows four to eight weeks later; although somewhat arbitrary, the pub date is the time by which the publisher hopes that books are on display in stores around the country; the publicity department requests that periodicals run their review of the book as close as possible to that date and it's the time when any promotional or marketing campaign will begin. Thus, with the addition of "lead time" (the time between the bound-book and publication dates), it does indeed take roughly nine months to produce the average book, just as the old saw says.

Nonetheless, schedules such as the preceding are always ideal and more honored in the breach than the observance. Many books are produced in less than seven months to bound book, without undue strain to the staff of any modern publishing house. Other projects take inherently longer to produce. For example, a juvenile picture book with full-color illustrations on each page will often take a year to produce, as will most college textbooks; lengthy scholarly projects have been known to take even longer.

When a work is still in manuscript form there is no foolproof formula for determining exactly how long it will take to convert it into a bound book. It must pass through several production and manufacturing stages, and it will require the attention of a host of individuals. Both conditions increase the chances that some unexpected development may sabotage the schedule. However, the typical scheduling director has developed a feel for what is difficult to copyedit or to set in type, what is easy, what will take months to accomplish, what can be done within a week or ten days. In other words, the director relies on a combination of experience, mechanical reckoning, and guesswork to arrive at a final projected date.

The scheduling director's biggest question mark is the time that will be required by the first stage—copyediting—and the intervals necessary for the author to review the copyedited manuscript and to examine the first-pass proofs. The staff must "turn around" or exchange the manuscript and its subsequent incarnations in type not only with the typesetter but also with the author, and it is the house-to-author-to-house turnaround that holds the greatest potential for unanticipated delays. The advent of overnight delivery services has eliminated most problems in getting material quickly to an author on the other side of the continent, but the scheduling director still needs to know if the author will have other conflicts—administering and grading final exams, for instance, or floating down the Amazon River to collect algae specimens. The scheduling director must make allowance for the inevitable delay or attempt to tighten the schedule at some other point.

The scheduling director's success also depends in part on her ability to reckon the intervals necessary for the mechanical and in-house tasks over which she has considerable control. In this respect, a competent editorial-production staff gives the scheduling director confidence that minor delays can be compensated for and unexpected obstacles overcome. In addition, once a book is well along in production, as in reproduction proofs, the time remaining until bound books can be estimated with a fairly high degree of reliability. The later the stage, the more mechanical the function, and consequently the less chance for errors in scheduling.

Abbreviating a Schedule. If your book is a crash project—if it simply must be out in five months' time or it will miss the Christmas buying season—the scheduling director simply accepts the publication date of November 15 as inevitable and works backward to establish dates for all the production stages leading up to it. Perhaps the most common way in which schedules are compressed is to tighten every phase (a week there, two days here) from copyediting and typesetting to the lead time before publication. Another quite frequent adjustment is to eliminate one stage of proof, so that only two passes are looked at in-house instead of three. It's possible, too, to arrange to pay freelancers higher rates to turn the project around more quickly. Any of the people working on your book (freelance or in-house) may be told to shelve whatever else they are working on to concentrate full-time on your book (someone else's work, then, gets bumped; but, as pointed out earlier, this can happen to your book, too). Typesetters and printers that get a large volume of work from a publisher are often willing to turn around priority projects faster; or the publishing house may be willing to pay them extra for rush service.

As author, you will initially be told of the season in which your publisher plans to bring out your book. There is almost no point in asking about the month until your manuscript is completely edited, or in asking about a specific week until you've returned your galley proofs. At that time, you may be told of the proposed publication date, but policies vary concerning whether you will be shown an actual schedule. Regardless of the point at which schedules are drawn up, they have a tendency to change once they are under way. For your part, when you receive your copyedited manuscript and later the galleys, it's vital that you do everything within your power to return them by the date the publisher requests. If you are a week or a month late, either the publication date gets pushed back by that same amount (or more), or the house staff starts working overtime to compensate for your delay. In the first instance, the delay could cause the book to miss its selling season; in the second, it could add to the book's cost and eventual price. Either way, it can spell reduced royalties for you, the author.

Copyediting

At this point it is assumed that, at least in terms of substance, your work is ready for publication. Having arrived on the managing editor's desk, the manuscript is now assigned to a production editor; she will be responsible for carefully checking the editorial content of the work as it undergoes the physical process of production. At some houses, this person may be called a project editor, a manuscript editor, or a staff copyeditor. We'll use production editor here, because it's the most common term and to avoid confusion with the copyeditor whom the production editor hires.

The production editor's first, and perhaps most important, duty is selecting and supervising a copyeditor to copyedit the manuscript. The copyeditor's stated task is to check and bring into line the internal consistency of the work at a number of levels. Supposedly he is not concerned with content and will set off in pursuit only of that elusive quality called style. In practice, however, the good copyeditor attends not only to the minute but also to the broad features of the work, and often comes up with criticisms of or suggestions about content that must be acknowledged and dealt with by acquiring editor and author.

Years ago, all copyediting was done by house staff. These days, most publishers send their manuscripts out to freelance copyeditors. Even those houses with copyeditors on staff frequently offer assignments to outsiders during peak periods. In all cases, the production editor will try to assign your book to a copyeditor whose skills are particularly well suited to the kind of job she, in consultation with your acquiring editor, thinks it needs.

Of all the functions in a publishing house, that of the copyeditor is perhaps least understood and easiest to underrate. The copyeditor enforces mechanical conventions—of spelling, grammar, punctuation, capitalization, abbreviation, and a host of additional stylistic matters—while knowing full well that conventions are not absolute and that they must be reinvoked and occasionally modified for each particular manuscript. If you have strong personal preferences about style, it is advisable to prepare a short memo before your manuscript is transmitted. The production editor will generally pass your recommendations on to the copyeditor to follow, even if they are contrary to the usual "house style."

Invariably the copyeditor will catch typographical errors, infelicities of style, errors of fact, and logical inconsistencies overlooked by all previous readers. He will normally correct as many of these as possible on his own. If he finds anything seriously troubling or if he feels a particular decision should be made by the editor or author, he will add a query. Most copyediting queries are written on small gummed tags (or "flags") attached to the side of the manuscript page; alternately, Post-its are used, or some houses ask copyeditors to type up lists of queries.

Like substantive editing, copyediting and editorial querying may be accomplished piecemeal or chapter by chapter, but it is generally done en masse. When the copyeditor returns the manuscript to the publisher, the production editor takes a quick look through it to get a sense of any major or overall problems; then she or the acquiring editor sends it to you for your review.

Your review of the copyedited manuscript is an important event in the publication of your book. Keep in mind that securing answers for specific queries is not the only reason for returning the manuscript to you, nor are the copyeditor's changes sacrosanct. Rather, they are proposed changes, and if they are shown to you, it is to gain your approval or disapproval, not to embarrass you or show you up. Admittedly, it is not always a pleasant experience to have an impartial mirror held up before one's grammar, spelling, and prose style. Nevertheless, the copyeditor's proposed substitutions and changes are intended to improve your book, not to detract from it. You owe it to yourself to take each editorial query seriously, to weigh it impartially, and to resolve it thoroughly.

If, for whatever reason, the copyeditor has changed a word, for example, and you disagree with the proposed substitution, the time to object is now, while the work is still in manuscript, and not when you see the new word later on in proofs and decide it should be changed back to the original. If made in galleys, such a change would be considered an author's altera-tion and you could be charged for it (see p. 181). Careful reading of the copyeditor's proposed changes throughout the manuscript can save a great deal of money in resetting type. In addition it is always preferable to make changes sooner than later, because it reduces the chance of errors creeping into the finished book.

Following a few simple rules as you review the copyedited manuscript will make it easier later for the production editor, the designer, and the typesetter. Make sure you answer all the queries addressed to you, but do not tear off or remove the query flags. If you write on the manuscript, use a lead or colored pencil—not a pen or a Flair marker—and write as neatly as pos-sible; some houses will even request that you not write on the manuscript at all, but only on query flags and Post-its (the pro-duction editor will transfer all your changes onto the manuscript page). If you disagree with any of the copyediting, do not erase it; instead, put a small check mark above the word or phrase in question, and write "stet" (meaning restore the original) in the margin. If you add any new material, clearly identify it (in a cover memo or with a Post-it). If you retype or re-output any pages, return the original versions as well, paper-clipped to the new versions. (If the house sends you other instructions with the copyedited manuscript, of course you should follow those.)

When you return the copyedited manuscript, the production editor will check through it to backstop all who have come be-fore (author, acquiring editor, and copyeditor). In the process, she will see that any missing material has been supplied, copyedit any new material herself (in the style the freelance copyeditor established for the book), and resolve any disagree-ments you have with the copyediting.

Part of the copyeditor's importance in relation to the quality and success of the book is that he is usually the last (and some-times the only) person on the staff to read the work in its en-tirety. Modern bookmaking procedures sometimes involve such pressures and short timetables that, as we have seen, the acquir-ing editor may never have time to sit down and reason about each line or paragraph of your manuscript. This responsibility may justifiably be delegated, and the buck usually stops at the copyeditor's desk. If he does not catch the anachronism, the potentially libelous remark, or the circular argument, such features may appear in the finished book, to the embarrassment of some and the potential revenue loss of all. While the production editor may read large portions of the manuscript after the author reviews the copyediting and while a proofreader will read it once it is set into type, the copyeditor is often the last line of defense, and his importance in this respect cannot be overestimated.

Another of the copyeditor's duties is to mark the manuscript in such a way that the text will require a minimum of alterations after it is set in type. If his marks are not clear to the typesetter, the publisher will have to pay alterations charges later on. By thinking of everything—or almost everything—the copyeditor performs an invaluable service in holding down costs. Either the copyeditor or production editor also keys (by marking with alphabetical symbols) the various headings and elements of the manuscript so that they can be readily identified by the book designer and the typesetter. In short, the team of copyeditor and production editor has a Janus-like role, looking back over what author and acquiring editor have done and ahead to what book designer and typesetter must still do.

If You've Worked on a Word Processor. You may be wondering what has happened to the diskettes you supplied with the hard copy of the manuscript. To answer that, we have to stop and look at how the publishing industry has responded to the computer age.

Publishers have used computers to great success in their so-called back-office operations (accounting, ordering, inventory, etc.) for almost two decades. However, in the areas of the house that you will come in contact with—the staff who edit, design, produce, and market your book—most publishers have been far slower to computerize than other businesses. Of course, there are exceptions: publishers of computer books (naturally), small entrepreneurial houses, and many textbook divisions and university presses have moved aggressively into using computers to help produce their books.

Nonetheless, for a number of reasons, a majority of trade

book publishers have been reluctant to take advantage of the new technology. Many book people have doubts about the possibility of maintaining their high standards of editorial excellence while working on computer screens. Management has hesitated to undertake the large capital expense of providing each worker with a personal computer and the necessary training. Many houses remember the bad experiences when they first tried to take advantage of the new technology, in the late 1970s—most of these experiments were disasters, and it has made publishers hesitant about trying even today, when many of the bugs have been ironed out.

As more and more authors work on word processors, more once-reluctant houses follow in the footsteps of those trailblazing computer-literate publishers. If you've been asked to supply diskettes with a hard copy of the manuscript, your publisher wants to take advantage of them in some way. The ways in which your diskettes are put to use vary considerably from house to house. But in most cases, it's at the copyediting stage that you may first notice a change from the more traditional methods described in the preceding pages.

The most technologically advanced publishers are having copyediting done electronically, on the computer screen. In a typical scenario, your diskettes are copied and then held aside. While the copyeditor is still sent a hard copy of the manuscript for reference, he does his work directly on the duplicate diskettes. When he returns the job, someone in-house prepares a new printout so you can review the copyediting. Both your original diskettes and the copyedited duplicate ones are run through a compare program and the printout shows both versions side-by-side, with some kind of highlighting. For instance, at one publishing house, wherever the compare program finds a discrepancy between the two sets of diskettes, the printout shows the author's version with a line through it (old) followed by the copyeditor's version with a light screen behind it (new). Editorial queries, if any, appear at the bottom of each page of the printout, keyed to a small superscript number (like a footnote reference) at the end of the passage in question.

The author is asked to review this copyedited printout (which also incorporates and highlights any line editing your acquiring editor or his designate did) along the lines of the procedures outlined earlier. When the author returns the printout, the production editor reviews the manuscript, and then she (or someone else on the staff or a freelancer) incorporates those additional changes you've requested onto the copyeditor's diskettes—those diskettes are now the master version. They will be passed on to the designer, who will add design codes and specifications (also electronically) before the production supervisor sends them (along with a hard copy, for reference) to the typesetter for first-pass proofs.

Other publishers may want to use your diskettes, but for one reason or another do not yet feel comfortable having the copyediting done on the computer screen along the lines above. In those cases, the traditional methods of copyediting on a hard copy are followed; the diskettes are held in reserve for now. We will discuss how they come into play in the next chapter.

Despite the slow rate at which they are adapting to the computer age, publishers are aware that this is the wave of the future. Increasingly user-friendly equipment and programs (such as a system called PenEdit, which allows editors to edit with an electric "pen") are being introduced each year. As these gain visibility and acceptance, publishers will become less skittish about using author-supplied diskettes.

Designing the Book

While the copyediting continues and the author then reviews the copyedited manuscript, work may also proceed on three distinct but related aspects of bookmaking: interior design, preparation of camera-ready artwork, and exterior or cover design. If the work is simple—a novel, for example, divided into chapters and having no illustrations or footnotes—such design tasks can often be carried out concurrently with the copyediting.

At small houses, there may not be any designers on staff, and the production department will freelance all of the design tasks to be performed. Even at larger houses, the house designers may freelance some of the work to outsiders. The policies of the particular house, rather than the nature of the book, usually determine the sequence or degree of overlap in the execution of design functions. In some houses a manuscript must be copyedited and keyed before interior design can begin; in others the design is created first, and preparation of the interior artwork begins at the same time as the copyediting. The exterior or cover design proceeds more independently, on its own schedule.

Interior Design. The designer is responsible for the technical specifications of the book: a set of practical, coherent, aesthetically pleasing dimensions and relations between figure (the printed text) and ground (the book page) that will guide typesetter, printer, binder, and cover artist. The second edition of Marshall Lee's *Bookmaking: The Illustrated Guide to Design/Production/Editing* (New York: R. R. Bowker Co., 1979) remains the best single-volume work available on the subject. If you are starting out to create a profusely illustrated or typographically complex book, it would be wise to examine this work and to read the chapters on composition, typography, and illustration.

Regardless of whether the designer is on staff or freelance, the production supervisor provides him or her with a copy of the manuscript or a sampling of its pages, originals or copies of the rough artwork and proposed photographs, and memos concerning the technical features already decided on at this point (especially the trim size and desired page length). The manuscript itself, if properly keyed, will call the designer's attention to levels of subheadings, indented quotes or extracts, lists, special type, formulae, and tables (at many houses, the production editor prepares a so-called design memo enumerating all the type elements in the manuscript that need to be designed). All this will be accompanied by additional memos from or conversations with the production supervisor (and sometimes the acquiring editor) concerning the general effect desired for the book: whether the design is to be conservative, modern, whimsical, hearts-and-flowers, and so on. Some designers specialize in one or the other, some are good with technical material, some have a touch for certain historical periods or intended audiences. An edited collection of essays about Matthew Arnold's views on industrialism, for example, would be likely to receive a conservative treatment. However, a book of essays by Tama Janowitz or Jay McInerney about nightlife in the Reagan years might require a more radical design approach.

In a week or two the designer provides a composition order (a list of the type specifications for the manuscript) and a number of two-page layouts. Layouts, which show typical pages in the book and special ones, can be prepared on artist's tracing paper or on a Macintosh computer. Together, the composition order and the layouts show the width and height of the page area within which the type is to be reproduced, the size and variety of all the type to be set, the space between the lines of type (called "leading") and surrounding the display type (called "white space"), and many other technical choices and details.

Once the layouts are approved by the house and the copyedited manuscript has been returned by the author and reviewed by the production editor, the designer then "marks up" the copyedited manuscript. Each time a new type element—chapter number, major subheading, footnote, table, and so on—makes its first appearance, the designer marks the exact type specification for that element on the manuscript itself. Thus the technical specifications of the design are repeated in whole or in part in three forms: marked manuscript, composition order, and layouts. Any one of these can be followed by the knowledgeable typesetters and makeup people who are about to create the page images in type.

If the manuscript is to become part of an ongoing series, it may not be designed in the manner just described. Instead, it may simply be marked up in the house according to a standing composition order. The design of an existing book can be copied or modified, too, and applied to your manuscript by an experienced production worker. In fact, the designer may not do the complete markup, which may be delegated to someone in the house when the design specifications are returned.

Sample Pages. A special situation worth mentioning here is the decision to ask the typesetter for sample pages. If your book is long and complicated or if for other reasons the publisher feels it is necessary, time may be allotted to test the proposed design by having only a few pages—usually between 3 and 12—set by the typesetter and returned for further study. When faced with a future composition bill that could run above, say, $10,000 (three times the cost for an average novel), the production supervisor will usually take the precaution of asking for sample pages; these cost at most only a couple of hundred dollars (and some typesetters will provide them free if they are going to typeset the entire book later). With sample pages at hand, the editors (acquiring and production) and designer can, if necessary, make further adjustments and refinements in the design before committing the house to the major investment of typesetting. Whether or not sample pages are ordered, once the design is sound and the copyediting and review completed, the marked-up manuscript is ready to be sent to the typesetter (again, we will discuss the use of your diskettes in the next chapter). Work continues, however, on other elements that will appear as part of the finished book.

Preparation of Artwork. To book workers, art refers to everything that is not set in type, whether it is a diagram of a petroleum pump, a photograph of Julia Roberts, or decorative design elements on chapter-opening pages. Each of these is identified not so much by content as by the technique with which it is reproduced. Thus black-and-white photographs become "halftones" and diagrams become "line art." There are further refinements involving screens (shaded areas), second colors, and overlays, but these need not concern us here. If there are illustrations of any kind in your book and you have followed the suggestions in this book for preparing them, the artists and graphics specialists will handle the technicalities.

The exact location of these artists is not important. The designer who prepared the interior design of your book may do the work, or it may be given to another staff person or a freelancer. At large textbook houses, there may be a separate department in charge of interior art, with art editors, photo researchers, illustrators, photographers, and other graphic technicians, all of whom are responsible for ensuring that the art appears "right" in the finished book. In a smaller house, the production editor or the production supervisor may coordinate most of these tasks with freelancers.

Whatever the arrangement, your roughs (pencil sketches or diagrams you have created or borrowed), glossy photographs, and illustrations taken from other printed sources will be examined, classified, sometimes redrawn, and eventually rendered in camera-ready form. An important part of this process is the "sizing" of art: reducing, cropping, or otherwise rearranging the dimensions of your figure so that it will fit attractively within the confines of the prescribed page area. Also important is the setting, placement, and checking for accuracy of the captions or legends that appear above or below the diagrams or photographs, and the similar checking of "call-outs"— the labels, letters, and numbers that appear within the figure proper. Such checking may be the province of a production assistant, artist, production editor, or all three in concert (if the finished, camera-ready artwork is relatively simple and straightforward, the acquiring editor and the author are generally not shown it).

Exterior or Cover Design. Since the exterior of the book is what a prospective buyer sees first, no other physical part of the book receives as much attention from the promotion staff—and possibly the author—as the cover design. (To simplify matters, we'll use the word *cover* here to encompass any graphic image on the outside of a book, whether it's on the dust jacket of a hardcover book, the cover of a paperback book, or the preprinted cover of a college textbook or children's picture book.) Every author is concerned, rightfully, about having an attractive cover on his or her book. Unfortunately this is an area where author and staff can come to considerable disagreement, if in fact the house even allows the author to see a proposed cover design. Most publishers have a standing policy against this, experience having taught them that the creation of such an important feature is something best left to the experts—in other words, the publisher's staff. The author, whose photograph may appear on the back of the cover or back flap, whose career may be described briefly in a "bio blurb," and whose life's work may be summed up in a paragraph or two on the flaps, rarely accepts the acquiring editor's assurances and sometimes tries to get in on the act by sending in sketches, copy, ideas, and ultimatums to have the final say-so about the cover. Such altercations merely slow down the book and contribute to everyone's ulcer, author's included. The ideal arrangement, as far as the house is concerned, is that the author simply provide, as accurately and completely as possible, everything the staff requests in the way of biographical information or responses to questionnaires, report any changes in this material, and reply to the copyediting queries. However, a few previously published, successful authors insist on the right—often written into the contract—to examine, criticize, pass judgment on, and even veto the proposed cover design and flap copy.

To begin the work on the book's exterior, the art director first discusses concepts with the acquiring editor and obtains preliminary specs from the production supervisor. If the text of the book is illustrated, a piece of the interior art may be adapted for the cover, or the featured artist may provide a sketch or sketches for a proposed cover. In other cases, the art director does the sketches or gives the assignment either to another artist on staff or to a freelance illustrator, photographer, or book designer who specializes in covers. Whether inside the house or out, the individual accepting the assignment will be given some general guidelines—the trim size, copy to appear on the front cover, and other material describing what the book is about—and will return, within a few days or weeks, two or three hand-lettered sketches of his proposal for the cover. These are circulated through the house and examined by practically everyone. The art director funnels back the various suggestions, criticisms, and counterproposals to the artist, who may further refine the most favored sketch or produce new ones if none of the first batch proved satisfactory.

If the sketch has been requested and approved far enough in

advance, the artist next waits until the production supervisor sends him "bulk specs"—a set of specifications giving not only the cover or jacket trim size and other dimensions, but also the all-important width, in inches or fractions thereof, of the book's spine. Normally spine width is not known exactly until the work has been entirely paged and no additional material (such as index) is still to come. If there is little time in which to prepare the cover or jacket, however, an experienced production supervisor can calculate and provide bulk specs in advance.

Type must also be set for the cover, sometimes under the staff's direction, sometimes under the supervision of the artist. With bulk specs and exterior type at hand, the artist can prepare and deliver a cover mechanical (known as a mock-up or paste-up elsewhere in the graphics industry). This is an assemblage of type and artwork pasted in place on a piece of large, flat illustration board; attached to it may be acetate overlays with some of the type and/or artwork pasted in place. Although photographed individually, the images on the board and the overlays are superimposed in the final printing process to create the finished multicolored cover. (Today, many covers are created on a computer diskette; color printouts are routed through the house for suggestions and approval.)

The cover is printed separately from the interior of the book—on a thicker, heavier paper, on a different kind of press, and usually by a different company. The time at which it is finished depends on the house policy and on the type and importance of the book. Trade houses in particular make extensive use of the image on the cover. Whenever possible, the proposed front cover is shown at a sales conference to the entire sales and marketing staffs, and their comments are among the most crucial for the art director and artist to take into account while revising the sketches. The salespeople are given a copy of the proposed cover—either a press proof (the front cover printed by the cover printer but without the selling copy on the back cover or the flaps), a photostat, or a full-color photocopy of the front cover—and show that in turn to the booksellers they visit. The publicity, advertising, and marketing departments also get copies to promote advance sales of the book. Having extra covers or jackets printed and available for distribution anywhere from three to four months before publication is even more important for illustrated children's books. In most cases, however, covers or jackets are printed two to four weeks before the bound-book date; extra copies are sent to the publisher as the balance are shipped from the cover printer to the bindery.

The development and execution of the exterior design, then, is concurrent with that of the text. While the exterior may be the work of those outside the production department, usually the acquiring editor—and occasionally even the editor-in-chief— keep close watch on the effect achieved. The involvement of production editor, designer, and artist will continue during the stages of typesetting, proofreading, printing, and binding to be described in the next chapter. As each successive task is completed, its results are sent back to the individual responsible for ordering it. This system of review and approval is followed during the remainder of the production and manufacturing processes.

6

How a Manuscript Is Turned into a Finished Book

> There are men that will make you books and turn
> 'em loose into the world with as much dispatch as
> they would do a dish of fritters.
> — MIGUEL DE CERVANTES

Your work has moved along in the weeks since you delivered the manuscript. Management and staff have made key decisions concerning the physical aspects of the book and even about its advance promotion (to be discussed in greater detail in the next chapter).

You have answered the copyeditor's queries, the interior design is finished, and a design sketch for the cover is on order. Momentarily the original, copyedited version of the manuscript rests in the production offices, where, if this task has not been accomplished already, it is marked up with the designer's specifications, preparatory to sending it to a typesetter.

Setting the Text in Type

In discussions with their editors, authors often ask "When are you going to send it [the copyedited manuscript] to the printer?"

Few stop to realize that the work must first go to a typesetter and that typesetting and printing are two very different operations. We will discuss printing later in this chapter. Fifteen years ago, almost every publishing house in the United States and Canada sent all its typesetting to outside firms. As with so many other phases of the publishing process, the arrival of the computer age has changed things dramatically. Typesetters (also known as compositors) have revamped their operations and invested hundreds of thousands of dollars in the latest sophisticated equipment, and many publishers now use desktop publishing (DTP) to do some or all of their typesetting in-house.

Therefore, a myriad of ways exist to take each book through the production process. If the publisher has substantial in-house desktop capability, the entire job could be done in the office or it could be done in-house to a certain point and then farmed out; or it can be sent to a typesetter in the conventional manner. Which method the production supervisor chooses for your manuscript will depend on its features (length, complexity, schedule), whether diskettes are available, the needs and schedules of other books the publisher is having typeset at the same time, and the capacity of in-house equipment.

Before we examine the impact of desktop publishing (both in-house and from vendors called independent service bureaus or disk management services), let's look at the more traditional route. If the publisher is sending out your manuscript to a typesetter, which one of the hundreds of such firms will get the job?

At the larger publishing houses, the production director (the head of the department) generally designates "preferred vendors"—three or four typesetters to whom the company has guaranteed a certain amount of work per year in return for a good price. The production supervisor has the leeway to pick one of these firms for your book, depending on schedule, the kind of typesetting job your book presents, and the quality the house is aiming for.

While at large houses only certain unusual typesetting jobs will be put out to several firms for bids, some publishers do this as a matter of course—two or three compositors look at duplicate copies of the manuscript and submit their bids. The production supervisor may not always accept the lowest bid, however. Here—as in his decision which of the preferred vendors to accept—the production supervisor makes his choice based on the experiences he's had working with typesetters for many years. He knows their shortcomings and their particular areas of expertise. He must consider the delivery date the typesetter promises, and he must weigh that against his own knowledge of the typesetter's past performance and reliability in meeting deadlines. Precisely who does get the job can affect not only the schedule but also the quality of the book, the remaining editorial tasks, and the manufacturing.

The production supervisor generally selects a compositor that will typeset the book through a film method called photocomposition. Although only a few houses still set a fraction of their books in the traditional hot metal process, the working methods of hot metal are the source of much of the terminology of the typesetting process. Thus, even though chances are that your book will be set in photocomposition (and possibly with the aid of a desktop system), it's still important to have some understanding of the elegant, old-fashioned way.

Hot Metal. Hot metal is another name for Linotype or Monotype composition—systems named for machines that, operated by skilled craftsmen, cast the characters of a text in molten lead either singly (*Mono*type) or in lines (*Lino*type). From such castings, ink impressions can be made on paper (these are called reproduction proofs, or repros), which are then photographed in order to make the plates for offset printing. When these "keyboardable" methods of setting type were invented in the late nineteenth century, they soon supplanted handset composition to become the dominant method of setting texts for books, magazines, and newspapers for generations. Linotype was more typically used for straightforward bookwork; Monotype, the more expensive of the two, was most often used for more complex typesetting, as in scientific or mathematical copy.

Both of these systems still exist today, and both are in use. But there is a tendency among book workers to speak of them— nostalgically—in the past tense. The houses that continue to set books in hot metal (poetry, some children's books, and the occasional novel or collection of essays by a major literary author who insists on hot-metal composition) do so only rarely.

Film (Photocomposition). Even as the advent of desktop is once again changing the complexion of typesetting, it's still safe to say that the majority of books are currently set by photocomposition. There are many photocomposition devices, but almost all of them share a common operating principle. Characters are typeset when a high-intensity light source is directed through a matrix, or grid, that contains film negative images of all the alphanumeric characters and other commonly used symbols. When the light passes through the film negative grid, it exposes the appropriate succession of characters onto either film or photosensitive paper, which is developed much the same as film from any camera. Proofs are then made from the negative.

Desktop Publishing. Personal computers can now generate relatively professional-looking proofs by using a laser printer with at least 300 dots per inch, or d.p.i. (photocomposition proofs are usually 1,200 d.p.i.). The diskettes of the copyedited manuscript may be run through a computer-processing language (such as PostScript) to put the desired text in a form understandable to both the computer and the laser printer. Then drums inside the printer generate the type in a nonphotographic method like the one used inside photocopying machines.

Desktop publishing can take many forms. The publisher may have its own desktop equipment. Many small operators have been able to go into business as outside service bureaus, competing with conventional typesetters. Publishers have discovered that they can reduce typesetting charges for their catalogs and other promotional materials tremendously, either through their own in-house system or by using an outside service bureau. When a publisher has the typesetting on an entire book done desktop, sometimes it is only for the proofs; the final reproduction proofs, which are sent to the printer to make plates, are run off by a conventional typesetter from updated diskettes incorporating all changes made in galleys and page proof. When typesetters are used for the repro stage, it's because the publisher feels the letter quality of the proofs it is able to obtain off the desktop system is not high enough for the extremely sensitive cameras used in preparing printing plates.

In short, any means of composition can be superior to any of the others on the basis of the combination of economy, quality, speed, and flexibility required for a given project. It will be up to the house production and manufacturing specialists to decide which method is best for your book. (The type you are now reading, for example, is 10½/12½ × 25 Century Book; it was set by Creative Graphics Inc. on a PC-based PostScript system.)

Effects of the New Technology on Bookmaking. The last two decades have brought about some extremely sophisticated variations in photocomposition, both in the desktop field and in computer-assisted systems. (Marshall Lee provides a good overview of such systems and their capabilities in Chapter 5 of the second edition of *Bookmaking.*) Since the state-of-the-art continues to change rapidly, the average author need not be concerned with the details and intricacies of particular machines. The author should be aware of the fact, however, that a technological revolution is still in progress, and that the bookmaking procedures to be described during the remainder of this chapter are themselves subject to considerable change under the influence of this technology. Like computers, typesetting and printing devices in the modern era will continue to breed new generations of machines; this, in turn, will invite further changes in the basic editing and proofreading methods described in this book. In general, more and more tasks will be performed directly employing a computer terminal.

The electronic revolution in typesetting and printing has been mostly "good news," but it has not been without its occasional "bad news." Let us look briefly at some of the developments during this transitional period, and consider their effects on the author and the manuscript.

One result of the rapid changes in composition has been to hold down typesetting costs. Relative to increases in the costs of paper, binding, and skilled labor, typesetting has held itself down, and a page of type costs little more today than it did in 1975, when this book was first written. This is because of the fierce competition among suppliers; not only do new suppliers continue to spring up, but each successive generation of new machines often has an additional time- or labor-saving advantage. All typesetting firms are pressured to bid low in order to keep their own machines busy.

On the debit side, the new machines have not meant greater speed in getting books through the publishing houses and out into the market. Photocomposition machines were originally developed for newspaper usage, and it took a few years for typesetters to iron out the problems in using these on books, where page formats can be more complicated, typographical conventions are stricter, and a greater variety of typefaces is used. This ironing-out process is now being repeated with desktop systems, which were originally developed to typeset résumés, newsletters, reports, and other simple materials.

One kind of book has shown great affinity for the new computer-assisted editing and typesetting systems. Catalogs, directories, and technical reference works or lists of spare parts are frequently updated, sometimes on an annual or even a quarterly basis. This reprinting process becomes considerably less expensive when the entire contents of each successive printing is keyboarded onto disks. The data can be called up for correction a column or a page at a time on the screen of an electronic editing terminal. With no pasteup, then, one can very quickly change nomenclature in particular lines—addresses, say, or stock numbers—while leaving the remainder of the book virtually untouched.

Yet such rewards have not been without their drawbacks. On another level, the proliferation of electronic machinery has created a "Tower of Babel" situation, with dozens of machines and devices on the market, and very few of them able to "talk" to one another by exchanging tapes or disks across manufacturers' lines. In other words, they do not interface well, not even in terms of the various "codes" written on manuscripts prior to their being keyboarded. Even those publishers who now have copyediting (and sometimes editing) done on the screen often need to put their authors' disks through a translation program, so the in-house equipment can read them (this is one area where outside service bureaus and disk management services do a lot of business, for typesetters as well as publishers). Despite some progress, there is still no electronic bible, a standard in which both buyers and suppliers of type can put their faith and trust for the next 80 or 100 years. As one book worker observed, "It's not the hardware that keeps going haywire. It's the software."

A generation of book workers who are comfortable with the new electronic systems is now in the making, but until that generation matures and begins gaining access to upper levels of corporate management, there will continue to be a certain amount of confusion in the publishing business about the best way to utilize the new technology. The slow rate at which publishers take advantage of these new systems means that the industry will be playing catch-up for many years to come. Keeping all this in mind, let's look again at how some publishers do work with an author's diskettes.

Typesetting Manuscripts from Diskettes. In the last chapter, we briefly discussed how a few publishers might copyedit your book via diskettes rather than on an actual physical manuscript.

Many others hold the diskettes in reserve as they copyedit in the conventional manner. Once the production editor has finished her work on the author-reviewed copyedited manuscript, and once the designer has marked up that manuscript in accordance with the text design, the diskettes come back into play. Sometimes the production supervisor will give the manuscript and the diskettes to a trained staff member or to an outside service bureau that will update the diskettes, incorporating all the handwritten changes on the manuscript. In other situations, the original diskettes are sent together with the copyedited manuscript directly to the typesetter; the production supervisor lets the typesetter judge whether it is more economical (in terms of both time and money) to update the diskettes to incorporate the editing or to ignore the diskettes and completely keyboard the manuscript into their own computers.

In all three cases (diskettes directly edited on, diskettes updated by someone other than the compositor, and diskettes updated by the compositor), the principle the publisher is trying to build upon is "capturing the keystroke"—since most of the individual keystrokes the author made remain the same throughout the editing, copyediting, and design process, it makes sense to use them. The typesetter need not have a member of its staff rekeyboard the entire text (as is done the conventional way), and thus there is no opportunity to introduce new errors.

What's in Store in the Future? The technology now exists to edit, design, make up a page, and add colored tints and screens, all on the computer screen. As we discuss the printing process later in this chapter, keep in mind that much of the preliminary work involved in printing can now be done by a skilled operator at a computer right in the publisher's office (or at a third site), who transmits data to a printer hundreds of miles away via a modem.

Small independent publishers have been particularly eager to experiment and attempt to produce books in nontraditional ways. It's also far easier for a knowledgeable author to "self-publish" a professional-looking book, now that desktop publishing has made these skills more accessible. The major stumbling block continues to be the lack of a common language, but it's almost inevitable that this problem will be solved within the next decade. At that point, those publishers that remain reluctant to take advantage of the new technology may find themselves in trouble.

In the meantime, authors should expect the unexpected here. If you're particularly well versed in computer technology, don't be surprised if your publisher is less so.

Reading the Proofs. Regardless of how the text of your manuscript is set in type, the resulting lines are proofread, or checked, character for character, space for space, to ensure that the original copy appears as it was edited. The first stage in which this is done is in galley proofs. The term *galleys* stems from hot-metal typesetting, where galleys were long sheets of paper containing the typeset material for as many as three book pages. Today, galleys are often called first-pass proofs, a reflection of the fact that they often look like page proofs.

The galleys are customarily proofread by one of the type-setter's proofreaders, corrections are made, and new, revised galleys are sent to the publishing house. (Because there is little chance to introduce new errors, this step is sometimes skipped in desktop or when a typesetter working in photocomposition uses diskettes the publisher supplies.) Once the galleys reach the publisher, the production editor hires a freelance proof-reader to read the master set (the set designated by the typeset-ter to be returned with all the requested changes clearly marked) against the manuscript. In some houses, especially those doing highly technical books such as law statutes or med-ical textbooks, proofreading might be done in-house by two in-dividuals working together—a copyreader, who reads aloud from the typeset galley, and a copyholder, who follows the manuscript and alerts the copyreader to discrepancies.

Meanwhile, a duplicate set of galley proofs is sent to the au-thor (some houses will send two sets—the second being for ref-erence once the first set is returned). Unless the book is exceptionally long, you will be given from one to three weeks to look at your galleys (about two weeks is standard), and you should do everything in your power to meet the requested dead-line. When you receive your galleys, remember that they are be-ing sent to you for your approval of both their appearance and their contents.

Make the effort to read your proofs closely, for several rea-sons. First, although the proofreaders already provided by the typesetter and the publishing house are trained professionals, they are, of course, only human—they can miss mistakes. In ad-dition, the proofreaders may not pick up the same kind of mis-takes that may pop out at you (as the expert on the material). Finally, the galley proofs are the last stage where it is *relatively* inexpensive to make changes—this will ordinarily be your last chance to update that reference to a name in the news or to sup-ply missing information (but, as we will explain shortly, a con-siderable expense is still involved).

As you look over your proofs, it is important to realize that not all the elements contained in your manuscript may be present. The artwork submitted in the form of roughs will not be there, nor may display heads (part titles, chapter heads, etc.), captions, and labels for the artwork. Also, complicated material like tables is usually typeset separately; these are grouped at the end of the galleys, with an annotation as to where they will be dropped into the text at the page-proof stage. Whenever you see such material, it deserves your closest attention: not to criticize and change unnecessarily, but to check for accuracy and to confirm.

While you are examining your galleys, additional sets are being looked at in-house for various reasons. In particular, the publicity department usually orders a set of galleys that is sent to an outside company to be cut up into approximate page lengths, duplicated, and bound with a plain paper cover. The purpose of these "bound galleys" will be discussed in the next chapter.

Finally, as mentioned earlier, galleys produced by the typical computerized method of photocomposition or by desktop are often called first-pass proofs. The type set on these photocopies is broken up into page length, but in first-pass form, such pages may still lack running heads, typeset folios (page numbers), and some or all of the display type. Regardless of the manner in which your galley proofs appear, they serve the purpose of allowing typographical errors and substantive discrepancies to be noted and changed. The intent of all persons involved at this stage, however, should be to make as few changes in the proofs as possible, due to the cost of changing lines already set in type.

Marking the Proofs. Regardless of how your galleys are generated and whether you are shown galleys or pages or both, the necessary changes or corrections should be marked in the same manner. And it is important to keep in mind that they should *not* be marked in the way you made corrections in your manuscript. A change in the latter, if it is properly double-spaced, is made directly on or over the affected word or letter, in lead or colored pencil, spelled out, with no symbols or abbreviations. Corrections for typeset material, in contrast, are always made in the margins, never within the lines of type. Instead, a small caret (∧) at the affected point is sufficient to let the production editor know where your marginal change applies.

Even if your proofs require only a few corrections, it is a good idea to glance over a list of proofreader's marks, as contained in almost any style manual or in the back matter of most good dictionaries. You are not expected to master all of these symbols, but it will help if you familiarize yourself with them and study an example of typeset material with corrections marked, as in *Merriam-Webster's Collegiate Dictionary*.

When you return your galleys to the publisher, the production editor will collate your corrections and changes onto the master set her proofreader has checked. She will be able to turn around the proofs quicker if you follow these additional suggestions. First, always write in the margin and, if possible, in one margin rather than both. Second, always write horizontally, never vertically or up the sides of the proofs. Third, do not write any changes you desire in script; print, using capitals and lowercase letters (not all capitals), as neatly as you can. Fourth, for corrections of a paragraph or longer, double-space them on a separate piece of paper; affix this "Insert A" (or "B" or "C") to the point on the proof where you also print "Insert A goes here." Draw arrows, if necessary, in order to be very specific about where Insert A begins.

The Cost of Alterations. As you begin to read through your proofs, you will encounter three kinds of errors—printer's (actually, typesetter's) errors, editor's alterations (actually, from anyone in the publisher's employ), and author's alterations—distinguished on the basis of the party responsible for making them. These categories have no significance for you now, and you should concern yourself only with making the changes you believe to be in order. When the production editor transfers your proposed changes to the master set of galleys, however, she will also add abbreviations corresponding to these three types of errors—*pe*, *ea*, and *aa*—so that it is clear who is responsible for what. If the typesetter has garbled a word that was spelled correctly in the manuscript, the typesetter pays for correcting that line (pe). If author and editor allow a misspelled word to stand in the manuscript and the typesetter dutifully sets it in its incorrect form, that is a house error, and the publisher pays for it (ea). And if you, the author, decide to change something that was correct in the manuscript but is not to your liking now, that is an author's alteration (aa). Let us consider how much it might cost to make these changes.

Compositors charge for changes in type not in terms of individual lines but on the basis of the materials, equipment, time, and skilled labor necessary to make them. Nevertheless, when the bill arrives, all changes made in proofs except for printer's errors (the cost of which the typesetter absorbs) are itemized on a per-line basis. At the present time, that cost ranges from $1.15 to $2.00. That may not sound like very much, but if you were to change three words (on three separate lines) on each of a set of 80 long galleys (equivalent to about 240 book pages), the cost could run as high as $480.

Moreover, if you were to add words, phrases, or sentences at places where they do not fit, without deleting material of equal length, it's possible the costs could double or triple. By adding a word to one line, you in effect push a word or syllable of equal length at the end of that line into the next line, and so on. This "bumping" of type only ends when the compositor has reset lines until the excess words run into a blank line space or the space at the end of the paragraph. Sometimes, by narrowing the spacing between words, the compositor can add the author's extra word and control the bumping effect within three or four lines. This is a more important cost consideration for books set in hot metal than it is when using a photocomposition or desktop method to typeset. Nevertheless, to restate the case for holding changes in typeset material to a minimum, if you were to insert the one-letter article "a" in the first line of a tightly set, ten-line paragraph, this could conceivably require resetting all ten lines, at a cost much higher than $2.00.

Everyone working on your galley proofs hopes that everything will be in order, that typos are few, and that you will not decide to rewrite or add new material. Some minor changes will invariably be made. However, if you insist on wholesale changes—

rewriting portions that call for the substitution of several lines and even paragraphs or sections—the work will be slowed down (by the time it takes the typesetter to implement and proof such changes), it will cost more (in editorial and production time, plus the typesetter's charges), and as a result the price of the book may have to be increased, making it less competitive in the marketplace. This in turn can mean fewer sales and diminished royalties.

For protection against this unhappy but all-too-familiar turn of events, most publishing contracts stipulate that the author may be billed for changes he or she introduces into proofs above 10 percent of the original cost of composition. In plain terms, if it costs $4,000 to set your book in type, and if in galleys, pages, or both you change lines so that the resulting bill from the typesetter shoots up to $5,000, and if the production editor and/or the production supervisor can demonstrate on the basis of the master proofs that there were few editor's alterations, then the publisher, unless it is extremely tenderhearted or dares not antagonize you because of your reputation and sales record for previous books, may arrange to have $600 of that extra $1,000 taken off the top of your royalties. Such a state of affairs— delaying the book and losing money out of your own pocket— need never come about if you submit a truly finished manuscript in the first place and cooperate with your acquiring editor, production editor, and copyeditor in the second.

Turning the Proofs Around. Depending on the nature of your book, its complexity, the success with which the schedule has been adhered to, and the imminence of the desired publication date, you may or may not see additional proofs after you have returned your marked set of galleys. For trade books, even those with lavish illustrations, the author may see only galleys. For scholarly or technical books, he will usually be sent page proofs, again to mark for errors and return by a certain time. An extremely important text, such as that of a classic American author issued by a university press, may go through five or six consecutive proofreadings (not to mention the Hinman collator, an elaborate and expensive mechanical comparer of printed texts) before receiving the seal of approval from the Center for Editions of American Authors.

When turning around page proofs, it is more important than ever that you make as few changes as possible, and then only word or line substitutions that will fit within the same spaces as the elements removed. The author who, having received page proofs, still attempts to rewrite and add new material, is only asking for further delay and unnecessary expense. If the changes proposed require refolioing (renumbering) the pages, the setback could be considerable.

Skipping Galleys. If pressed for time, the house may decide to "go directly to pages." In this case, the first form of proof seen is not galleys but proofs of made-up pages. (Unlike the first-pass proofs that merely *look* like page proofs, these made-up pages include running heads, folios, display type, and the proper amount of space allotted for artwork.) Unless expense is of no consequence, these cannot be changed or corrected to the degree that galley proofs (or even first-pass proofs) can, but they have the virtue of eliminating the time necessary for proofreading and turning around galleys. Skipping galleys saves time for the publishing house, but it does not appreciably decrease the typesetter's costs or the composition and makeup time. Although the scheduling director would usually prefer to resort to this option only when he knows the manuscript presents so few typographical problems that it can go directly to pages without creating headaches further down the line, it's becoming more and more common.

There are times, however, when skipping galleys is not a good idea—for instance, if the space requirements for the art have not been carefully determined down to the last pica, or if the manuscript has been written hastily, so that many corrections are likely to be proposed by the author and acquiring editor. Regardless, if you are told that the rush to get your book out is so great that galleys are being skipped, take that as a sign that page proofs—if you even get to see them—are almost sacrosanct.

Making an Index. Whether or not your book is to have an index is something that will have been decided months ago, perhaps even at the time the contract was signed. Before you reach the production stage of page proofs—the earliest practicable point at which an index can be made—there are some important issues for you and your acquiring editor to discuss.

First, what kind of index does your book require? For a study of Pentagon spending policy, an index of persons, places, things, and key concepts should be sufficient. For a collection of critical essays on South American literature, you might also want the index to include the titles of literary works referred to, as well as the first lines of poems quoted in translation. A gourmet's guide to the Far East might offer an index listing not only the names of the significant Asian restaurants and markets but also the exotic dishes and foodstuffs for which they are famous. Some scholarly or highly technical works might even benefit from two or three separate indexes; for example, a literary anthology might have a second index of first lines of all the verse included. Remember that the index will be for the anonymous reader's use, not your own. If you cannot form a clear notion of what the index should do for the reader, discuss the nature of the index with your editor, or leave it all in the publisher's hands.

In fact, the basic decision you and your acquiring editor must make is whether you or the house will prepare the index. It is important to remember that most publishing contracts assign the responsibility for providing the index to the author. It is, in other words, an inherent part of the original manuscript, although not immediately deliverable. In practical terms, you as author can prepare the index yourself or you can hire an indexer of your own choosing. Most authors, however, prefer to have the publishing house arrange to do it for them; the production editor will then hire an experienced freelance indexer. Here, too, you will still pay, but the cost will most likely be taken out of your future royalties.

Since it is coming out of your own pocket or your own time and energies in any event, the decision might well rest on other factors—for instance, do you have the time to do it yourself?

(Since the preparation of the index comes near the end of the production process, schedules are usually very tight.) Do you have the inclination, and the know-how to do it yourself? Are you too close to the material to index for a lay reader's use? If you do decide to prepare your own index, there are a number of small, economical pamphlets on the market that will guide you through such a project. Sina Spiker's *Indexing Your Book: A Practical Guide for Authors* (Madison: University of Wisconsin Press, 1954) remains one of the best. *The Chicago Manual of Style* (14th edition) devotes an informative chapter to the techniques of making an index; the chapter is also available separately in pamphlet form. In addition, the publisher will provide guidelines for preparing the index—approximately how long it can be (based on the number of pages allotted for the index in the back of the book), how the index should be typed, and so on. The production editor will be able to answer specific questions for you.

The argument against authors making the index for their own books parallels that of attorneys traditionally advised against defending themselves in court. By the time your work reaches page proofs, you may find that you have temporarily lost all objectivity about what it says. Furthermore, although you may be able to create an acceptable index for your own book, a professional indexer can usually do a better job, in less time, and in a form more convenient for the production editor and the typesetter.

But if you decide to take the responsibility yourself and hire your own indexer, what will it cost? Figure on about $225 to $275 per 100 book pages. If your book is highly technical or loaded with proper names, that figure can increase to $350 to $400 per 100 pages. Most publishers pay professional indexers by the hour; the going rate is $15 to $18 an hour. (Some houses pay by the length of the index or by the length of the text, but the charges wind up almost the same as paying on an hourly basis.) Freelance indexers use all the shortcuts available, and for the average nonfiction book seldom bill for more than $1,250. If you decide to let the house arrange for preparing the index, you may want your editor to provide an estimate of how much it will cost. To help him make an accurate estimate, be as specific as possible about the kind, the form, and the purpose of the index your book should have.

Repro Proofs. Set in type and circulated in proof form, your work has been checked by your own eyes and by those of the acquiring editor, production editor, proofreader, designer, and indexer. When all of these readings are finished, pages have been made up, and requests for any last-minute changes have been noted in the margins of the master set of page proofs, that set goes to the typesetter for what the house hopes will be the final time. If there are many changes to be made, the typesetter may send back revised proofs for yet another check by the production editor. When these go back, the typesetter is now ready to prepare "repros" (reproduction proofs). These are camera-ready proofs from which the printer's negatives for making the printing plates will be made. While these usually come in the form of high-quality photocomposition images on dull-coated white paper, some typesetters will supply film negatives as well.

Corrections can be made in repros by "patching" (pasting over) an offending word or letter with a replacement cut from a duplicate set of repro proofs, but with luck, very few such patches will be necessary. Positive prints of sized, camera-ready line drawings or graphs may be pasted down in the blank spaces already provided for. Photostats of sized photographs will be pasted down in the spaces allotted and marked "for position only"; the original continuous-tone photographs themselves will be sent to the printer with the repro and incorporated onto the page during the next step in the process.

The production staff still has a bit of work to do at this stage, but the work of the editorial staff is virtually finished. Similarly, the author will normally have nothing to do with the remaining manufacturing steps of preparing the plates, selecting the paper, printing the sheets, binding the signatures, and warehousing the finished book. Nevertheless, the well-informed author should have some knowledge of these steps, if for no other reason than to calm his fears during the six- or eight-week interval it will require to accomplish them.

Preparing the Plates

The company selected weeks or months ago to print your book may have one, two, or a number of presses of different sizes and capabilities at its disposal. The dimensions of these machines affect the range of possible trim sizes originally contemplated for your book. Standard sizes throughout the industry—4⅛″ × 6⅞″ (mass market paperback), 5⅜″ × 8″, 5½″ × 8¼″, 6″ × 9″, 7½″ × 9¼″, 7″ × 10″, and 8½″ × 11″—achieve the maximum efficiency of press time and leave the smallest amounts of waste trimmed away from the standard-sized sheets or rolls of paper. In addition to trim size, the printer and its various estimators and schedulers also must think in terms of signatures: sequences of 8, 16, or 32 pages formed by folding large rectangles of paper printed on both sides and trimmed open at three edges.

Signatures in turn, when collated into sequence, form the book proper, with pages running consecutively from 1 to the end. If one counts the front matter and the blank pages that may be present at the end, the total number of pages is usually a number divisible by eight, the smallest practicable signature for most modern printers. So that sheets or continuous rolls of paper may be printed, cut, folded, gathered, collated, and eventually bound together to form a book with all pages in proper sequence, either the individual repro proof pages or the film pages must be positioned accurately in relation to one another before printing plates are made. Grouping them together is called stripping and the resulting pattern, called an imposition, is predetermined by the number and size of the pages relative to the size capabilities of the press.

Camera Work and Stripping. Let us return momentarily to your book as it exists in the form of individual repro proof pages. After they have been checked and sent to the printer, they go to a camera room, which might be the printer's own or which might belong to a supplier several hundred miles away. Here the pages are photographed (shot), several at a time, with a large, high-quality industrial camera; the film is developed and then sent to the stripping room. Meanwhile, if the book has halftones, screened negatives of the original photos are made to the correct size. In the stripping room, the screened negatives for the halftones are stripped—cut into and taped to the larger text negatives arranged in their proper positions. Imperfections in the text negatives are painted out with opaquing fluid. Elements of type or art may still be shifted slightly at this point, but the restripping process is expensive and time-consuming. (Once again, the later changes are made in the sequence of manufacturing steps, the more expensive they become.)

The negatives of the individual pages, the negatives of the art, and the negatives of the halftones have been stripped together in a predetermined pattern of imposition to create the larger negatives—each containing from 8 to 12 pages per side—from which the printing plates will be made. But before platemaking, these large negatives are put through a machine that produces positive contact prints known as blues or blue lines (also called silver prints, van dykes, or ozalids). These final proofs can be folded, cut by hand, and assembled in sequence, so that they resemble very closely the finished book in unbound form.

The blues are returned to the publisher for approval; the production department often gives them to the production editor and the designer for checking. Authors almost never see them. Except for the coloring, blues show the book pages and every element, every line of type, every illustration or accent mark as they will appear in the finished work. They are checked for overall appearance and for the accuracy with which they match the book's technical specifications: Are the gutter margins correct? Are the folios in proper sequence, the running heads correct right and left, the illustrations right-side up? If everyone has done his or her work, they are. House approval of blues gives the printer authorization to print. It may have directed the making of negatives and blues in its own shop, or it may now receive the negatives from a firm specializing in such camera and stripping work. The printer sends the negatives to its platemaking department, where, with arc-light exposures and carefully controlled chemical baths, the image of each large "flat" of page negatives is burned onto a specially prepared aluminum plate.

Selecting the Paper

Except for very small runs, printers do not normally provide the paper on which your book is to be printed. Instead, someone in the production or purchasing department of your publishing house orders the necessary quantity of paper from a paper distributor and makes sure that it reaches the printer's plant sufficiently in advance of press time. Estimating paper needs and placing orders is a complicated business; it is also an extremely important process, since the cost of paper, which fluctuates wildly, is usually the most expensive element in the manufacturing process and since certain kinds of book paper are difficult to obtain.

The purchasing agent must order the paper for the text and possibly for the paperback cover or the hardcover jacket. The bindery that is contracted for the work typically supplies most of the additional materials necessary to create casebound books. The production supervisor provides the bindery with specifications concerning the cloth, vinyl, or paper material that will constitute the case, the type of boards enclosed by such material to give rigidity to the case, the headbands, and the stamping die with which title and author's name are stamped on the spine of the case. Of all these, what probably concerns you most, as author, is the paper on which your text is to be printed. Its selection, like most other things in publishing, is determined by a variety of factors.

To begin, the purchaser must know if the book is to be printed by sheet-fed or web offset press, or on the Cameron press (these will be explained shortly), as well as the exact dimensions of such presses. He must know the kinds of images that are to be printed (e.g., halftones, four-color illustrations, or a second color of ink). He must know how the sheets will be folded after they emerge from the press. And he must know whether the house plan calls for the book to be beefed up (by the use of thick, bulky paper) or slimmed down (by the use of thin, low-bulking paper). Finally, he must know the number of copies to be printed. After some mechanical reckoning based on these figures, the purchaser can draw up the order.

Most text paper is made from wood pulp containing many additives (titanium for opacity, bleach for whiteness, dye for color, acids to improve water resistance, and so on). Because the acids contribute to the deterioration of the paper within 50 years, a controversy arose in the 1980s over the use of such paper. Today, most publishers have agreed to provide acid-free paper where economically feasible, in order to extend the life of your book. It is definitely advisable to confirm this with your publisher. (In actuality, "acid-free paper" is a bit of a misnomer, since pulp from many trees contains natural acids; acid-free really means that enough alkalines have been added to pH-balance the paper.)

Aside from that, your role as author in this paper-selection process is minimal. If you do have a suggestion or special requirement, be sure to communicate it to your acquiring editor. For example, if you have written a manual for beginning typists, such books are often printed on tinted paper, such as light green or blue, to reduce glare from overhead lights in the classroom. The point is certainly worth bringing up in preliminary discussions about your book. But be prepared, too, for the possibility that cost limitations may modify some of your original plans or hopes. You may have envisaged color photographs scattered throughout each chapter, near their references in the text. Your editor might decide, however, that if these are slightly reedited and grouped on glossy (coated-stock) signatures of 4, 8, or 16 pages, the rest of the text may be printed on more economical, lower-bulking paper. Listen carefully, then, if your editor comes up with a suggestion that could result in savings for both you and the publisher.

Printing the Sheets

The printing presses involved in bookmaking are so complex and the workers operating them so highly skilled that press time is not only expensive, it is also rigorously scheduled. The printer's management makes every effort to ensure that its presses are continually busy, sometimes around the clock. This in turn means that their sales representatives must work closely with production and manufacturing people in the publishing houses. When both sides agree that finished books will be ready to ship from the printer's warehouse dock by November 10, they are also agreeing implicitly to a succession of camera, stripping, platemaking, and printing dates that will make that final shipping date possible. If the plates are not ready when the job is scheduled to go on the press, the printer may have a standby job ready. But if the plates are not ready because the publisher's representatives have been derelict in delivering camera-ready copy, or if the paper is not delivered as promised, the printer faces potential revenue loss due to the unexpected idling of its equipment—and the publisher may lose its press time. The book may have to wait days or weeks until suitable time is available again on an acceptable press, or the printing plan may have to be modified for a different press. In other words, procedures and schedules in contemporary commercial printing plants are virtually inexorable. The huge capital investment in the machines calls the tune, and everyone associated with the enterprise dances accordingly.

Offset Printing. There are two kinds of photo-offset presses: web (where a roll of paper is fed continuously through the press) and sheet-fed. Each has its advantages, each its drawbacks. Books printed in two or more colors of ink or containing full-color illustrations are more likely to be printed on sheet-fed presses for runs of 10,000 or under. In some such presses, each sheet of paper must be run through the press one time to print one color of ink on one side of the sheet. More sophisticated sheet-fed presses are able to print two colors consecutively in one pass of the sheet through the press. Some machines, called perfector presses, can print on both sides of the sheet during one pass. Multiple-color jobs call for multiple negatives and plates—one set for each color of ink used. Aligning (registering) these plates with one another is a complex, time-consuming job, especially for four- or five-color offset printing, which yields illustrations in "full" color. In the larger printing establishments, web presses can be set up to run two or more colors, but in the main they are used for the straight printing of one color only.

The web photo-offset press derives its name from the fact that the paper issues continuously from a large, man-sized roll, feeds through the printing surfaces at high speeds, and is chopped and folded into sheets as it emerges from the opposite end of the press. For runs above 5,000, it is economically superior to the sheet-fed method. For much larger runs—up to 100,000, for example—new rolls of paper can be spliced to the ends of previous rolls without shutting down the machine.

With both sheet-fed and web photo-offset presses, the printing plates do not come into direct contact with the paper. Instead, after the plates are inked, the image is "set off" in reverse (or mirror-image) form, onto a matching rubber-coated roller called a blanket cylinder, which transfers a right-reading image onto the paper passing through the press at high speeds. This offsetting method has the effect of reducing wear on the metal plates and extending the quality and life of the run.

Cameron Printing. A substantial number of trade books are currently printed on a Cameron belt press. This press has the great advantage of combining printing and binding: Paperback books emerge completely finished at the end, and hardcover books need only to be jacketed. The Cameron press uses a web roll of paper, and it prints books in signatures of 12 pages. The printing itself is a direct-impression method—a camera shoots the repro to make flexible plastic plates, but unlike the photo-offset presses, these plates actually come in direct contact with the paper.

Cameron printing does have some disadvantages. It can print only in one color. Some particularly elegant typefaces do not reproduce well, nor do halftones, so the Cameron press is generally avoided when a book has halftones, fine line illustrations, or screens.

Other Printing Methods. A few other ways of printing are not currently used much in bookwork but still are worth mentioning.

Letterpress. Letterpress is a traditional method that is simply too expensive and inefficient for contemporary commercial usage. It can be used only when books are set in hot metal. With this method, a relief plastic molding is made of the printing surface of each grouping of pages. Each mold in turn is used to cast a metal or plastic printing plate, the raised surface of which will receive ink and transfer or press it directly to the surface of the paper passing through the press. The camera has no part in the preparation for letterpress printing. Book people are often as nostalgic for letterpress as they are for hot metal, but except for a few hardy individual craftspeople it has gone the way of the horse and buggy.

Gravure Printing. If your work is to be a large, expensive book containing high-quality photographic illustrations or reproductions of fine artworks, gravure printing may be used. Photogravure is more complicated and more expensive than sheet-fed or web offset, since its intaglio printing plates are difficult to prepare. Although quality gravure printing is obtainable in North America, a considerable amount of it is done in Europe and the Far East, adding more time to a schedule. It's only on large press runs (200,000 or more) that gravure printing is no more expensive than offset printing, so it is used mainly by magazines and Sunday newspaper supplements.

Ink-Jet Printing. This relatively new method of printing has the potential for bringing about still additional changes in the typesetting and printing of books. The bed of an ink-jet press consists of thousands of tiny dots, each of which squirts out a controlled quantity of ink on command from a typesetting computer activated by a tape or disk (imagine the huge light screen at a major-league ball park reduced to page size and emitting ink instead of light to create its patterns). This process has great appeal, since it eliminates the need for both camerawork and platemaking; books set via desktop could be sent by modem directly to the press. Ink-jet is not yet economically competitive, but some production specialists consider it the wave of the future.

Photocopying. The do-it-yourself publisher, the volunteers issuing a community cookbook, and the PTA program committee have been using photocopiers to print their short runs for many years. With the development of new generations of sophisticated copiers, paste-up lines rarely show and color printing is possible. While large commercial publishers will not print this way—they can get better prices and quality from an offset or Cameron press—photocopying continues to be a viable alternative for small operations, one that yields a more professional-looking product with each year.

Binding the Signatures

When your book is printed by any method except the Cameron press, the printed sheets must be taken to other locations and fed through a series of mechanical folders, gatherers (collators), and trimmers before all of the pages appear in proper order and correct trim size. Printed separately and in advance, special picture inserts on glossy stock are introduced mechanically during the gathering process (they are occasionally glued in place by hand). A sample set of these folded and gathered sheets (commonly called F&Gs) may be requested by the production supervisor; in juvenile picture books, multiple sets of F&Gs are used by the publisher in sales and marketing. The largest complete book manufacturers may offer all the necessary printing, folding, gathering, and binding equipment under one roof. Smaller plants may have to ship the printed sheets to another location or even to another company to be bound. This shipping time, of course, is "dead" time that adds to the overall time necessary to produce the book.

The intended market for your book will determine the kind of binding it will get, whether casebound or paperback (or both), and this will sometimes be spelled out in the contract. Beyond that, you will have little to do with the details and mechanics of binding. Here, too, in the last phase of manufacturing the production supervisor must choose one of several different methods.

Sewn (often called Smyth-sewn, after the manufacturer of the most widely used equipment). Signatures are sewn together with thread and then glued so that the case can be applied. The oldest, most traditional method of binding, sewing is very time-consuming and expensive and is rarely used these days.

Notch or Burst. In this method, notches or bits of paper are pierced out of the back of the signatures, and then glue is inserted into the notches. While much more economical than sewing, the finished book can be opened almost as easily as a sewn book.

Perfect or Adhesive. The assembled signatures are held tightly while rotating knives slice away about an eighth of an inch of their spines. Next, a durable adhesive is applied to the spine, and the cover or case is wrapped around and joined to the spine with the same glue. Rather than signatures of 16 to 32 pages, the book now consists of, say, 128 separate pieces of paper held together by the glue along one edge. Twenty-five years ago, random pages of a perfect-bound book frequently fell out, but the strength of the glues used today result in a binding as durable as a sewn book. Cameron presses, which bind as well as print, use perfect binding.

The preceding are the three most commonly used methods to bind a paperback or casebound book. Other binding options include saddle-wire, where the center of the fold is stapled like a comic book (used only for paperbacks of 64 pages or less); spiral or comb binding (generally used for engagement calendars and for some cookbooks and computer manuals, where the pages must lie absolutely flat); and side-stitching, which is primarily used for the reinforced library bindings of juvenile books.

If your book is a trade hardcover, there's one more step to go through after the binding is complete. By now, the jackets have arrived at the bindery from the jacket printer; they are applied to each book either by hand or by automatic jacketing equipment. At last your book is ready to be cartoned and shipped to the publisher's warehouse or distribution center.

To the Warehouse

Your finished book is stacked in cardboard cartons designed to hold the maximum number of units of that particular trim size. For marketing purposes, some books may first be individually shrink-wrapped in clear plastic or inserted into a slipcase. The full cartons are stacked on a pallet for forklift handling, and the pallets are consigned to the warehouse. (Some publishers forgo cartoning all or some of the press run of a book, stacking them directly on pallets and then carefully shrink-wrapping the entire pallet to hold the books securely.)

Sometimes, although 5,000 copies of your book may have been printed, only 3,000 were bound. The F&Gs or flat sheets with the additional 2,000 are held at the supplier (printer or binder) until needed.

From among the first few finished copies, the bindery supervisor will take sample copies requested by the production supervisor and send them to the publishing house. There they will be distributed to key personnel, with a couple of copies going to you, the author, as soon as possible. Additional author's copies—the amount depends on your contract—will arrive later (often, your editor's assistant has to fill out one more form to request them from the warehouse). You will also be allowed to purchase more copies, if you need them, at a considerable discount, ranging from 15 to 50 percent.

When that first package arrives, and you begin to leaf through your book, remember that no one is perfect—not you, not the people who work at the publishing house. If "they" have mis-spelled the name of a friend or colleague in the acknowledg-ments, or left an atom off the spiral of a particular DNA mole-cule in one of the illustrations, such minor errata can easily be fixed if and when your book reprints. For now, some congratu-lations are in order: You are a published author. By means of a wide range of techniques and procedures, some of which date from Gutenberg's day, some of which are products of the latest computer technology, your manuscript has been turned into a book. The process did not, after all, turn you into a nervous wreck; and it just might, with a bit of luck, pay for your trip to Europe next year. Like everything else in publishing, it all de-pends. Congratulations anyway.

7

How a Publisher
Markets a Book

My publisher, Schmeitzner in Chemnitz, is in the
wrong profession. . . . He is a genius at intrigue
and my books are his greatest secret. In eight
years he has spent nothing—not one pfennig—on
publicity. He has not sent out one copy for review,
nor placed one book in one bookstore. So you will
not find my books in any Viennese home. So few
have been sold I know the names of most pur-
chasers. . . .

—FRIEDRICH NIETZSCHE in *When Nietzsche Slept*,
by Irvin D. Yalom, M.D.

Of all the major industries in the United States, surely book publishing is the most primitive, the most disorganized, and the
most haphazard. Consider the following: What other industry
would launch a national campaign for an untested product
whose life span is usually less than a year and whose chances of
recouping its investment are worse than one in three? What
other industry would manufacture so many competing products
with only the barest notion of which of them might succeed in
the marketplace? What other industry would sink a hefty percentage of its capital into a variety of mechanisms designed to
stimulate sales, knowing full well that the most effective
method—that elusive "word of mouth"—is totally beyond its
control? In many ways, a publisher acts like a Hopi shaman
praying for rain: They both execute a number of rituals designed
to convince themselves and their followers that they can control
uncontrollable events, and then go home and cross their fingers.
If rain doesn't fall, they blame themselves or their acolytes for

not adequately performing some of the rituals, thereby angering the gods and spoiling the magic. "Go out and get some really smooth stones this time," they say, "and let's try again."

The limit of most authors' interest in the sales, distribution, publicity, advertising, and promotion of their books seems to boil down to two questions: Why haven't they advertised my book in the *New York Times*, and why can't I find my book in any #*!?# bookstore? Both legitimate questions have two sets of answers, one simple, one complex. The publisher's simple answers are: The advertising budget allocated for your book (provided there is any budget at all) can be more effectively spent in other media, since a full-page ad in the *New York Times Book Review* costs $18,220, and the reason your book isn't in the store is that the store owner didn't stock it because he didn't think it would sell in his store, or because the store hasn't paid for the last shipment of books sent, so the publisher is, quite reasonably, refusing to ship more. Presuming that your curiosity is not satisfied by these answers, an exploration of the various methods employed in both stimulating interest in your book and providing the opportunity for someone to buy it will help to answer these questions in a more complex fashion. Nevertheless, an air of mystery and uncertainty will still remain for some vital questions such as, what makes a best-seller? After all, a successful book isn't quite like a better mouse trap. Would you have predicted, for example, that *Harvey Penick's Little Red Book*, a book about how to play golf by an obscure (at least to nongolfers) golf pro, would make it to the top of the best-seller list?

Marketing a book consists of the following basic functions: publicity, that is, getting the word out (call it free advertising); sales, whether overseas, directly to the consumer, or to libraries, wholesalers, or retailers; distribution, how a book gets from a publisher to a bookstore, newsstand, or library; advertising, either to the trade or to the consumer; and sales promotion, that is, helping the retailer to sell the book. Each function overlaps and reinforces the others, and most are performed simultaneously, so that it would not matter with which we began our discussion. In fact, the marketing of a book commences long before the book is off press; it begins with the delivery of your final manuscript to the publisher.

Author's Questionnaire

Because authors generally feel helpless about doing something to facilitate the sales of their book once they have delivered the manuscript, they may find solace in filling out the author's questionnaire. At least it is something to do. The questionnaire is in part designed to provide the publisher with biographical background material on the author. The data will be used to provide copy for the dust jacket, the publisher's catalog, ads, and even for copyright forms. Some of it will be used to help sales reps promote and sell the book, and it may also alert the sales or publicity department to other potential markets or audiences in which to promote the book or the author. The author's web of professional, vocational, and personal associations are all possible sources for publicity or sales.

Even more important than the author's background are his or her suggestions to help publicize and sell the book, and equally important, the author's own efforts to promote and sell the book. Too many authors prepare these questionnaires hastily, not fully realizing that the information only they can provide can help determine whether the book will be a success or a failure. Nor do they realize that once the final manuscript has been delivered, it is no longer the editor who is the key figure in nurturing the book, but the publicity director or someone else in the publicity, sales, or marketing departments. (Consider it a transition from the obstetrician to the pediatrician.) Therefore, it is important to establish a relationship with someone in this department, preferably in person, but at least by mail or phone.

Blurbs. The author's questionnaire should request the names of people you know (or don't know) whose opinion would carry some weight in helping to publicize or sell the book, that is, people who might provide an endorsement or testimonial that praises the book. These remarks are generally called blurbs, and it is acknowledged that they can and do influence the reception of the book. While your editor will know some ideal people to query, you should be the source of the best leads.

These endorsements may be used on the dust jacket, in trade and consumer ads, in the press release, in the publisher's catalog, and in fliers or brochures. Their influence, however, extends to wholesalers, bookstore owners, reviewers, and book-club and paperback reprint editors in addition to the consumer. While few of these people will admit to being seriously influenced by blurbs, there is little doubt that they operate as a signal and can draw attention to a book struggling for recognition among thousands of competitors. The inner circle, those 1,000 or so writers with national reputations, are usually going to have their books reviewed and ordered by bookstores, with or without blurbs. The same will hold true for books by or about celebrities. But another 10,000 writers and their books will struggle for recognition, and endorsements by either noted authorities in relevant fields or by persons whose names or opinions have national clout may just provide the added nudge for the reviewer or book buyer to at least take a closer look at the book.

Therefore, in supplying names for possible blurbs, try to estimate carefully the potential impact of the endorser's statement: Will it really help draw attention to the book? You may have to be callous about dredging up tenuous relationships with people whom you might normally not dream of "bothering." After all, the fact that they will be asked for a blurb doesn't mean they have to or will respond. Besides, if they do like your book, and find the time to look at it, they will probably be glad to help— many "notables" deem this kind of request a professional responsibility, and successful authors in particular are aware that they did (and sometimes still do) need this kind of publicity. Don't be disappointed if fewer than half respond; some luminaries are inundated by requests. Preferably, this list will be a mix, comprised of people directly in the field or on the periphery of it, and just plain VIP's. The intended audience for your book will suggest the range of endorsements that can help: The broader the potential appeal of the book, the farther you can range outside of its specific intended audience. For a novel, for instance, just about anyone with a "name" will do.

For the average book, the publisher will generally have anywhere from 10 to 100 "bound galleys" manufactured. These are cheaply bound sets of pages with a paper cover, a portion of which the publicity department will send out, generally accompanied by a letter; several other departments use some for other purposes. (I say they are cheap only in the sense that they look like cruder versions of an actual book. In fact, because they are printed and bound in such small quantities, they usually cost the publisher more in unit costs than the book itself.) Sometimes the editor herself takes care of sending these copies out, and will help prepare a list of possible endorsers. The letter might be signed by the publicity person, or by the editor. If you think a personal letter from you would be helpful, suggest this to your editor and provide her with one if she agrees.

Beyond this prime list, the writer should supply the names of from 25 to 50 people whose opinion of the book will influence that elusive word-of-mouth campaign. Not just specialists, but anyone who would read the book and is in a position to spread the word, from the local president of the Rotary Club to your college alumni director. These people will be sent bound copies of the book as soon as it is off press.

Two more lists are needed: the names of publications that might review the book, and the names of ideal media in which to advertise the book. The publicity department has its own extensive file of review media, not only a basic list, but a whole series of special-interest lists as well, such as periodicals for sports fans, history buffs, and animal fanciers. But there are always a considerable number of specialized or particularly regional media that only the author might ferret out. You may sell more copies of your book from a review (or an ad) in a local newsletter with a circulation of 2,500 than from a review in the *New York Times*.

Since the author cannot generally expect a national advertising campaign for the book, a list of carefully selected media catering to those readers who constitute the most clearly identifiable market for the book may sway the publisher to place more than the token ad(s) most books generally get. Preferable to a mere list is a letter to your editor or contact in publicity, stressing both the potential value and the reasons for suggesting ads in those particular places. In addition to an ad, perhaps a brochure or flier sent to members of an organization or subscribers to a journal can also be justified. If you belong to or have a connection with an appropriate organization or association, you will want to inform and assist your editor with a potential "special sale." A book about minor league baseball, for example, might be purchased in quantity by a baseball team as a giveaway at the turnstile for a game on a Tuesday night. Sometimes a large special sale can be a significant money maker for author and publisher alike, and it may be only through your connection that such a sale is even considered or pursued.

Generally, the publicity department's knowledge and experience will be instrumental in deciding the most effective means and methods of promoting your book, but a letter from you accompanying your author's questionnaire, with a variety of *specific* and intelligent suggestions for promoting your book, can sometimes make the difference between success and failure. With a nonfiction book, the chances are that no one knows the book's audience or market better than the author; not to exploit this knowledge as carefully and as thoroughly as possible is a mistake many writers make, assuming that the publisher is the expert and knows exactly what to do. One word of caution, though: Don't overdo it. Incessant letters or phone calls will have a negative effect.

Publicity

The number of people in the publicity department can range from a single department manager and combined secretary-assistant, to eight to ten members, some of whom may specialize, such as in radio and television promotion, or author's tours. The role of the publicity department in affecting the ultimate success or failure of a book cannot be overestimated. All other considerations aside, a crucial problem for a trade book is to gain the attention of the consumer as well as the appropriate people within the media and the publishing industry. Though more than 20,000 trade books a year are clamoring for this attention, only upward of 5,000 or so will get enough to make a difference in sales. Just as an example, the *New York Times Book Review* receives about 40 books a day, or 12,000 a year, out of which they review roughly 1,500. This discrepancy between the number of books published and the amount of space available—whether on bookstore shelves, in libraries, in review media,* on interview shows, and so on—is the essential marketing problem for every publisher, and the effective coordination and efforts of the various departments are the means of tackling it. Even if one accepts the truism that word of mouth is what sells books, it is rarely fruitful unless the groundwork is supplied by the publisher.

In recent years, the publicity department's problem has increased due to the shrinkage of review and first serial media. Magazines buy less first serial material than they once did. Many newspapers that reviewed books have now ceased to exist, and many that remain either never reviewed books at all, or have cut back on their reviews. Even the *New York Times*, which once reviewed at least one book every day, now skips the Saturday review. Some magazines in part compensate for this trend: Many special-interest magazines, with new ones starting all the time, include book reviews—from magazines like *Entertainment Weekly*, which offers brief reviews mostly of best-sellers, to popular magazines catering to devotees of sports, parenting, wildlife, music, and dozens of other subjects, to a proliferation of specialized academic journals, which print extensive reviews of scholarly, professional, and (more rarely) textbook titles. Still, general trade books can be squeezed out when it comes to getting a review where it will be widely read.

---

*According to A.A.P. statistics, fewer than 15 percent of published books get reviewed; conventional publishing wisdom has it that bad news (i.e., poor reviews) is better than no reviews at all.

Early Review Copies. Bound galleys (sometimes called "Cranes" or "Cape Cods" after the name and location of one of the companies that makes them) represent the first set of review copies to be mailed out. If the publisher anticipates that this is a "big" book—big in sales, that is—special bound galleys with four-color covers may be made, making the package almost indistinguishable from a trade paperback book. Occasionally, other imaginative promotional tricks are played: Random House, for example, sent out the galleys of a racy novel, *Vox*, in a plain brown wrapper.

These bound galleys are sent out about three months in advance of publication date to trade publications such as *Publishers Weekly*, *Library Journal*, *Booklist* (these last two are library trade magazines), and *Kirkus Reviews*, which are read by librarians, reviewers, bookstore and wholesale book buyers, and mass market and book-club editors. Not only are these reviews the first indication of the critical reception of the book, but the select audience that reads them has a significant impact on the fate of the book. An enthusiastic review in *Publishers Weekly* will usually result in a greater number of consumer reviews, more nibbles for potential rights sales, and higher prepublication bookstore orders. A good review for a middling book in *Library Journal*, for example, will usually ensure the publisher of a library sale of at least 1,000 copies, provided the book is not too specialized; a rave review can boost this figure to 3,000 to 4,000 copies. Reviews in these journals are so important to librarians that some libraries cannot buy a book unless a favorable review from one of the library trade journals is attached to the purchase order. Early trade reviews or sub-rights sales can influence the publisher itself, both in the decision on the quantity of the first or second printing (sometimes ordered even prior to publication date) and on the advertising budget for the book. And, of course, these reviews, if favorable, can provide good copy for the first or second set of ads for the book. Poor advance reviews, on the other hand, have a negative psychological effect on the publicity department as well as on sales reps and others in the house. This can short-circuit the kind of enthusiasm necessary for the whole house to push the book. Just as the number of titles in the marketplace competes for the consumer's attention, the number of titles each house publishes every season competes for the attention of everyone in the house.

A number of sets of the bound galleys—anywhere from just a few to more than a hundred sets are made, depending on the publisher's expectations for that particular book—is sent to consumer review media. Some of the major daily newspapers, such as the *New York Times*, the *Chicago Tribune*, the *Wall Street Journal*, as well as the syndicated book reviewers, need copies well in advance of publication. (Bound galleys are generally ready four months before publication date.) Some of them will also be sent to Sunday supplements and national magazines such as *Vanity Fair*, *Newsweek*, *People* magazine, and *The New Yorker*. Of course, the audience for the book will determine where some of these sets are sent: A biography of John Adams would be sent to *American Heritage* magazine, and so forth.

Some of the remaining sets of galleys are used for the sale of subsidiary rights, which we will discuss later on in this chapter. Others may be sent to the sales reps and even occasionally to wholesalers and chain-store book buyers.

Bound Books. When bound books are ready, the publicity department will mail out 25 to 500 review copies (this latter figure would be for an anticipated blockbuster) though the average number sent is about 100. Working from your list, combined with their general list and supplemented by a hand-picked list particularly suited to the subject of your book, these copies will be sent to newspapers, magazines, journals, and syndicates, and sometimes as well to radio and television programs that discuss or review books or interview authors.

The publicity director and others on the staff do not rely merely on mailing out review copies. Part of their job is to talk with those in charge of delegating reviews at major magazines and newspapers, usually by taking them out to lunch. Armed with the fall or spring catalog, they will try to generate enthusiasm for some of the books, focusing on those that might particularly appeal to that reviewer or that publication as well as on the major books for that season. They may also on occasion diplomatically suggest someone who might be a natural to review a certain title.

There are a variety of overt as well as covert criteria that determine whether, where, and how a book is reviewed, above and beyond the actual merits of the book. It should surprise no writer that two dozen or so major trade houses may account for more than half of the reviews in the national media. The larger houses have the staff and money to actively promote their titles, spend their advertising dollars in these media, and attract the more glamorous and best-selling authors. Payola, beyond expensive lunches and free books, can be discounted. It is, at most, a rare event. There is, however, a sort of eastern publishing establishment fraternity that is self-perpetuating, and its members, · which include authors, do scratch each others' backs. A certain amount of justifiable paranoia grips smaller publishers, who feel that many of their good books are unfairly ignored, and especially "alternative" publishers, that feel they are fundamentally excluded from access to traditional review media, though in the last few years both are gaining more attention for their books. By and large, reviewers and book editors at magazines and newspapers are merely subject to the same crunch as every other channel in publishing, limited space, and it is to their credit that works of scholarly or literary merit, rather than simply what may be assumed the public will buy or read in huge quantities, are generally given a fair amount of review space.

Obviously, other divisions in publishing are equally active in sending out review copies, though on a smaller scale.

The Press Release. Simultaneous with or prior to sending a review copy, the publicity department usually mails out a one- or two-page press release; though publishers are now cutting back on this practice, and many books now get only a "pub slip," containing author, title, publication date, and price. Like any press release, whether it is from a politician or a laundry detergent manufacturer, the publisher's press release provides factual information with a purpose: to put across a point of view. Thus a book's press release delivers the facts: title, pub date, an author biography, and some idea of what the book is about, but it is usually "enriched" with blurbs and other promotional statements. One of its functions is to identify the publication date, so that newspapers and other media can review or announce the book at approximately the same time, presumably to coincide with the book's arrival in the bookstore. In reality, publishers try to get the book out to the stores a month or more in advance of publication date, partly in hopes that it may take hold before it is reviewed, just in case the reviews are negative. While most newspapers and magazines will attempt to honor the publication date, the squeeze for space and the problems of scheduling prevent them from doing this except for a limited number of titles. Most reviews will appear anywhere from a month before to six months after publication date, especially in magazines. Journals are notorious for reviewing books a year or two after publication, sometimes after the book makes its appearance on the remainder tables.

Many more press releases than review copies will be distributed. Not only are they much cheaper, but they can stir up advance interest in the book and permit the review media, which are inundated with written information and books, to decide whether to follow up when the book arrives or to request a copy if none is forthcoming. As many as 1,500 or more releases may be sent to: book editors at 500 or so newspapers and magazines, radio and television book contacts, newspaper syndicates, libraries, sales reps, and others. Since some books are newsworthy, copies may be sent to feature editors, news commentators, columnists, and a variety of "opinion makers." The publicity department will attempt to generate news coverage for the book, often racking their brains for a local or national angle.

As many local newspapers do not have their own book reviewer and do not subscribe to a syndicated review, they may use part of the press release itself for a review, particularly if the book has local appeal. For a hometown author, this may be supplemented by an interview, editorial, or feature story, which is generally accompanied by a photo of the author. Don't be reticent about sending in a photograph with your author's questionnaire. Even if you do not want it to appear on the jacket, it can be a useful tool for the publicity department.

News Conferences, Press Parties, and Publishers' Parties. If the appearance of a book coincides with a current event; if the book is particularly topical, political, or worthy of a feature story; or if the book is written by a celebrity, political figure, or notable author, the publicity department may schedule a press or publisher's party or call a news conference. Generally these convocations are limited to "hard" news or celebrities; a publicity director who arranges a non-newsworthy happening for reporters soon finds himself in the same position as the boy who cried "wolf."

Television and Radio Interviews. There is some dispute about which TV shows sell books the best, but an appearance on *Donahue, Oprah, The Tonight Show,* or *60 Minutes* is a coup for the publicity department, a windfall for the sales department, and a consummation devoutly to be wished by many authors. Unfortunately, few authors get on the top shows, or on any shows at all. There is no doubt that an author who shines on one of the top-rated shows can catapult his or her book onto the best-seller list within a week; but just as easily—and unfathomably—an appearance can create no ripple in sales at all.

Some local or cable TV shows will feature a hometown author, but most national television shies away from them unless the author is a notable personality, or the topic of the book either has broad appeal (such as dieting, gardening, or raising pets) or timely popular interest (a current political scandal, or a recent lurid crime). Novelists, even best-selling novelists, are rarely interviewed on television unless they happen to be personalities as well, such as Stephen King or John Grisham.

Be prepared for at least two auditions if a television appearance becomes a possibility: Someone in publicity will covertly give you the once-over to see if you would go over well, and someone from the program itself will interview you either in person or by phone. If you pass muster, you may be primed with some printed or verbal instructions on technique, which will include such trenchant advice as "Glance through the book before interview if book has been out awhile. See if book is on set."

Recently, radio has attracted more attention from the industry as an effective tool for selling books. There are more than 75 radio stations around the country that delight in interviewing authors, and many of these stations have more than one show that does so. National Public Radio has proven particularly effective, so much so that HarperCollins, Random House, and Farrar, Straus have all become corporate sponsors of the network. Publicity firms that serve the publishing industry increasingly use radio "tours"—tape cassettes of interviews distributed to radio stations, or live phone interviews with the author—to promote their clients' books. NPR's "All Things Considered," "Morning Edition," and "Fresh Air" are all considered powerful sales stimulators by publishers and booksellers alike.

Since media exposure can often sell a lot of copies of your book, it pays to suggest to the publicity department that for specific reasons you think your book will appeal to a certain local program or interviewer, and that an audience will find you witty, charming, and articulate. Even if you think your book has a narrow audience, you might find that certain anecdotes about the topic or what happened to you while researching or writing the book are funny, interesting, or whatever. A book on scrimshaw, for instance, whether a how-to or an illustrated history, might appeal to a television interviewer if you had a sufficiently interesting collection for show-and-tell.

Generally, unless you or your book patently appears to be a natural for radio or television, nothing will happen unless you make the first move—all the more reason to establish a relationship with someone in the publicity department.

Authors' Tours. The bane of many a successful author's existence is the author's tour. Unless you enjoy hopping from city to city and from motel to hotel—you will not enjoy a promotion tour. There is also the frustration of finding that in several of the cities in which you appear not a single copy of your book can be found. (The publicity director told the local sales rep you would be in Omaha on November 16, and he did call the local bookstores and got additional orders, but the warehouse shipped them late, and they will arrive next week when you are in San Francisco.)

Only rarely will a publisher sponsor a national author's tour; it's costly and therefore generally limited to authors of anticipated best-sellers; for smaller books, the costs exceed the benefits of a tour. There are other kinds of tours, however, besides the ones where the author moves physically from one city to another across the country. By using the broadcasting possibilities made possible by communications satellites, a TV satellite tour can be set up. The author sits in a single TV studio and is interviewed, in five-minute segments, by as many as 20 TV stations, one after the other. Such arrangements are expensive enough to be reserved for the top titles on a publisher's list, but they are still much less expensive than a city-by-city tour, which can cost more than $20,000. Even less costly than TV satellite sessions are the radio tours described earlier.

You may have the time or resources to sponsor your own publicity or lecture tour, locally or out of state, even if it's only to coincide with a vacation. Certainly your hometown and home state will welcome lectures and appearances at local clubs and organizations, and local radio stations and newspapers will be happy to interview you (in the largest urban centers, of course, you may not be welcomed so eagerly; the competition is keener). You can motivate the publicity department to send press releases and copies of the book, as well as to send letters and make phone calls if you indicate your own enthusiasm for cooperating and assisting in arranging these events.

Autograph parties at local bookstores can be arranged, but remember that you run the risk of having no one but your friends and relatives show up for the party. If you don't want to risk that embarrassment, it is still always useful to visit stores wherever you travel and offer to autograph copies of your book that are on their shelves, which may entice the manager to display them more prominently. Often the publisher can be persuaded to place some local cooperative ads in newspapers (the publisher pays 80 to 90 percent of the cost, and the bookstore pays the rest. It's really not a big deal, and the publicity department knows exactly how to go about it, but without any prodding on your part, the possibility may never be raised. Generating this campaign effectively requires the full cooperation of the sales rep for that territory; get to know the rep, and go out of your way to cultivate his or her good graces. It's advisable to plan appearances at least six weeks in advance so that you can manage, if possible, to take a month or so off, and so that publicity and sales can comfortably coordinate the arrangements—which will include seeing that books are there when you are (if you drive, put 50 copies in your trunk for insurance).

If you travel out of state on a vacation or can arrange to do so for any reason at all, and are willing to pay for your own expenses (you might ask for a partial rebate), the publicity department will generally assist you as just described. Appearances, media interviews, lectures, and autograph parties at either bookstores or in department stores are an effective means of publicizing and selling your book, but they are often avoided by authors out of fear, timidity, ignorance, or inertia, or shirked by the publisher because of commitments to the major titles on that season's list—or merely because other authors have been more vocal about their interest in publicizing their book and their willingness to cooperate in doing so.

Though authors' tours and other elaborate methods of promotion are usually reserved for that small percentage of books that the publisher thinks have a chance of "taking off," it sometimes happens that a modest book will begin to gain momentum, whether through unusually good or widespread reviews, by word of mouth, or by other means, and sales will dramatically increase months after publication. The publisher may then decide to initiate some of the publicity devices he had skipped, such as an author's tour. Or he may hire an independent publicist to plan and execute a special promotional campaign.

Publicity for Hire. *LMP,* under a section called "Public Relations Services," lists more than 100 individuals or companies who can perform a variety of publicity functions for a onetime fee or an annual retainer. Publishers can decide to call them in at any of several key stages in the life of a book: before publication, upon publication, or thereafter. A small house may find itself with a potential best-seller, feel that it lacks the clout or human resources to follow through, and judiciously invest some of its publicity budget in getting this outside help. These freelance services are also available to authors. If, for instance, your book unexpectedly gets a rave review on the front page of the *Los Angeles Times Book Review*, and you jubilantly phone your editor to find out how the house intends to capitalize on this serendipity—as happened with one of my authors recently— you may find that even though the editor is equally excited, the house has decided to "sit tight" and "see what happens" (meaning it is probably just going to enjoy the extra sales, but may not try to parlay the terrific publicity, as it should). If you can afford to spend $2,000 to $5,000 to hire one of these freelancers to promote you and your book, in the long run it would probably pay for itself and then some, in additional sales (i.e., royalties). The additional publicity might also, for instance, double the value of a paperback reprint sale. Before committing yourself to such an expensive step, you would want to discuss it with your editor, who will take it up with the house. In most cases, the house will cooperate with you and the freelancer, and even if it will not share the cost, it may consider some supplementary advertising, or be willing to compensate you for some of the cost if the campaign clearly results in additional sales for the house. It is an option certainly worth discussing.

Other Publicity Department Functions. Aside from the obvious need of publicity to help coordinate the general promotion of a title by working in conjunction with the editorial, advertising, and sales departments, they also act as both the "custodian" for the publisher and public relations spokesperson.

Being custodian means keeping any information concerning the author or title in its files, whether it is reviews, advertisements, the author's questionnaire, newspaper clippings, and so forth. Virtually all publishers subscribe to one or more clipping services, and each week the current file of reviews will be passed around the house. Generally a photocopy of each review is forwarded to your editor, who will pass it on to you. Some editors are less diligent than others about this, and a good relationship with someone in publicity will permit you to ask that copies be sent directly to you.

The publicity department makes sure that the trade journals and newspapers are kept apprised of internal changes of personnel, as well as providing newsworthy items about the house, such as a big rights sale, an acquisition of an "important" title or author, or a merger. Finally, in conjunction with the editor, publicity will submit appropriate titles for literary prizes. Do not neglect to inform your editor or someone in publicity if you think your book might be eligible for a certain prize. Generally the more famous contests, such as the National Book Awards or the National Book Critics Circle Awards, do not solicit submissions, but there are hundreds of awards and prize contests that do. Your publisher's publicity department has lists that detail the requirements for submission, and you should ask for them.*

From the variety of tasks that the publicity department performs, two conclusions can be drawn: first, that many of its functions are not just routine, and an imaginative and diligent director or department member can make a big difference in getting the word out (and that does usually mean more sales); and second, that the author who can skirt the line between being a nuisance and a confrere is able and welcome to cooperate and assist in affecting the amount and quality of publicity for his or her book.

What You Can Reasonably Expect. Unless the house has predetermined that the book is going to be one of their big books for that season—about 10 percent get this designation—either because of the author's track record, his or her celebrity, or the topic of the book, most authors are going to be disappointed; they generally expect more than a publisher can deliver. They are not going to try to get you on the *Today Show*, and they are not going to send a copy of your book to every Phil, Geraldo, and Oprah who might talk it up. They will probably not throw a

---

*PEN's *Grants and Awards Available to American Writers*, now in its 18th edition (Summer 1994) contains a description of most of them; it's available for $8, postage included, from PEN American Center, 568 Broadway, New York, NY 10012.

press conference or a publisher's party, nor send you on a national tour, invite you to speak at their sales conference, or ask you to autograph copies of the book at the annual American Booksellers Association meetings. All the more reason for you to be active and cooperative within the scope of your possibilities. Complaints of inadequate or ineffectual publicity generally bear no fruit, while diplomatic suggestions and a note of thanks for tasks accomplished can produce unexpected efforts and results.

Many authors, and even editors, having struggled through the one to five years needed to write and see the book produced, sometimes feel and act as if its appearance is the final curtain for them; it is now out of their hands. One must overcome this inertia; the public does not yet even know the book exists. External developments, impressive early sales, or enthusiastic reviews can all be the occasion for renewed or stepped-up publicity efforts, and it is up to the author as well as the publisher to stay on top of things and be responsive to continuing publicity opportunities.

What You Can Do Yourself

As I have stressed repeatedly, each author faces severe competition of one form or another at every stage in book publishing, from the initial submission to the book's appearance—God forbid—on the remainder table. To try to avoid this denouement, you must see yourself as an active partner in the entire process, rather than as a passive observer of an event over which you have no control and into which you have no significant input.

Filling out the author's questionnaire in detail is just one of many other steps you can and should take. You can generate local publicity on your own by sending notes to local newspapers suggesting an interview with a "native son" author, by writing to local book reviewers, and by doing the same with local radio and TV stations (of course, you will notify the publicity department about what you are doing, and inform it of your success). By generating interest and sales in your community, you may perk up your publisher's interest and effort. Arrange as many lectures as you can for yourself, and don't be timid or lazy about traveling farther afield.

Identify potential "special sales" for your editor (or find out who handles this at your publisher's and establish contact with this person). Is there an association that you belong to which might sell the book through its magazine, newsletter, or even a special mailing piece, which you or the publisher will provide? Is there a mail-order catalog it would fit into? A manufacturer who might give it away as a premium? An organization or club, local or national, whose members might want to buy and read your book? Are there specialty stores that might carry it? No one knows your book's potential audience as well as you do. If there is any chance at all for a special sale, write a separate letter exploring the possibilities, and make sure to supply the names and addresses of the appropriate people your publisher can contact.

To help interest the publisher's sales reps in your book, since it is unlikely many of them will read it, you can prepare a one-page fact sheet for the sales conference, pointing out what is unique about your book and why it should sell well. Help your editor come up with a "handle," a short, catchy, one-sentence description that either sets the book apart from the competition or links it with a previous best-seller (*The Tumultuous Years* does for adolescence what Gail Sheehy's *The Silent Passage* did for menopause). You may also be able to identify specific areas of the country where your book is likely to do particularly well.

For the sub-rights department, you will want not only to suggest the magazines which might be interested in reprinting a section of the book, but you can pick out the chapters most suitable for the individual magazines, or suggest how certain sections might be adapted or linked together to form a suitable article, or even suggest spin-off articles that overlap with your book's contents. Look over the list of more than 200 book clubs in *LMP* and see whether one or more of the specialized clubs—which might be overlooked—is a possible market for your book.

Finally, since it is unlikely that your publisher will fully exploit the potential sales or publicity for your book, considering the limited time and budget any publisher has to expend on a single title, you can consider hiring your own publicity agent (talk to your editor first!) and you can place your own coupon ads in specialized magazines (or even in classified sections), filling the orders yourself with copies you've purchased at a significant discount that, if it is not already stated in your contract, you can arrange with your editor.

With any of these tactics, you will want to be diplomatic, generous in praise for efforts on the publisher's part, and careful not to nag, annoy, or overdo it. By providing as much information as you can, and by supplementing rather than interfering with the publisher's role, you will generally find that your help will be accepted and appreciated. The publisher is as anxious as you are to see that your book is a success, even if he doesn't always seem to be.

Publicity in Other Divisions. Paperback originals—whether quality, oversized, or mass market—are generally publicized by the same methods as are used for trade books. In spite of the recent and continued growth in originals, paperbacks still have a harder time getting reviews in the media, though improvements, such as a paperback page in the *New York Times Book Review*, are taking place. As a consequence, the publicity dollar is more likely to be spent in advertising or sales promotion. For mass market houses in particular, the problem is compounded by having a small staff turn out a huge number of titles each month, so that it is logistically impossible to expend much effort in publicizing most individual titles. Because of the greater number of consumer outlets for these paperbacks, the built-in market for category books, the lower prices, and, in the case of reprints, the fact that publicity has already been initiated by the trade publisher, publicity is not considered as vital to the success of most books, except for a limited number of blockbuster titles.

Textbook houses tend to restrict themselves to putting in appearances at academic conventions and to sending out copious quantities of complimentary (examination) copies of each book. From 250 to 2,500 or more free copies may be sent to professors teaching a course in which they might adopt—require their students to buy—the book. Publicity and advertising are normally combined as a single function, as when the publisher sends out a mailing piece to 75,000 professors who teach Introductory Sociology, extolling the virtues of its textbook (with some blurbs here, too) and urging the teacher merely to write in for a free copy. Textbooks are hardly ever reviewed as such, so that publishers compensate by advertising in academic journals.

Professional book publishers also rely almost exclusively on advertising and sales promotion to get the word out. Primarily through mail-order brochures, using mailing lists purchased from magazines and organizations as well as their own list of previous customers, by space advertising in technical and professional journals, and by displaying at academic and professional conventions, these publishers are able to zero in on their potential customers.

Advertising

The rule of thumb that most trade publishers use to determine their advertising budget is to allocate 10 to 12 percent of the anticipated net sales for any given season or year, and then to apportion that amount among individual titles based on the sales expectations of each particular title. By and large, the major books for a given season claim the major portion of an advertising budget, and the amount of money left to advertise middling titles would never satisfy the expectations of *any* author. An author's concept of advertising is generally limited to consumer space ads, such as in the *New York Times Book Review*. Since a full-page ad there currently costs $18,220, a book with an anticipated first-year sales of 7,000 copies would blow its entire budget on about half a page. Aside from the fact that no publisher is convinced this kind of ad will sell a single copy of a book, it would leave no funds for advertising to the trade, the most vital initial market for your book. Very simply, if your book is not on the shelves of a bookstore, there is little point in spending money to attract people to the store to buy it. Of course, a clamor for your book at stores will generate orders, but generally the books will arrive when the demand has passed. The function of advertising, then, begins with an appeal to the trade: to bookstore owners or buyers and wholesalers. In fact, the advertising dollar must be spent in a variety of ways, many of which are unseen by the author, such as on the publisher's catalog, posters, circulars, and on ads in several different trade magazines.

Depending on the size of the publisher, the house may employ a single advertising manager and a secretary, or a department with a staff of up to ten or more people. The advertising manager works in close conjunction with publicity and sales and acts as the liaison between the publisher and the ad agency (some small publishers continue to perform the ad agency's job themselves, but even medium-sized houses use an agency). Working generally with an information sheet on every title, which contains a description of the book, background on the author, and material from publicity, such as blurbs, this department is also generally responsible for supplying jacket copy, catalog copy, copy for mailing pieces, circulars, and sales letters, as well as supplying book information and suggestions to the ad agency, helping to determine mutually the kind and format of specific ads, the media in which to place them, and the disbursement of the budget in order to get the most mileage from each dollar spent. In doing all this, the advertising manager must take into account and reflect in the ads the ideas of the editorial and sales department, as well as those of executive management.

While the author conceives of advertising as a means of persuading the consumer to buy her book, there are actually several other equally important goals to be accomplished. The wholesale and retail bookseller is the most important link in the chain between the publisher and the public, so that advertising to the trade, primarily through trade journals such as *Publishers Weekly* and *Library Journal*, is the most important first step. Each summer and winter, these two magazines publish their "announcement" issues, in which most trade publishers take full-page (or more) ads to announce all their titles for the forthcoming fall or spring season's books. During the rest of the year, some of the individual issues are devoted to other specific

categories or divisions, such as religious, juvenile, or professional publishing, or examine other segments of the industry,
such as regional or international publishing. Throughout the
year publishers advertise heavily in trade magazines—and generally provide more specific information about the book than is
found in consumer ads: the size of the first printing, the sales
record of the author, subsidiary rights sales, publicity, sales promotion and advertising budgets and plans, why the book should
sell well, and so on. Presumably the bookseller is informed both
by the size and number of the ads, as well as by the information
in them, of the extent to which the publisher is getting behind
the book—"$50,000 National Advertising Campaign!"—and will
be influenced to stock the book in commensurate quantities.
The slant of ads in *Library Journal* and other magazines and
journals for librarians will, of course, be more oriented to the
quality of the book rather than just its marketability. Successful
advance or early sales for a book will usually result in follow-up
ads in *Publishers Weekly*—"Third printing! 20,000 copies now in
print!"—to encourage the bookseller to reorder.

In addition to stimulating wholesale and retail book sales,
early advertising in both trade and consumer media is expected
to have an influence on subsidiary rights sales. Both book clubs
and paperback reprint houses are the main targets: The more
advertising splash for a title, the more attention is drawn to the
book, the more likely it is to be considered for a subsidiary
rights sale. Each sale that does take place may be the occasion
for another ad—"Main selection of the Literary Guild! To be serialized in *Cosmopolitan!*"—in order to stimulate further subsidiary rights sales as well as wholesale or retail bookstore orders.
Ideally, the publisher is hoping for a snowball effect: that each
event—whether a rave review in *Publishers Weekly*, a first serial
sale, a second printing, or a book-club sale—will generate more
interest, excitement, and publicity, which will in turn result in
additional orders from bookstores and wholesalers, another subsidiary rights sale (perhaps an option for a film), greater consumer sales, and finally an appearance on the best-seller list.
While advertising cannot in itself generate this activity, it is an

effective means of parading it and keeping the title alive in the minds of all concerned.

Reviewers, of course, are not totally immune to advertising either. Trade ads, which support the efforts of the publicity department, bring titles to the attention of prospective reviewers. The more splash a publisher makes for a book, the more likely a reviewer is at least to consider reviewing the book. Nor are agents and authors unresponsive to ads. While the effectiveness of advertising, particularly in consumer media, cannot be measured—except for coupon ads, which can be quite effective for how-to and self-help books—authors still believe in it, probably because it is so much more visible than publicity and sales promotion (ads placed primarily to please authors are called tombstone ads). Many successful authors will consider moving from one publishing house to another either because they feel slighted due to the low number of ads for their book or because some other house is heavily advertising its authors and they want some of the same. Agents respond to advertising not only because they know it makes their authors happy, but also because it lets them know which publishers are doing what, occasionally suggesting why and where they might submit their next manuscript.

Each book on a publisher's list requires a different advertising strategy or campaign. If the book is not slated to be a major book for that season and thus does not have a generous budget, the problem of deciding how to reach the greatest possible number of potential customers for the least amount of money is even more crucial. The amount of circulation for a particular magazine, journal, or newspaper is usually not the decisive factor: The publisher wants to reach the hard-core book buyer, not the casual reader. A lengthy biography of John Foster Dulles is obviously much more effectively advertised in *The New Republic*, which has a circulation of 100,000, than it is in *People* magazine, which has a circulation of more than three million. With more than 1,700 daily newspapers published in the United States, more than 8,000 weekly newspapers, and more than 10,000 magazines, the problem of targeting the prime audience for a "general" book is all the more acute. It is difficult to say what the "average" ad budget for a first novel would be—some first novels (usually about one or two a year from a given publisher) are published with great fanfare and at great expense in publicity and advertising, but most get little beyond inclusion in the ad that announces the season's list in *Publishers Weekly*. Sometimes a first novel will be advertised in a large-circulation magazine or newspaper whose audience includes "serious" readers, but the effectiveness of such ads is doubtful.

Many nonfiction books have a more clearly identifiable audience, so that advertising in the magazines and journals that cater to this audience can be effective. Your suggestions in the author's questionnaire or in a letter to your editor for advertising media will be considered; you may know the market and the most appropriate media in which to advertise your book better than anyone in the house, especially if the topic is quite specific, such as a hobby, a craft, or a vocation.

One cost-effective method for the publisher is a "P.I." ad (per inquiry). A magazine will run a full- or half-page coupon ad, for which the publisher pays the magazine 30 to 50 percent of the receipts the ad draws. Or the magazine will list or review books that might interest its readers on a "bookshelf" page, and—acting like a book club—will offer these books at list price or for a small discount, while buying the books directly from the publisher at a standard bookstore discount. For both special-interest and new magazines, this helps to inflate the number of advertising pages and brings in some additional revenue, whereas for the publisher it is basically a free ad, since he is still selling his books at a normal discount.

While advertisements in major national newspapers are generally most effective for books with a wide appeal, a book by a local author or a book with regional interest (such as *Libraries of New England*) may warrant ads in a regional newspaper. Publishers may try to coordinate these ads with local interviews, appearances, and autograph parties at bookstores.

Television advertising is costly and thus used very sparingly. Mass market publishers now occasionally use TV to advertise books with anticipated sales of a half million or more copies, or for series of highly successful romances, for example. Sometimes the chain bookstores will share the cost of TV advertising with some trade publishers for specific "major" titles. Cable TV has allowed publishers to choose audiences with more precision—they can reach specific groups with specific titles by advertising on CNN or MTV or the Black Entertainment Network. Late-night or early-morning nonnetwork advertising is sometimes used, but even before paying for the air time itself, the production cost alone for a modest TV ad can range from $15,000 to $50,000. High cost and the inability to measure its usefulness have limited publishers' interest in TV advertising. A television ad tie-in, however—promoting or advertising a book that is simultaneously appearing as a TV film or series—is an opportunity most publishers will exploit when possible.

Radio advertising is less expensive, and the number of programs that feature authors is higher, so that books are more commonly advertised on radio. Some programs, for instance, will run a prerecorded interview of an author for a price. In general, though, only a very small proportion of nonfiction books are advertised on either radio or television, since it is felt that hard-core readers can be reached more inexpensively through magazines and journals.

The use of mailing pieces, which might just as readily be identified as a sales function, is particularly effective for professional or highly technical books. These books are generally more expensive (so that the cost of mailings is offset by the higher net receipts), the specific audience is easier to reach, and the percentage of book buyers, per capita, is much higher than for the general population. Trade publishers, who also often publish books for specialized audiences, will use mailing pieces as well, especially when they publish a series or a number of books in a specific field. Textbook publishers generally confine their advertising to journals and use mailing pieces—frequently with coupons attached—to solicit requests for examination copies.

A coupon ad, conversely, may be most effective for a book with wide appeal, directed toward an audience that does not consist of hard-core book buyers. A book on how to stop smoking or books on dieting or self-help are examples.

The library market is so vital to the juvenile division, professional publishers, and university presses—as well as to the trade division of many houses—that a separate budget may be set aside for library promotion, which combines advertising, sales promotion, and publicity. There are more than a dozen publications specifically for librarians, such as *Library Journal* and the *A.L.A. Booklist*, and in addition to advertising in these special media, publishers may produce separate catalogs solely for the library market.

Since the ad budget for most books is so limited, publishers frequently resort to group ads, in which several or more titles are combined, sometimes featuring one or more titles and merely listing the others. This holds true for both trade and consumer ads and mailing pieces, whether the book is directed to a broad audience or a narrow one. Authors tend to overlook the group ad when complaining about the lack of advertising for their book.

If you consider the publisher's expectation of selling roughly 6,000 copies of a "middling" book and recognize that money allocated for advertising must also pay for trade ads, catalogs, and a variety of unseen costs (cost of preparation of the ad by the ad agency, for example), the author should not be disappointed to learn that only a handful of ads or less have been scheduled for his book. The time to complain is when no ads at all are placed for your book, which is not that uncommon. As in all businesses, the advertising department often finds itself over budget before the year is out, and the middling book is the one most likely to be short-changed. Also, unforeseen expenses—additional ads for a book that starts to take off or gets rave reviews—may cut even deeper into the yearly budget. If the advance sales exceed the publisher's expectations, if a hefty subsidiary rights sale is concluded, if the book gets excellent reviews in trade journals or large-circulation consumer magazines or newspapers, or if the bookstore orders or reorders are heavy, then the publisher will generally follow up with some additional ads. In other words, it is often only when the book succeeds in spite of minimal advertising that the publisher increases the budget for the book, though, of course, a major book will already have a substantial budget. The main reason for this Catch-22 is the publishing lottery: The major books aside, most publishers are still producing more books than they can effectively promote, either through publicity, advertising, or sales promotion—in spite of the periodic trimming of lists at many major trade houses—partly because it's impossible to know in advance which ones will sell and which won't. The only certainty is that fewer than half will have to support the rest.

Sales, Sales Promotion, and Distribution

Shaky economic times in recent years forced many publishers to cut back on their inside-the-house sales forces and increased the use of "commission reps." Smaller sales staffs are now the rule. Publishers also learned to control the itineraries of their sales staffs more carefully, and to concentrate sales calls on those stores or areas with greater sales potential. The slack has been taken up by increased telephone sales. In selling by mail or through coupon ads, publishers are trying to target the audiences more precisely, and are using test mailings or ads more frequently, in order to make sure that a larger campaign is worth the expenditure.

Obviously, no department is more vital to the life or death of a publishing house than sales, and any economic pressure is felt most keenly here. Publishers are trying to boost sales by opening up more nonbookstore markets, from sporting goods stores to hardware stores to garden supply stores. And special sales, such as selling to manufacturers that may give away a book as a premium, are being pursued with renewed intensity.

One additional result of these pressures is stricter attention to the budget, not only in marketing, but in all the other departments in the house. As a consequence more power and decision making has passed into the hands of the accounting department and the financial people—a trend helped along by conglomerate policies—and so in some ways publishing is beginning more and more to resemble conventional industries, such as those that manufacture and sell soaps or cereals.

The Sales Conference. The cycle for selling trade books officially begins at the sales conference. Even though the sales manager may have had a decisive voice in determining whether or not to sign up a book and in estimating how many copies it might sell, it is not until this semiannual conference is held that the sales reps are actually presented with the next season's list. In the last decade, more and more books have come to be published during the summer and winter months, so that the traditional fall and spring lists are actually spread out over 12 months. Even though some houses now have three lists, with sales meetings usually held in April, August, and December, the practice of holding two meetings a year—in May for the fall list and in December for the spring list—is still widely followed.

The conference lasts from one to four days and is generally attended (sometimes by means of videotape) by all the editors and by sales reps, as well as by representatives from publicity, advertising, and other departments. The main objectives of the meeting are to inform the sales reps of the next season's books, to outline the publicity and advertising plans for the list, and, in general, to fire up enthusiasm. In addition to the seasonal catalog, sales reps are supplied with dust jackets, if they are ready, copies of forthcoming ads and circulars, press releases, blurbs, backlist information, and sometimes copies or page proofs of one or more of the anticipated major books for the next season.

A medium-size house may publish up to 40 or 50 books a season, not to mention the juvenile titles, which are also generally presented at this meeting. As a consequence, each editor is expected to spend no more than three to four minutes presenting one of his or her books, providing a brief description that emphasizes the book's merits, discusses its potential audience and market, distinguishes it from the competition, and points out salient facts about the author. Lest you should feel overly dismayed that four minutes hardly do justice to your book, observe that when the sales rep presents the book to the buyer, she will probably average less than a minute per book. In an attempt to overcome this handicap, the editor will try to provide a "handle" for each of his books, a one-sentence pitch designed to arrest the attention of the bookseller by pinpointing the book's main virtue and its theme. For a while, "This book does for _____ what Tracy Kidder did for computers" was popular, but then it began to appear that the line was hurting more books than it was helping. Thinking up a striking handle (or a good title for that matter) is an art, and editors often have to limp along with something like "the new novel by the master of medical suspense."

As the books are presented, questions and comments arise, from "That cover will kill the sales on the West Coast; can't you put some red in it?" to "They won't go for Russian cooking in my territory; nobody's ever heard of borscht in Alabama." The editors' presentations are followed up by a report of the publicity and advertising campaigns that are planned for the forthcoming books. A certain amount of time will also be devoted to the current list and the backlist: What's selling well and what isn't; what additional ads, sales promotion, or publicity are intended; what so and so's appearance on the *Today Show* has done for her book; which books are going into second or third printings; which books have been taken as book-club selections or been sold to a paperback reprinter; and so forth.

A major feature on the last day of the conference is the setting of quotas by the sales manager for "advance sales." Taking into account the original estimate for the first year's sale of a book, the amount of the first printing, the comments of sales reps and others on each title during the presentations and the rest of the meeting (including palavers over lunch and dinner), the initial success of specific subsidiary rights sales, and finally his own educated hunch, the sales manager will set a specific quota for each title of the total number of copies he wants, hopes, or expects the entire sales force to sell on their first trip into the field. Furthermore, he will allocate a specific portion of that quota to each sales rep or territory. For a first printing of 7,500 copies, for instance, he may set an advance of 2,500 copies: 250 for California, 300 copies for the southeast, 400 copies for New England, and so forth. The quota may be influenced by the previous regional sales of that author's book, the subject of the book, the author's location, or the nature of the advertising and publicity campaign.

While this quota is obviously as much a fantasy as the estimate of the first year's sale of a specific title, it often takes on the potency of a self-fulfilling prophecy. The higher the quota for a specific title, the more time, effort, and attention each salesperson will devote to that title, so that the sales manager's prediction influences the sales rep's exertions, which in turn influences both the bookseller's expectations and his or her order for that title. While many books manage to break the initial mold that is cast for them, either doing better or worse than has been prophesied, the prepublication quota is often a vital determinant in the success or failure of many books. The rationale, and often the result of these quotas, is the oft-mentioned competition for time and space. In this instance, each salesperson knows that a bookseller has only limited shelf space for the 20,000 new trade books published each year, and that the seller can be turned on by only a handful of titles on that publisher's seasonal list. Thus, the bulk of the sales pitch is confined to the major books; the rest go out on a wing and a prayer. However, as the advance sales are sought prior to actual book publication, an unexpected enthusiastic response on the part of buyers, that is, bigger orders than were anticipated, may not only increase the size of the first printing, but may influence the house to spend additional money on advertising, to expend more time on publicity and sales promotion, and to urge the reps to increase their efforts for that title.

The Sales Staff. There are two categories of sales reps in trade publishing: those who work solely for that house, and those who work exclusively on commission and represent several publishers. The former are salaried by the publisher, work exclusively for that house, and generally also get a yearly incentive bonus based on their sales and quotas. The latter are independent, work exclusively on a commission of roughly 10 percent of sales, and may represent from 5 to as many as 40 publishers. While the bigger houses usually employ house reps, and the smaller houses commission reps, many publishers work with a combination of both. Overseeing the staff is a sales manager, whose other prime responsibilities are to see that accounts are serviced properly and regularly and that major customer relations problems are solved, to set house policy on returns and discounts, to work with other departments for a smooth coordination of overall marketing strategy, to advise on decisions about signing up books, and to see that the sales reps are supplied with any requisite new information or materials that filter in from day to day. The sales manager will also personally take care of, or oversee, the selling to the large chains. B. Dalton has more than 1,000 stores. Barnes & Noble (which is now owned by B. Dalton) has 938 stores, of which 168 are "superstores." Waldenbooks has more than 1,200. Crown, Kroch's and Brentano's, Books-A-Million, Loriat's, Borders, and Waterstone's are also significant chain bookstores, though none of them is nearly as large as the two leaders.

Publishers usually estimate that for most trade titles, as much as 20 percent of the sales will be through Dalton and Walden. This kind of sales power can have a significant impact on some publishing decisions. That the chains almost never take literary first novels, for instance, is partly responsible for their diminishing numbers. And trade houses are sometimes swayed for or against a book by the answer a buyer at either chain gives during a phone call asking whether or not he or she thinks a book on X, Y, or Z will or will not sell well.

Each house will divide the country into territories, whose size is determined both by the number of salespersons employed by the house and the volume of business in a specific territory. The biggest houses may have as many as 100 representatives, and a single territory may be no larger than ten square miles, whereas a smaller house may have one man or woman covering a territory as large as New England.

Most sales reps will service roughly 200 accounts, which may include individual retail bookstores, chains, wholesalers, and sometimes library systems. On an average, each visits her bookstore accounts four times a year: once before the fall and spring lists are published, and once during the season to check stock and take reorders. At the two extremes are large accounts, such as wholesalers or chains, that may be serviced every month— and once a week by phone—and the smaller retail stores that are visited but once a year, or which may never see a sales rep and are serviced by phone or mail. Armed with a kit—catalogs, dust jackets, ads, circulars, and so on—the sales rep may spend one to three weeks on the road, though, as most of them live in the territory, they generally do not have to be away from home more than a week at a time. In addition to selling the new list, they usually check stock to see which current titles have sold out and ought to be reordered, and will also see to it that perennials on the backlist are on hand. As an average sales call may last two hours, of which half an hour may be spent in checking stock and another half hour on the backlist (a book goes on the backlist the day it is published), the sales rep may have only an hour or less to talk about the 25 to 50 new titles. (A commissioned sales rep, who represents several firms, may be taking orders for more than 200 new titles.) From past experience, she generally knows what kinds of books are stocked or go over well for that store and will concentrate on pushing the major titles and a smattering of the others.

To retain credibility, a judicious salesperson will neither oversell her books nor exaggerate the potential sales of a title—nor will she push more books on that store than she thinks it can reasonably sell. Since the returns policy of virtually all publishers permits the store to send back all unsold books for full credit up to a year after purchase—and now more commonly for as long as the book remains in print—the temptation exists to overload the store by pointing out that "you can always return what you don't sell." But the paperwork for processing returns is time-consuming and complicated (partly to discourage returns), the store's shelf and storage space are limited, and some publishers require that the buyer pay the shipping charges on both the incoming order and the returns, which can eat up slim profits. Thus the buyer exercises restraint for these reasons, and the sales rep, who will visit the store several times a year, ideally controls her impulses to oversell so that her advice and suggestions are respected on future calls.

The Bookstore. How many bookstores are there in the United States? It depends what you mean by a bookstore. There are

20,000 outlets that carry some kind of hardcover book—including religious, medical, secondhand stores, college and department store concessions, and the chains. Of the 9,000 or so stores that sell new trade books, only about 2,500 stock a fair sampling of trade publishers' front and backlists. The remaining 6,500 carry only staple titles—dictionaries and other reference books, maybe a few classics, some long-selling titles like *What Color Is Your Parachute?*, and some remainders. Most of the chain stores carry only about 15,000 or so titles, which means you're not likely to find the one you want there. There is a promising new development in the "superstores" that have been opened in recent years. These are stores run by the chains—Barnes & Noble has the majority of them—that stock more than 100,000 titles each. The 200 or so superstore outlets accounted for more than a half billion dollars in sales in 1992, so they may prove a significant force in bookselling during the coming years. Still, with only a little more than 2,500 serious bookstores in the country, it's no wonder that most books are printed and sold in such small numbers.

Wholesalers and Jobbers. Though the bookstore may not order your book from the publisher's representative, it does have access to another supplier. The major wholesalers or jobbers, of whom there are about 15 spread around the United States, will stock a huge inventory of trade books from most commercial publishers—not only the major titles, but the middling and backlist books, too. These 15 or so are backed up by almost 1,000 smaller regional wholesalers, many of whom are flourishing because they provide personal service and direct sales calls, which publishers are now supplying by computer or phone. Often in competition among themselves, the small wholesaler may be more imaginative and aggressive in opening up and servicing nonbook outlets, such as toy stores. Some jobbers primarily service trade book accounts; others specialize in library and school sales; most service both. If a customer requests a title that the store doesn't carry or has run out of, the store can generally get the book from the wholesaler within three days, no matter where the store is located. A bookstore in Montana might have to wait three to five weeks to get a shipment of books from an eastern publisher. They may order forthcoming titles from the publisher's representative, but once the season is started, they will generally rely on the wholesaler to supply them with current books. The wholesaler often works closely with the publisher to provide the local store with other materials and assistance: He may supply advice on forthcoming titles, copies of book reviews, or a list of best-sellers, and help coordinate promotional appearances of authors.

S.T.O.P. As big an inventory as a wholesaler may carry, he cannot possibly stock copies of each of the approximately half million titles that are currently in print in the United States. The Single Title Order Plan, sponsored and administered by the American Booksellers Association, permits the bookstore to order one or more copies of any single title and still receive the publisher's usual trade discount (which varies depending on the publisher), though prepayment must be included with the order. Many publishers have individual plans for single-copy orders, but S.T.O.P. is the most widely used service. Single-copy orders are often inefficient—it can sometimes take anywhere from three to five weeks or more to get a single book through S.T.O.P. or the publisher—and it is one of the prime examples of the inability of the publishing industry to provide adequate distribution of its products.

Mass Market Wholesalers. While many wholesalers now also stock mass market paperbacks, the major suppliers for the more than 100,000 paperback outlets—that include drugstores, airline terminals, magazine stands, variety store chains, and supermarkets—are the 550 or so "independents," whose primary business includes magazine distribution (only about 350 carry books). Sales reps for mass market publishers service both bookstores and independents, but since the majority of outlets are businesses for whom paperbacks are a sideline, so that no one on the staff is likely to have or develop the expertise to select paperbacks judiciously for their particular outlet, the book selections are often made by the publisher or the independent distributor. As consumer buying patterns tend to vary, depending on both the regional location and the type of outlet, some independent distributors have paperback experts who choose and prepack a representative selection and quantity of new titles, based on the previous sales history and volume of business for a particular outlet. Some distributors are novices, choose stock carelessly, overstock their outlets, and service the book racks with minimum attention to what's moving and what isn't, what should be returned and what reordered. This accounts in part for the staggering industrywide average returns for mass market paperbacks.

Publishers also have a variety of automatic allotment systems for both nonbookstore outlets and independent distributors who are either less knowledgeable about current paperbacks or don't have the time or personnel to buy carefully or prudently. Keeping track of the bewildering array and huge output of new titles, not to mention the backlist, is not a task for the dilettante.

College Textbooks. The textbook sales rep has a special moniker, college traveler, perhaps in recognition of the fact that her job is more public relations than salesmanship. The largest houses employ upward of 60 sales reps, while the smallest may rely on catalogs and other mailing pieces to promote and sell their books. Each traveler's itinerary consists of a territory in which she visits a specific number of community and four-year colleges and universities. Most textbook houses publish both basic texts—single comprehensive books that presumably cover the entire syllabus for a one-semester course, such as an Introduction to Psychology textbook—and a variety of anthologies or supplementary texts (usually in paperback editions).

The traveler's task is to help persuade professors to adopt a textbook for their students, that is, to place an order through the bookstore for as many copies of the book as will cover the anticipated enrollment for their forthcoming courses. For virtually every standard course in the curriculum, whether undergraduate or graduate, there are anywhere from 4 or 5 to 40 or 50 competing basic texts. Because most professors generally know much more about the subject matter than the traveler, her role is essentially to see that teachers are apprised of forthcoming texts in their field from the traveler's firm and to prevail upon them to examine a free copy. Prior to the 1970s, required courses with large enrollments, such as a two-semester survey of American history, may have been taught to as many as 2,000 or more students per semester in a single school, and it was common practice for a committee of several teachers to choose a single text for all sections of this course (this is known as a blanket adoption). An adoption of this size did encourage salesmanship, high-pressure tactics, and occasionally fomented departmental politics and factionalism. In the 1970s, however, not only did individual course requirements diminish, but most professors, and even teaching assistants, were free to choose their own texts, thereby reducing the traveler's role as salesperson while simultaneously driving college bookstore managers to distraction— imagine 40 different instructors ordering four or five different paperbacks for their Introduction to Literature class. But now the pendulum has swung back in the other direction: more required courses, more basic texts, less use of supplementary paperbacks, and more blanket adoptions.

Concomitantly, a more independent attitude on the part of undergraduates is reflected in higher returns of textbooks, as students no longer purchase all the books assigned by the professor. Returns now average 30 to 50 percent. Students also are now more inclined to sell their textbooks after the course is over, so that secondhand sales (controlled by a few large used text outlets) cut heavily into the textbook market within a year after the book is published. Partial results are a decline in the number of books signed up, an increase in list prices, and more frequent revisions of successful basic texts.

In addition to the use of travelers, sales are pursued through frequent mailings of catalogs and fliers and by displays of texts at annual academic conventions. Since 1970, telephone sales have become a conventional means of selling textbooks. Instead of sending a traveler from school to school, which costs a publisher roughly $18,000 in salary and close to $12,000 in expenses, he can hire an inexperienced clerk with a pleasant voice to call individual professors or committee members and make a pitch over the phone. In this way, the publisher can reach more schools at a much lower cost per sales call. The use of commission sales reps to sell texts is also a growing phenomenon.

There has been some movement in recent years on the part of trade paperback and mass market publishers to promote to the educational market. Some paperback publishers have put out a barrage of catalogs and mailing pieces, free sample copies of books that might be adopted or recommended, and elaborate displays at educational conventions. Two mass market houses, the Dutton Signet division of Penguin, and Bantam, have the lead in this area, and other paperback publishers are also aggressively pursuing these sales.

In the 1990s yet another new competitor for the textbook dollar has surfaced: the "coursepak." This is a collection of articles, chapters, and the like, compiled by a professor to use in place of a textbook. It is photocopied in quantity, then spiral bound for student purchase at the local Kinko's. This customized book of readings is made possible by relatively inexpensive photocopying, and facilitated by new, streamlined procedures for clearing permissions. Upper-level humanities and social science courses are the current primary users of coursepaks. Coupled with the huge market in secondhand textbooks—few students fail to recycle their $42 *Introduction to Economics*—text publishers have been forced to retrench, become lean and mean, merge or submerge.

Professional Book Sales. Books specifically written for professionals, academics, or specialists are primarily sold by mail order. The three basic markets are individuals, libraries, and foreign sales (which accounts for a surprisingly high 20 percent of total sales). By means of the house mailing list and of lists purchased from journals, professional organizations, and companies that sell specialized mailing lists, the publisher is able to direct its sales efforts to prime potential customers.

There are many professional, reference, and technical book clubs. Newbridge Communications, for example, runs about a score of highly specialized clubs, from the Library of Speech-Language Pathology to the Nurse's Book Society to the Architects and Designers Book Service. These types of book clubs now account for a hefty percentage of professional sales.

Library, academic, and professional conventions provide another outlet for the professional or reference publisher to display and sell its list. However, further library budget cutbacks in the 1990s have caused a considerable decline in library sales, not only in the United States, but worldwide (most of this genre is not translated, but read in English around the world). Another factor implicated in decreased library sales is the development of computerized information sharing: a major university that once bought six copies of a professional book now buys two, and has electronic aids to circulate portions of the book. Alternatively, the university may buy on-line reference material, so that a single disk or program suffices for all users. Whereas many professional book publishers could count on selling 3,000 copies to libraries here and abroad, the sale to this market is now reduced to 500 to 600 copies. Therefore, in many instances first printings that used to be 1,500 to 2,000 copies are now reduced to between 800 and 1,000.

Discounts and Distribution. The discount schedule in publishing is so far from uniform that the American Booksellers Association annually provides a thick looseleaf collection of hundreds of different publishers' discount schedules for its members; in fact many publishers offer different discounts on different books, or offer different discounts on the *same* book on different occasions, regardless of the quantity ordered. The gremlins introduced into publishing by the computers are usually responsible. Similarly fragmented are the archaic and confusing means and methods of book distribution, ordering and returning procedures and policies, combined with the lack of an industrywide systematic method of inventory control that would link the publisher, the wholesaler, and the retailer. Contributing in no small way to this problem is the staggering number of books now in print and available to order (400,000). Automation has yet to deliver this branch of publishing from the Middle Ages, though it certainly will someday, since the lack of a comprehensive, uniform, industrywide system for marketing books is costing every publisher more than he would care to admit—if he were able to figure out what it was costing him. Merely to note the average returns of unsold books—15 to 30 percent for trade and text publishers; as high as 40 percent for mass market publishers—is sufficient proof of the seriousness of the problem.

Most publishers offer larger discounts to bookstores if they agree to take the books on a nonreturnable basis. The notion of selling all books on a nonreturnable basis gets some support from time to time, but it has never really taken hold as an industrywide policy. The reasons go beyond the scope of this book, but it seems likely that this gigantic and costly headache could be mitigated by giving bookstores larger discounts, and having them remainder those books that they might normally return.

Many in publishing feel that the distribution system is now more efficient, with electronic ordering and wholesalers who can deliver books to bookstores within 48 hours. Both publishers and bookstores have become more aware of realistic business practices, and the number of bookstores has grown significantly in the past decade.

With regard to distribution, technology is now making some inroads into these massive problems, and most publishers are eagerly incorporating new methods and systems of distribution, which are helping to increase the standardization of practices in the industry. The use of machine-readable symbols on books, for instance, supplemented by the use of scanners—such as those now seen in many supermarkets—will provide useful data for both the publisher and the bookseller. Publishers know what they sell to bookstores and wholesalers, but they are often unaware of what these companies are selling to *their* customers. By knowing more quickly what titles are moving in the stores, publishers can more efficiently and rapidly decide which titles to reprint; guesswork has been one reason for big returns. Computer-to-computer communication via tapes of orders, invoices, and price changes, between publishers and their customers, will not only expedite orders—so that sales are made rather than lost because interest waned before books arrived—but will reduce the number of human errors in billing, filling, and shipping orders. The laptop computer, with which more and more sales forces are now equipped, speeds order entry, cuts down on errors, and helps to produce more accurate first-print projections. Some publishers may jointly use or sell computer systems which will provide more standardized, readable, and informative royalty statements; many of the current ones are confusing, cryptic in detail, and not uncommonly contain simple mathematical errors. During this transitional period, as publishers increasingly employ automation, authors (and publishers) may find that the problems created are equal to the problems solved, but in the long run it is assumed that the computer's ability to store and retrieve large amounts of information will benefit all the players in the industry.

The professional book publisher does not get its wares displayed in general bookstores, not primarily because the audience is limited, but mainly because the publisher offers books to the bookseller at a "short" discount, that is in the 20 to 33⅓ percent range (depending on the individual publisher and the quantity of titles ordered). Booksellers feel that the markup is not high enough to warrant having the book in stock. Textbooks, which are generally sold to the bookseller at a 20 percent discount (although 25 percent is becoming increasingly common), are therefore also excluded from general bookstores and are only stocked by college bookstores when a professor adopts a title.

Trade books, however, as well as mass market books, are sold at a "long" discount, which ranges from 40 to 50 percent, again depending on the publisher and the quantity ordered. A typical trade discount schedule would be:

40 percent on 5 or more assorted titles

42 percent on 50 or more assorted titles

44 percent on 250 or more assorted titles

46 percent on 500 or more assorted titles

The wholesaler and the independent, who order from publisher in larger quantities, receive higher discounts, ranging from 42 to 50 percent for trade books and going as high as 55 percent for mass market paperbacks. Of course, the individual bookstore or outlet must pay for the convenience of buying from the wholesaler instead of the publisher by receiving a lower discount, which averages 33⅓ percent, though it may go as high as 40 percent for large orders. In other words, the wholesaler stays in business by buying at an average of 47 to 50 percent discount and selling at an average 37 to 40 percent discount; what he lacks in margin he makes up in volume.

Library and Institutional Sales and Promotion. The revenue from library sales is so important for virtually all categories of publishing that often a separate department or school and library consultant devotes full time to this market. This department promotes and sells its books both to the library and to the el-hi (elementary-high school) market. The reasons are twofold: The teacher (and department chairman and principal, or the district curriculum committee) have a say in what books are purchased for the library, and some of the books—particularly juveniles—may be used in the classroom. We are not talking about textbooks per se. The el-hi publisher or division is separate and has its own sales staff and methods of sales and promotion. *Educational sales* in this context refers specifically to the spillover into classroom use of juvenile and trade titles, hence the combining of library and educational sales efforts. This spillover has stimulated the sales efforts and even refocused the editorial policies of some mass market publishers during the last decade. Many mass market paperbacks are now written for and adopted in the el-hi classroom. Juvenile publishers also issue many of their titles in paperback, sell paperback reprint rights to mass market houses, or initiate paperback originals themselves.

There are about 9,000 public libraries (15,000, counting all the branch libraries), 10,000 special libraries (law, medical, religious, business, armed forces, government, etc.), 49,000 elementary school libraries, 13,000 junior high school libraries, 19,000 public and private high school libraries, and 4,000 college and university libraries. Combined, they buy a lot of books! Total library budgets, including school libraries, add up to about $4 billion, which sounds like quite a healthy sum. But, while book prices have barely kept up with inflation over the past decade, journal prices have soared. It isn't unusual to find a quarterly journal whose subscription price is $200 a year—$50 per issue. In many college, university, and other research libraries, 60 percent of the acquisitions budget goes to buying journals, leaving the rest for book purchases. This has the predictable effect on the quantity of books libraries can buy. The professional book publisher that used to be able to count on selling 1,500 copies to libraries (which for certain kinds of books was the difference between profit and loss) is no longer sure of selling even 500. About 80 percent of juvenile hardcovers, 25 percent of university press and professional books, and between 10 and 15 percent of trade books are sold to libraries, so this is a significant part of the market for many publishers.

It is apparent that many publishers could not exist without library sales. University presses in particular have felt the squeeze over the last decade: Some have folded, most have cut back their lists, and many are now passing up marginal scholarly books, regardless of their quality or potential contribution to scholarship. Instead, some are now signing up trade books— nonfiction with a wide potential audience and even fiction.

Surprisingly, more than 75 percent of the orders for libraries are filled by jobbers and wholesalers. The explanation is simply that publishers give libraries discounts of 10 to 20 percent, whereas wholesalers—some of whom specialize exclusively or primarily in library sales—offer discounts as high as 39 percent. Nevertheless, both the publisher and the wholesaler are active in promoting books for library sales.

The publisher exerts his sales efforts in several ways. Direct sales calls to wholesalers and to library systems are supported by a variety of catalogs, mailing pieces, and even newsletters. Because the library represents the major market for most publishers of juveniles, many will prepare separate library and educational catalogs, broken down by subject, grade levels, or both. These catalogs and mailing pieces will be sent not only to librarians, but to school principals, district-level media specialists, curriculum committees, and others. A variety of prepackaged "standing order" buying plans for groups of books is available for both the school and library, and the practice of sending a free review copy to the committee or buyers for a school or library system is conventional, since some systems purchase up to 100 copies of a book. Classroom adoptions of juveniles, of course, can run into the thousands. Multiple-order library purchases are often made six to eight months after publication, since librarians either wish to review the books themselves first or want to see reviews in the various specialized journals and magazines, such as *Library Journal*, *School Library Journal*, or *Booklist*, before making their decisions. Advertising for this market is concentrated in these magazines and journals and in ads and listings placed in wholesalers' catalogs. The publisher's library consultant may clip and send out copies of good reviews, along with notices of awards and prizes or nominations for them—the coveted Newbery or Caldecott juveniles awards may boost an anticipated 10,000-copy sale up to 40,000 or 50,000 copies.

The publisher, but even more consistently and effectively the wholesaler, will also provide the library with Library of Congress catalog cards and check-out cards and will put shelf numbers on bindings, though for these services and higher discounts most wholesalers require an exclusive contract with a library system. In fact, for most trade publishers, the sales and promotion efforts encourage libraries to buy from wholesalers. The cost of the paperwork involved in billing and shipping the individual orders and in servicing library accounts is more headache than profit. The task is obviously more efficiently managed by wholesalers, who can supply an individual library with titles from a wide variety of trade publishers.

Finally, a number of annual national and regional conventions, whether for professionals, academics, teachers, or librarians, provide the publisher—whether juvenile, professional, trade, mass market, or university press—an opportunity to display, promote, and sell to the library and educational markets.

Special Sales. One method of compensating for high costs, reduced net profits, and diminishing sales figures is to open up new markets. Special sales are those made to any outlet other than a bookstore or library. While this method is not by any means new to publishers, there is now an intense and renewed effort made to exploit these markets more thoroughly and systematically. Hitherto most publishers merely filled requests that came in unsolicited, such as when a mail-order house would ask for quotes for multiple copies of a book it wished to offer through its catalogs. Now some publishers are either hiring someone to go after these sales, assigning the task to someone in-house, or setting up a separate department to handle them.

Premium sales are both the most difficult to make and the most potentially lucrative of special sales. Manufacturers, banks, insurance companies, or any other firm with a product or service to sell to a huge number of customers may be a suitable market. Warner Books, which published the paperback edition of *How to Prosper During the Coming Bad Years*, noticed that the author recommended stocking up on dehydrated food. The editor contacted one manufacturer of such foods, who wound up taking thousands of copies, which were offered through its catalog; more than 30 other manufacturers later followed suit and contacted Warner's to order multiple copies.

The other major avenues for special sales are mail-order catalogs, special-interest stores (health, sports, crafts, gourmet, computers, and the like), associations and their publications, and direct-mail campaigns initiated by the publisher, either through its own mailing lists or those rented outside of the house.

Publishers will now be particularly receptive to authors' suggestions on where and how to make a special sale for their books. While selling novels this way is a slim possibility, many nonfiction books are appropriate, particularly how-to and craft books. By writing a letter to your editor, accompanying the author's questionnaire, and by identifying the potential "special" audience, you may be able to turn your modest book into one that unexpectedly sells thousands of additional copies. Remember that premium sales depend on large volume: royalties on premium sales are in the range of 7½ percent of net receipts on hardcover sales and 5 percent of net on paperbacks.

International Sales. A publisher markets books outside the United States in two ways: either by exporting the English-language edition in the "open market" throughout the world, or by selling British or translation rights (which we will discuss shortly). To interest foreign publishers in their wares, many U.S. publishers attend the large international book fairs held annually in Frankfurt, Bologna, Jerusalem, London, and other locations. The American Booksellers Convention has also become a place for publishers from all countries to get together to do business in foreign rights. Some of the larger U.S. publishers have their own subsidiaries or representatives in foreign countries which sell and distribute directly to foreign wholesalers, libraries, and bookstores. And some actually sell books direct to European wholesalers and bookstores. HarperCollins, for example, has a European rep who visits bookstores and wholesalers all over the Continent to sell HarperCollins titles. Most publishers still rely on the handful of companies that act as intermediaries which specialize in overseas sales. The largest of these is Baker & Taylor, the giant American distributor that also sells abroad.

The percentage of total sales that foreign sales represent for any publisher varies considerably and is directly related to the type or category of books published. For university presses and professional book publishers, foreign sales represent an average of about 8 to 10 percent of total sales, whereas for trade publishers, the amount averages about 5 percent, and an additional 10 percent in Canadian sales. Foreign mass market and college text sales, surprisingly high, fall somewhere between these two. The complexity of marketing English-language books throughout the world—consider bill-collecting problems with a New Zealand firm, for example—makes obvious the benefit of local representation, and a company like Baker & Taylor either has its own local sales agents or offices or is in partnership with a variety of wholesalers in foreign countries. For an average 10 percent of list commission and exclusive territorial rights for designated countries, they sell, distribute, ship (sometimes), and bill for more than 200 major U.S. publishers. By means of sales reps, mailing of catalogs, appearances at foreign book fairs and exhibitions, an export representative markets books in much the same way as do U.S. publishers. The cost of the export representative's commission, as with the added operational costs of U.S. publishers' own foreign sales subsidiaries and representatives, is reflected in the author's reduced royalty rate for export sales.

Canadian sales are generally excluded from the open-market territory; U.S. publishers invariably employ Canadian wholesale distributors, most of whom are publishers in their own right, and they sometimes publish a separate Canadian edition of a U.S. book. But the export representative does sell the book in the rest of the British Commonwealth—provided the author or her representative has not retained this right and the U.S. publisher has not sold rights to a British publisher—and in virtually every other English-speaking and non-English–speaking country. Even Eastern Europe and China are now opening up to English-language books. For Eastern Europe now, the stumbling block is no longer access to markets, but the lack of hard currency. Most business with Eastern Europe has been in professional books, technical books, and English as a second language titles. American trade books are still a tough sell there. Hong Kong is a growing market, and there is some small amount of business now with mainland China as well.

Remainder Sales, Out-of-Print Decisions, and Reprints. Since the advent of the computer in publishing, weekly printouts permit the publisher to maintain precise inventory control, that is, to know how many copies of your book still remain unsold in the warehouse. At some predetermined level of inventory depletion, a symbol on the printout (or some similar procedure) will indicate to the sales manager that a decision must be made to reprint the book or to let it go out of stock (or out of print) by continuing to sell it until the last remaining copy is gone. Or the publisher's inventory may remain at a high level because the book, for whatever reason, is not selling or selling very slowly. Then a decision may be forthcoming to dispose of all or most of the remaining copies at a much reduced price, with the books subsequently sold to the public as "remainders," or "overstocks."

Several factors determine whether and when a publisher decides to remainder or to let a book go out of print, and these factors vary depending on the category of publisher. Keeping any book in print involves certain ongoing costs: warehousing, record keeping, royalty reporting, and such, not to mention reprinting. After the first year, as sales diminish beyond a certain point, the publisher must decide whether the anticipated future sales warrant keeping the remaining stock and justify the aforementioned costs. If a trade book has been sold for paperback reprint rights—in which case the paperback edition is generally issued one year after hardcover publication—the publisher knows the sales of the cloth edition will plummet close to zero once the paperback appears. Whether the cloth edition has been successful or not, the publisher may be stuck with 500 to 10,000 or more copies at that point (book clubs can also overprint and be stuck with potential remainders). Because determining the first print run and predicting first-year sales are based on educated hunches, many books do not live up to initial expectations. Good reviews or big advance sales, for instance, may prompt the sales manager to hastily order a second printing, but once the book is actually sent to the stores, it may not sell well; returns may be heavy, and the second printing may go begging. Christmas books are particularly vulnerable to this calamity. Since the shelf life for most trade books is often less than three months, and since the appearance of the paperback will cut off future sales, the only sensible option in many cases is to remainder the book if the warehouse inventory greatly exceeds anticipated sales over a one- to three-year period. Paperback reprinters, incidentally, may stipulate in their contracts that a book cannot be remaindered for at least six months or a year or more after the appearance of the paperback, since the remainder price may be lower than the paperback cover price and cut into sales. However, even if all the clothbound copies are remaindered and none are available for sale, the existence of the paperback means that the book is still in print, so that the author usually cannot reclaim the rights.

Even if no paperback reprint right is sold or the publisher himself has no intention of issuing a paperback, he is still faced with a similar decision: Will future sales warrant keeping the book in print? The publisher's backlist, the titles that he keeps in print over a period of years, is a vital source of revenue, and it keeps many publishers afloat. The books require no publicity, scant advertising, promotion, or sales efforts, and the cost of reprinting each copy is often only two-thirds as much as the cost of the original edition, since all plant costs have been paid off. So a publisher's first preference is to keep your book in print.

Current tax laws are a potent factor in putting many slow-selling books out of print, or in considerably reducing stock on selected titles. Inventory is now considered an asset, and each year publishers must pay taxes on their end-of-year total assets, creating a strong temptation to jettison "excess" inventory to lower these tax payments.

But there are the costs we mentioned, and the additional problem of higher unit-costs for smaller reprint orders. Because the unit-cost for reprinting a book is dependent on the size of the print run, most trade publishers do not find it economical to reprint fewer than 2,500 copies at a time, but a run as low as this means a high unit-cost. Furthermore, the lower the list price of the book (and thus the less net income per sale), the more likely the publisher is to consider that keeping the book in print is not worth the costs. This means that whereas on a $10 title he may consider 2,000 copies a year the minimum number it must sell to warrant stocking and reprinting, on a $20 title he may consider 1,000 copies sufficient. Other factors in the decision may be: keeping a house author happy, stocking a classic or important book as a "service to the profession," or the anticipation of a revival of interest. Unfortunately, the recent trend is toward a decrease of backlist-title sales, which have dropped from a high of about 50 percent of net sales during the 1960s, to the current average of 20 percent.

Other categories of publishers use different rules of thumb. Mass market houses will generally not keep a book in print unless they can sell a minimum of 5,000 copies a year, and will not reprint less than 15,000 copies; quality paperback houses (or lines) generally not less than 3,000 copies for either sales or reprintings (though some go as low as 1,000 and some as high as 5,000). Both these amounts are for absolute minimum numbers of sales and reprintings. Many paperback houses have higher standards. On the other hand, juvenile divisions commonly expect the life of the book to stretch over 10 to 20 years, so that reprinting in smaller quantities is a way of life, so to speak; however, owing to inflation, the cost of printing juveniles in low quantities has become prohibitive, and many of these publishers are letting slow-selling books go out of print. Professional book publishers and university presses may be content to reprint as few as 500 or 1,000 copies. The cover price is generally high, the sales normally tend to spread out over a number of years, and the publisher's operation is geared to expect and handle a smaller volume of sales. One option, most frequently exercised by textbook publishers, is to revise the book and publish a second revised edition. Bringing certain kinds of books up to date often breathes new life into diminishing sales. The keen competition for introductory-course adoptions often necessitates a revision every three or four years; an expected fringe benefit is that it temporarily eliminates the secondhand market.

But if the sales of a book in any category have gradually trickled down to under 500 or so copies a year and there is no reason to expect that matters will improve, the publisher will normally declare the book out of print once his stock is exhausted, or do so upon remaindering the copies left in the warehouse. It's not a general public declaration, he just discontinues listing it in his catalogs, does not file the title with annual bibliographies such as *Books in Print*, may publish a list of discontinued titles in the classified section of *Publishers Weekly*, and will return requests for the book by stamping letters or invoices "out of print." He may not, in fact, as we mentioned in Chapter 3, even notify the author.

If sufficient stock remains to warrant remaindering, the publisher has the choice of selling the stock at reduced prices directly to bookstores, or selling it to a "remainder house," a specialized wholesaler that deals exclusively in remainders.

The remainder business has been quite healthy in recent years. A huge market exists for those clothbound books that the average consumer is unable or unwilling to pay $15 to $50 for, and many bookstores now thrive on remainder or "budget" sales. Though the bookstore usually makes only a 40 percent markup on these books (many remainder houses offer the bookstore an additional 10 percent discount provided it is spent in advertising these titles), the sale tables often draw in the nonhabitual book buyer and build traffic. *LMP* lists more than 40 firms that specialize in remainder wholesaling, and some of them—such as Outlet Books, a division of Random House—now also buy "cheap cloth edition" reprint rights from the original publisher. When the $19.95 edition, which has been remaindered for $9.95, is sold out, the wholesaler can reprint 10,000 to 25,000 copies on cheaper paper, with inexpensive bindings, and put a list price of $7.95 on the book or put a list price of $12.95 on it and mark it down to $7.95. A number of publishers have traditionally done this. Others have recently caught on to the gambit and will reprint their own cheap edition to sell on the remainder table. Art books and illustrated film books are the prime candidates. Best-sellers, though, are rarely reprinted in cheap clothbound editions because of the inevitable appearance of the later paperback edition. The author, unfortunately, does not receive a fair share of profits from this second life. The convention is to pay a 5- to 6-percent-of-list royalty for the cheap cloth edition, even though the costs and profits would permit the publisher to pay a higher royalty.

Once the publisher has decided to remainder the stock for several titles, he will generally notify a number of different remainder houses by mail, listing the titles and number of copies available, and solicit a bid, either for specific quantities or titles or for the entire list. Some titles may be sold in bulk directly to bookstore chains, because the publisher generally gets a higher price from the chains than from the wholesaler. Or, as is happening more recently, the publisher will merely remainder his titles through his own sales staff and with mailing pieces. Instead of soliciting bids, he will set a wholesale remainder price on the book so that individual stores can buy in any quantity they wish.

The remainder wholesaler, in turn, will market the book in several different ways: mailing catalogs to retailers, inviting buyers to a showroom where samples are on view, and by means of direct sales calls. For some individual book outlets throughout the country, but particularly for variety stores and supermarket chains, the "prepack" is popular—buying in quantity a preselected mix of remainder titles. Some remainder houses, such as Barnes & Noble, have retail bookstores, act as remainder wholesalers, and sell remainders directly to the consumer by mail order. Professional-book publishers and university presses will occasionally hold a warehouse or clean-out sale and remainder their books directly to the professional or academic consumer by mail. Obviously remainders are sold by a variety of overlapping methods and companies.

How do the finances work? Based on market savvy, the kind of book, and the quantity available, the remainder house may, for example, bid as low as 10 cents or as high as $4, depending on the original list price and the salability of the title. Then, considering both what was paid for the book and what the traffic will bear, the remainder is offered to the retailer at a wholesale price with an implicit retail price.

The $20 book for which the remainder house has paid 50 cents may be offered to the retailer at $2.50, and then sold to the consumer at anything from $3.99 to $7.99—or whatever price the retailer feels he can get. Since it is the intermediary here— the remainder wholesaler—who is profiting, and the publisher is (usually) making little or nothing, publishers now try to bypass the remainder wholesaler by offering "markdowns in place." They simply refund money to the bookseller for titles already in his store, allowing him to "remainder" them without paying either a shipper (by returning them) or a remainder wholesaler. And some publishers have gone into the remainder business themselves, selling remainder stock directly to bookstores.

Authors may have reason to complain about the business of remainders. On remainder sales (*overstock* is the euphemism in the contract) the author generally gets 10 percent of the amount received by the publisher, but only if this amount is higher than the publisher's manufacturing costs—that is, his manufacturing unit-cost per book—which it usually isn't. In other words, if the unit-cost of your $20 book was $3, and the publisher sells it as a remainder for $2.50, you receive no royalty or share of this sale. Obviously, the publisher isn't making any money on this sale either—he's just losing less than he would by destroying the books. The publisher cuts his losses, the remainder wholesaler and the bookseller each make a profit, and the author makes nothing.

One More Reprinter. Authors should make sure that their contracts permit them to reclaim the rights to their out-of-print book, in the event that at a later date some publisher may express interest in reprinting the book. Particularly in the area of professional and scholarly books, a book that is either in the public domain or has been out of print for many years may find a small and select library professional market when reissued by a reprinter that specializes in this type of book.

Generally this reprinter publishes books in series, such as in the history of science or volumes of eighteenth- or nineteenth-century legal documents or classics in British and Scottish folklore. By reprinting as few as 250 copies, charging extremely high prices (from $20 to $50 for books that may have originally sold for from $5 to $10), and by mail-order marketing to libraries and select lists of professionals, some of these companies have been able to earn huge net profits because of their low overhead costs. In recent years, many new reprint houses have appeared, some of which expanded their concepts of a typical reprint to include more recent nonfiction books and fiction classics or oddities (e.g., early nineteenth-century romances by women). Even some of the remainder houses branched out into this area of reprinting. But because of reduced library budgets, and perhaps a now-oversaturated market, these kinds of reprint sales have declined.

Sales Promotion. The word *promotion* is bandied about so much in publishing that it is difficult for the casual outsider to get a fix on it. Nevertheless, *sales promotion* refers to the material the publisher or wholesaler supplies to help the retailer at the point of sale to the consumer.

A variety of free display materials may be furnished to the retailer, most of them reserved for the major titles: posters, bookmarks, window stickers, counter cards, blow-ups of dust jackets, and sometimes even buttons, bumper stickers, and shopping bags. Many retail stores have mailing lists of steady customers, particularly for use during the Christmas season, so the publisher and wholesaler supply a number of different mailing pieces with the bookseller's name and address imprinted on the material; however, these fliers are mostly for "general market" or expensive gift books. The mailing pieces may range from a statement stuffer—a one-page flier that is included in the customer's monthly bill—to an elaborate four-or-more-page circular (already prepackaged for mailing) that has been test-marketed for its drawing power.

With rising costs and declining sales, publishers have become more and more imaginative in finding ways to gain attention and additional sales with promotional gimmicks. Dutton Signet, for example, launched a recent book on dating, *Guerrilla Dating Tactics*, by manufacturing keychains with a little box attached that contained a condom, and distributing them to key accounts. The same publisher recently launched a new romance line with the help of the model who posed for the jacket of the books; they produced bookmarks, notepads, and calendars with his picture on them, and then had the model make promotional appearances at bookstores.

Examples of other materials available to the bookseller include, for instance, a retail chain catalog called *Book Chat*, which is distributed bimonthly to more than half a million consumers; individual publishers may purchase space ads in the catalog for recent titles. A variety of similar mailing pieces and catalogs are available to bookstore owners from both publishers and distributors. Some publishers are active not only in supplying promotional materials to wholesalers, but in educating them on how to reach and expand their markets.

Display racks for books, primarily for paperbacks, may be offered to the bookstore either by the publisher or the wholesaler, and the rack jobber—the independent mass market paperback distributor—will supply racks for variety and chain stores, supermarkets, and other outlets carrying paperbacks. Or publishers and distributors of mass market books may give new bookstores a "rack allowance" of 60 to 70 cents per "pocket," depending on the percentage of titles the store will carry from that particular publisher or distributor. For instance, a new store with 10,000 pockets may intend to fill about 400 with Zebra paperbacks and thereby have $240 deducted from its first bill(s). Some quality paperback publishers will extend the same offer. Dump-bins—cartons of books that can be opened and folded out to be used as both a display and a container for best-selling paperbacks—are widely furnished by paperback publishers. Because publishers and wholesalers are competing so keenly for display space in bookstores, it is obviously to their advantage to be imaginative, generous, and diligent in suppling a variety of free promotional materials to book outlets.

Subsidiary Rights

The day-to-day operations of the subsidiary rights department are belied by glamorous tales of the million-dollar paperback-reprint sale that is followed up by the sale of movie rights to Walt Disney Productions for a sum "in the high six figures," as the trade magazines like to say. These highlights are infrequent events at most trade houses. The reality is that many trade books do not get sold for a single subsidiary right, and most of those that do ring up considerably more modest revenues.

Permissions. The rights department generally includes permissions under its aegis, that is, granting either an author, a publisher, or a magazine the right to excerpt a passage, paragraph, page, chapter, short story, or poem for use within another work. If the use is incidental or for critical purposes, such as using a stanza for an epigraph or quoting a paragraph to make a point, then permission is generally granted gratis. Though many of these requests are covered by "fair use," permission is often solicited anyhow. A request for permission to reprint a poem or a short story in a textbook anthology, or a chapter from a nonfiction book in a collection of critical essays, will require a fee. The permissions person generally works from an informal and flexible house "going rate," which is based on several factors: the reputation of the author; the manner of publication intended, whether cloth, paper, or both; the size of the extract; the territory requested, whether United States and Canadian, English-language or world; and what the traffic will bear. These are postpublication requests, and you may not be consulted if permission to use an extract from your book is requested and sold, but will find out only when the sale is listed on your royalty statement and your 50 percent share included in the royalty check.

But the major task for the subsidiary rights department is the attempt to sell first serial, book-club, paperback reprint, and foreign rights. Radio, television, film, and dramatic rights are generally not aggressively pursued, since the great majority of writers whose works might naturally be attractive to those media have agents who have retained these rights for their clients. However, when they do have these rights and the book seems particularly suitable for a "performance" rights sale, they may use a sub-agent (usually one on the West Coast) to handle them. Some smaller houses don't have their own sub-rights department, but use instead one of a handful of independents who specialize in rights sales.

Subsidiary rights possibilities are discussed at the time the decision is made to sign up the book. Occasionally the house will canvas a mass market reprint house before signing the book if the author or agent is asking for a very large advance, but generally the sale of these rights does not begin until the completed manuscript is in-house. If expectations for rights sale are high, the department may begin sending out photocopies of the manuscript even before it has been copyedited. Magazines, in particular, require considerable lead time in order to serialize a book in several installments, so that a major women's novel, for example, may be sent to *Cosmopolitan* the same week it arrives in-house. Book clubs and paperback reprinters generally work from bound galleys, but there is no hard and fast rule: Any stage from manuscript to galleys to page proofs to bound books may be used by the subsidiary rights department. The ideal schedule is to sell first serial rights, then book-club rights, then paperback rights, and then film rights—all accomplished before the book is in the stores—using each one to help stimulate interest in the next, as well as to boost the price. Most books do not follow this pattern, though, and a rights sale for a paperback edition after book reviews appear is conventional. In the case of a very few books, most of which are agented, first serial, paperback, foreign, and even film rights may be sold just as soon as an outline has been accepted by a trade house, but these are rare exceptions.

First Serial Rights. The halcyon days of serializing books for huge sums has come and gone, such as when *Life*, *Look*, and *The Saturday Evening Post* bid for William Manchester's *Death of a President*, which *Life* scooped up for an immodest $650,000. Not only have prices come down, but so has the amount of space available in large national-circulation magazines; many more have folded than have arisen to take their place. The major women's magazines, such as *Ladies' Home Journal*, *Redbook*, and *Glamour*, rarely serialize novels, preferring to buy a chapter, often as a second serial (after publication), and that only rarely. Occasionally *Time* and *Newsweek* (now sometimes joined by *People* or *U.S. News & World Report*) will pay into the six figures for a sure best-seller like Norman Schwartzkopf's memoir, but the average price for excerpts usually ranges between $3,000 and $25,000. Other magazines, such as *Playboy*, *Esquire*, and *The New Yorker*, pay in the same range, with *Reader's Digest* going a little higher. The *National Enquirer* used to be a good bet for a certain kind of book, but they pay less now than they used to. The actual condensing, whether of a chapter or an entire book, is generally performed by an editor on the magazine's staff. If serial rights for a condensation of an entire book are sold to one of these magazines, the publisher will generally shift the book's publication date, if necessary, so that the book comes out shortly after it has appeared in the magazine. Most people in publishing circles, by the way, do not feel that serialization severely cuts into sales of the book. The additional revenue and the wide exposure are considered to more than compensate for any loss of sales.

The bulk of first serial rights, however, is sold to magazines with modest circulations and payment rates. The topic of your book will generally determine whether the rights department will send a chapter(s), though there are so many specialized and small-circulation magazines to keep track of that any suggestions from you may be useful. In the case of those magazines or journals that do not pay, you may be better off suggesting to submit the chapter on your own. Obviously, even if the fee is small or nonexistent, the author is getting free publicity; any first serial publication is worth your time and effort, if not the publisher's.

Second Serial Rights. Some magazines are now more active in acquiring postpublication rights, particularly since the going rate is half the price or less. *Cosmopolitan*, for example, now commonly serializes novels after publication. Newspapers almost always serialize after publication. The rights department may sell these rights directly to a newspaper or, as is more common, to a newspaper syndicate, which will in turn sell the book to individual newspapers. The fees are nominal: Even a large-circulation newspaper may pay as low as $50 to $100 per excerpt. The syndicate takes 50 percent for its services, and your publisher takes half the rest, which leaves you with 25 percent. Still, it can add up if the book is widely serialized, and the exposure is generally believed to increase sales.

Book Clubs. Even though the number of bookstores has increased in recent years, and despite the presence of the large superstores that stock more than 100,000 titles, book clubs still flourish. It is still true that many people do not have easy access to a bookstore that stocks a wide variety of hardcover titles. Book-club sales now account for between 6 and 7 percent of the total book sales in the United States, a market share that has decreased only slightly in the past decade.

There are almost 200 book clubs in the United States, catering to both a mass readership and an astonishing diversity of special interests—free-market capitalism, arts and crafts, gardening, cooking, natural history, psychotherapy, quilts, erotica, golf, birding, chemistry, architecture, airplanes, bodybuilding, and many others. The Thomas More Book Club, which features books on Catholicism, claims no fewer than 8,000 members, and many of the clubs are much smaller than that. The giants—The Literary Guild and Book of the Month Club—have more than 3 million members each in a variety of clubs that each owns. Newbridge Communications is another large company; it owns almost two dozen different clubs. Rodale has five clubs, with just under half a million members.

Most clubs have a board of judges that selects the main and sometimes the alternate selections after all of the submissions have been winnowed down by the editorial staff to a manageable number of recommended titles. About 13 to 15 times a year each club offers a main selection, 2 to 5 alternates, and up to 100 additional titles. The bigger clubs print their own books, using plates or negatives supplied by the publisher, whereas the medium- and small-sized clubs usually join in on the publisher's first print run—or occasionally buy stock directly from the publisher if the decision is made too late for the first print run.

A typical main selection will be bought by about 10 percent of the members of The Literary Guild and Book of the Month Club. This means that as many as 250,000 copies of some books can be sold as main selections. For smaller clubs, the numbers decrease proportionately. Most book clubs pay a guaranteed advance against a 10 percent of book-club-list-price royalty, which the publisher shares equally with the author. (The Literary Guild pays an average of 7½ percent, whereas *Reader's Digest*, since it includes four books in one volume, pays 2 percent per book.) Royalties for premiums for the four-for-$1 type are reduced to 5 percent of the book-club list. Advances are negotiable. If the two major clubs are bidding for the exclusive right for a main selection, the advance can go as high as $250,000, but commonly the advance will average $85,000 for a main and anywhere from $13,000 to $25,000 for an alternate. For medium-sized clubs, the average advances for main selections are in the $5,000 to $10,000 range. Obviously the amount of an advance varies considerably, depending on whether the book is a main or an alternate and on the size of the club.

There are two schools of thought in publishing regarding the influence of book clubs on trade sales and the author's income. The major school feels that the added exposure, advertising, and sales are a boon for both publishers and authors. The minority dissenters point out that the book club cuts heavily into trade sales and the author's royalties (which are reduced *and* split 50/50 with the publisher) and fosters the notion that publishers are ripping off the public. When a $25 dictionary is offered as a premium for $2, it is hard for the lay person not to conclude that she is being gouged by the publisher. But the income for the publisher is irresistible; not only is he guaranteed before publication to recoup all or part of his investment, but even a small sale increases the size of his print run and thereby reduces his unit-costs.

At one time the naming of a book as a main selection of The Literary Guild or the Book of the Month Club could turn it into a best-seller. But today the big clubs are much more reluctant to take chances on their main selections. Usually, the main selection is a book that everyone knows will be a best-seller anyway. Since main selections get printings of up to 300,000 copies, the reluctance of a book club to gamble is understandable.

Paperback Reprints. The big paperback auction is the rights sale that gains the most attention in publishing circles. A typical scenario goes something like this: Copies of galleys, or even the manuscript, have been sent to the eight major paperback reprinters, followed up by intermittent letters from the publisher announcing that first serial rights were sold to *McCall's*, that Book of the Month Club has taken the book for an alternate, that additional printings have been ordered to meet the huge prepublication demand, and that *Publishers Weekly* has given the book a rave review. Finally the closing date is announced (i.e., the date for the actual bidding) and a $100,000 "floor" or minimum bid is set. Ballantine calls a week before the auction date, offers the minimum bid, and is given "topping" privileges, the right to take the book for 10 percent higher than the last best offer. The day of the auction the phones are buzzing; five out of eight reprinters want the book. Having bid $175,000 at 11 A.M., Avon finds that by 4 P.M. they will have to bid more than $300,000 to stay in the running. At 5:45 the game is still on, and it is carried over to the following day. The editor-in-chief at Bantam thinks the bidding may go as high as $750,000 and calls the company president—who is sunbathing in Jamaica—to get an authorization to go that high if necessary. By noon the following day, Pocket Books has offered $560,000, Bantam decides to pass, and Ballantine declines to top the final bid. The subsidiary rights director and the editor-in-chief go out for a $150 lunch after calling the author's agent, who in turn calls her client. To say he is stunned is an understatement.

The final deal includes the following extras in addition to the $560,000 advance: another $50,000 if a movie sale is consummated; $20,000 additional if the cloth edition appears on the *New York Times* best-seller list, plus $5,000 to $100,000 for subsequent appearances on the list, depending on the number of weeks and the book's position on the list (these are called escalators).

Obviously, 99 percent of the reprint sales do not follow this pattern. In fact, most reprint sales, both for mass market and quality paperback, fall in the $5,000 to $10,000 range, even though most of the books are auctioned off, or offered to a number of reprinters at the same time. The conventional royalty the mass market house pays is 6 percent for the first 150,000, 8 percent for the next 150,000 copies, and 10 percent thereafter; for a quality paperback, 6 percent for the first 15,000 copies sold, 7½ percent thereafter. Both are negotiable, and books with high-priced auctions or by well-known authors will generally command higher royalty rates. The originating publisher generally licenses the reprinter for a period of five, seven, or ten years, after which the reprinter may have to renegotiate the contract if he wishes to continue to carry the book or may just be given the nod by the publisher to carry on.

Several recent developments have cut back the number of high-priced auctions and have somewhat altered the way mass market paperbacks deals are done. The world in which there were hardcover houses on the one hand and mass market houses on the other has become much more complicated. First, hardcover houses started buying mass market paperback companies. For example, New American Library was bought by Penguin, Pocket Books by Simon & Schuster, and Avon by William Morrow (technically S&S and Pocket are both owned by Paramount Publishing, and Avon and Morrow are both owned by Hearst). Then later, some paperback houses began to develop hardcover lines of their own—Warner and Bantam are examples of this phenomenon. Next, some hardcover houses started mass market paperback lines de novo: HarperCollins and St. Martin's both did this recently. To complicate matters even more, some mass market houses which had been previously bought by hardcover houses began to develop hardcover lines of their own: Pocket Books, for example, now has its own hardcover imprint. Where one company owns both a hardcover and a mass market paperback house, or publishes in both formats, that publisher can buy "volume" rights (i.e., it will publish the book in both formats without selling any reprint rights, and even in a third format, "trade paperback," if demand warrants it).

Another kind of deal has developed in which the paperback house does a "reverse" rights deal, selling hardcover rights to a hardcover publisher, which publishes the book under a license prior to the paperback publication. And finally, although it is now less common, sometimes a hardcover and paperback house will set up an ad hoc joint venture to share the costs of buying both hardcover and paperback rights. Arrangements in which volume rights are sold to a single publisher are particularly advantageous for successful authors with track records, because they receive full royalties on both editions—instead of sharing the revenue from an auction sale with the originating publisher—and they still receive a six-figure advance.

British and Foreign Rights. Most publishers employ agents overseas to represent them in British and foreign rights sales, though some of the larger publishers handle these rights themselves. Often the publisher or the author's agent will send galleys overseas to sell British rights, so that the British publisher can get in on the print run, since only a few minor typesetting changes are necessary. If the book, as is more common, is sold once bound books are ready, the British publisher will buy negatives or positives from the U.S. publisher, paying an offset (shooting) fee of approximately $4 per page, in addition to the advance and royalty. British advances, as you might expect, are generally lower than U.S. advances: A book that commanded a $10,000 advance here might be sold for $5,000 for British rights, though royalty rates are roughly equal. In fact, the British publishing scene is quite comparable to that in the United States, insofar as general operating procedures and subsidiary rights are concerned. One anglicism is the banding together of several trade houses to set up their own mass market paperback subsidiaries, thereby paying the author a full royalty on paperback editions.

Translation Rights. Here, too, most U.S. publishers and literary agents use foreign co-agents to represent them. Sending bound books, rather than galleys, is generally the rule, though for the major books, manuscripts or galleys may be sent. Publishers follow these overseas by attending the Frankfurt Book Fair, held once a year in early October, in order to negotiate deals in person with editors from foreign book publishers. Though foreign publishers buy and translate our books in much greater proportion than we do theirs—so that on an Italian publisher's trade list, for example, 10 percent of the books may be translations from various languages, whereas most U.S. publishers can scarcely point to more than one book a year—the amount is still negligible when compared to the number of books published in the United States every year. When a book is sold, discounting the blockbusters which may be auctioned off for big sums as they are here, the advances are quite low, averaging $1,500 to $4,000, and the royalties are also reduced, starting as low as 5 to

7 percent, to compensate for the additional cost of translating. (In the United States, most translators are still paid coolie wages, averaging $55 per 1,000 words, whereas overseas the average rates for translators are almost double.) Foreign publishers generally ask for and receive a two-month option in which to consider a U.S. book.

Television, Film, and Dramatic Rights. In the world of the visual media, your book is known as a property, perhaps because fidelity to its contents is so rare that it might as well be identified as a parcel of land, distinguished only by dimension rather than substance. The conventional advice from agents and subsidiary rights directors is to "take the money and run," since most authors are dismayed to see the final results, over which they have little control even if they are hired to write the script. The greatest number of rights sales are for options, that is, the right to hold on to the property for six months to two years just in case enough money can be raised by the producer to put it into production or, in the case of television, to sell the idea to an independent packager, network, or sponsor. Often the author's agent, or the subsidiary rights director, will join forces and split the commission with a dramatic agent, many of whom are based on the West Coast, because these specialists are more adept at threading their way through the eccentricities of the show business subculture.

Options are purchased cheap for TV productions—the going rate is anywhere from $1,000 to $10,000. Movie options are higher, usually between $30,000 and $100,000. The vast majority of options are never exercised, but when they are the price for the average movie is somewhere between $100,000 and $300,000; for a TV production it's rarely more than $100,000. Best-sellers or otherwise hot properties can command much higher figures, especially if several producers or studios are bidding for the rights.

Electronic Rights. As this book goes to press, the disposition of electronic rights remains one of the great unfinished stories of book publishing. "New Media" is the phrase on everyone's lips, but many agents and publishers still don't understand what electronic rights are exactly, and even among those who do understand, few can guess exactly what these rights are worth. Most people know by now that storing information magnetically on floppy disks or compact discs for use in personal computers has created a new way of reading and using books, but no one knows what this will mean for the future.

Most books available now on CD or floppy disk are reference titles, since these books lend themselves to the medium: You look things up in them rather than reading them cover-to-cover. The ability of computers to search a disk for a word, a phrase, an article, or even a motion picture makes a reference book on disk a real improvement over one on paper. *Compton's Family Encyclopedia*, for example, contains, on one disk, 26 complete encyclopedia volumes, including 31,000 articles and 10,000 pictures, a world atlas, a dictionary, music, speech, and sound—and you can find anything at the touch of a computer button and then print it out on your printer. Even at $295, this may be a good buy. *A Survey of Western Art*, *The Software Toolworks World Atlas*, *The CIA World Fact Book*, *The Guinness Disc of Records*, and *The College Handbook* are typical CD titles; prices range from about $40 up to $400. The advantages of this medium when it comes to fiction and narrative nonfiction, however, are less clear, and, although disks containing illustrated children's books are available (*The Sleeping Beauty Multimedia Storybook*, *Beauty and the Beast*, *Peter and the Wolf*, and many more), the idea of reading a child a bedtime story from a computer screen hasn't yet become widely accepted. As in any technology associated with computers, financial expectations are high. But there is no guarantee that they will be realized.

When publishers control electronic rights, the normal split has become 50/50 with the author. Agents sometimes want to reserve these rights, but many publishers are insisting on controlling them, and the pressure to turn them over to publishers may be too great to resist. As far as the author is concerned, the real question is whether the publisher or the agent will be more successful in exploiting the rights. And the answer depends upon which publisher and which agent you are dealing with. Some agents have aggressively pursued these rights, with some of the larger agencies hiring specialists whose sole function is to market them; others have left it to publishers. Publishers' attitudes have varied similarly: Some are quite interested in buying and exploiting electronic rights along with other subsidiary rights; others are indifferent.

It is almost impossible to say what a typical advance and royalty arrangement would be for electronic rights, or even how those rights will ultimately be delineated. Some agents are trying to reserve the rights not because they know of a specific market for them, but because they are unsure what they are worth. And publishers want to acquire the rights for much the same reason. Even the term *electronic rights* remains vague. Does this mean only the use of the actual text of the book as a text file on a computer disk? Does it include the pictures? Does electronic rights include use of pieces of the text in an electronic anthology with pieces of other books? Has the purchaser of these rights also bought the right to add sound and pictures to the book for use in a CD multimedia production? Can he or she put the book on-line on a service like Prodigy or Compuserve so that computer users can reference it and download it by modem? And of course it would only be after all these questions are answered that a rational discussion of advances and royalties could begin. Sorting all this out will not be easy, and publishers, agents, and authors will have much to discuss over the next few years before the answers are found.

Audiocassettes. The audiocassette industry operates quite differently from book publishing. There are two basic products and markets: the larger market is for books that are *abridged* (the text is adapted by freelance specialists into a script of roughly 125 double-spaced pages) and normally sold in a double-cassette pack for $16 to $18, although four-cassette packs at prices ranging from $23 to $30 are increasingly common. The other and smaller market is for books that are recorded *unabridged* and sold in sets that contain from 4 to as many as 16 cassettes. Incidentally, abridged and nonabridged rights may be licensed separately, for the same book, though audio producers want a

12- to 18-month publication lag between formats. More than two-thirds of abridged sets are sold through bookstores, supermarkets, and, more recently, video stores (primarily rentals), airports, and even truck stops. On the other hand, more than 50 percent of the unabridged sets are sold to institutions—such as libraries, schools, and nursing homes—and through mail-order sales. In addition, the cassette *rental* market is a major source of revenue for distributors of unabridged sets.

Major publishing houses, including Simon & Schuster, Random House, HarperCollins, and Bantam Doubleday Dell, have audio divisions and license rights from other publishing houses, as well as recording their own authors. A half a dozen or so major independent audio houses, such as Dove, Recorded Books, Books on Tape, and Audio Renaissance, license audio rights from publishers. The large independent producers, and especially the smaller audio producer/publishers (of which there are now more than 1,000) often sell via mail-order catalogs not only their own tapes, but those produced by other audio companies. Generally, the licenses are for five, seven, or ten years, usually renewable either by mutual consent or with payment of a new advance against royalties. A decade or more ago, when books on audiocassettes were first introduced, the licenses to produce them were normally *nonexclusive*, so that two or more audio houses might record and distribute the same book. But now most licenses are exclusive, though cassettes made from books in the public domain may be recorded and sold by more than one company. The Grand Dad producer of spoken cassette sets is Caedmon Records—now owned by HarperCollins—which produced Dylan Thomas's *A Child's Christmas in Wales*, in 1952.

The run for an unabridged set may be as low as 15, though 50 to 200 is more common. Of course, thousands may be produced if the anticipated potential sales (or rentals) is higher. On the other hand, the first run for abridged sets—with a much larger potential audience—is normally in the 1,000 to 5,000 range. The average abridged title sells 5,000 to 12,500 units, whereas a bestseller might sell about 30,000 units in a year, with blockbuster novels selling as many as 100,000, as do novels by Judith Krantz and her ilk, and inspirational nonfiction titles by the likes of Leo Buscaglia. One of the most successful audio titles, *Creative Visualization*, a New Age tape from California, has sold more than 200,000 sets; its progenitor sold more than 1 million copies in hardcover. The largest audience, as you might surmise, is the commuter.

When books are licensed to an out-of-house producer, an acceptable author/publisher split for an abridged book is 75/25 (for unabridged rights 50/50), though, like most other rights, it is negotiable. For the average title, the book publisher will normally negotiate a modest advance from the audio producer—in the $500 range for an unabridged set, and $2,500 to $4,000 for an abridged set—against an escalating royalty of 4 to 7 percent of list price. More common now is a 5 to 10 percent escalating royalty based on *net* receipts (the same royalty percentage is paid whether the cassette is sold or rented). The reasons for these lower-than-book royalties are that discounts are higher (averaging 50 percent rather than 44 percent for books), and a royalty is also generally paid to the performer. Advances do rise for books with bigger sales potential, and may go as high as $25,000 to $35,000 for anticipated best-sellers. Audio producers want to buy rights as soon as possible after a publisher signs up a book, in order to release the cassettes simultaneously with the book. This practice seems to increase cassette tape sales, while not, some say, cutting into book sales.

When the originating-print publisher produces the cassette tape, typically no money changes hands, and the author receives all of the income from the royalty rates mentioned, rather than half. However, agents customarily retain audio rights on behalf of their authors. If the originating-print publisher has its own audio division and wants to retain this right, an agent may try to negotiate an additional advance payable at the time the book is signed up or if and when this right is exercised. Or, the author's agent may insist that the publisher license or auction the right, with its own audio division bidding at arm's length. Other permutations are possible, as with any other subsidiary right.

The astounding growth of the audiocassette industry in the past ten years is slowing down somewhat, though annual sales exceed $1 billion and some quarters report both dollar and unit sales increases. For the past few years, the $16 to $18 price bar-rier (for the two-cassette abridged set) has kept profit margins slimmer than for books, whereas books have steadily increased in price. Also, the economies of scale that decrease the unit price as the book publisher increases a print run do not apply to cassettes: for more than 2,500 sets, the unit-costs remain virtu-ally the same (on the other hand, it is economically feasible to run off only 50 or 100 sets at a time and thus maintain low in-ventories). Even more problematic is the fierce competition for limited shelf space. In 1985, when *On Cassette* was first pub-lished, there were 11,500 titles in print; in 1992 over 53,000 titles were listed, and they are being added at the rate of about 5,000 per year. Yet bookstores, which generally stock at least several thousand different book titles, normally stock no more than 200 to 300 separate audiocassette titles.

Veteran audio producers predict slim profit margins, and over-production may result in the same implosion that occurred in the computer-book market in the mid-1980s. In that instance, ex-cess output caused horrendous returns and minimal sales for many new titles (one of my clients' first royalty statements listed a one-copy sale; the book never sold another copy).

A sign of coming problems—or new solutions—may be the appearance of low-priced lines, such as Random House's recent list of abridged novels on cassette selling for $8.99 per set. An-other solution, some say, is to exploit specialty markets and niches in nontraditional ways, for example, producing cassettes from books on fly fishing and selling them to sporting goods stores.

8

Alternatives:
Small Presses, University Presses, Vanity Presses, and Self-Publishing

> Literature is like any other trade; you will never sell anything unless you go to the right shop.
> —George Bernard Shaw

In spite of the vast number of trade books published every year, you may find, to your dismay, that your manuscript or proposal is rejected out of hand by every commercial publisher you approach. Some writers give up more quickly than others, succumbing to defeat after four or five rejections, while others have stronger egos. As an agent, I have sometimes submitted the same proposal to more than 30 publishers before giving up, when I firmly believed in the merits or sales potential of the project. At other times I have desisted after eight or nine submissions, primarily because the editors were consistent in their criticism, and I was finally persuaded that their cumulative intuitions were more accurate than my own. Each writer has to decide when it is time to stop, but to curl up in despair after three or four rejections is a sign of being in the wrong field.

Too small a market or a poorly conceived and executed idea are probably the most common and justifiable reasons for the failure to find a publisher, though you might not think so from scanning the shelves of a bookstore. But the competition in every phase of the publishing industry is fierce, and nowhere more keenly experienced than in passing the first hurdle. If you are trying to place your first book, particularly a first novel or collection of poems, the odds are heavily stacked against you, no matter what its literary merits or potential market. At some point, you will sit back and take stock. The proposal or manuscript has been turned down by a dozen or more publishers, two years have passed, and you have had it. Before considering some of the alternatives to commercial publishing, perhaps it's time to try a different gambit.

If the manuscript is a novel, a book of poems, or a collection of short stories, you should try to publish an excerpt or selections in magazines or journals before approaching a publisher. Almost every book editor will be more receptive to fiction and poetry that has been accepted for publication elsewhere, even in small-circulation literary magazines. The number of these publications that exist and the quantities of material they use provide much better odds for getting published; if you cannot get a story or a poem published in a magazine or journal, you probably have little chance of finding a commercial book publisher. The references that have already been mentioned—*Literary Market Place*, *Writer's Market*, and the *International Directory of Little Magazines and Small Presses*—contain the names and addresses, and the latter two clearly identify the type of material used, the preferred manner of submission, and other helpful information.

The same advice holds for nonfiction. There is generally at least one chapter in any nonfiction book that is suitable as an article, even if it requires some editing, cutting, or adapting. Approaching a publisher with an offprint or copy of an article, which is culled from a proposed book or is appropriate as the genesis for one, immediately increases the writer's chances of at least being taken seriously, even if he or she is not ultimately offered a contract.

But though you succeed in publishing an excerpt, some poems, or a piece of fiction, you may still eventually find the doors of commercial book publishing closed to you. Assuming that the fiction or poetry is imaginative and worthy, or that the nonfiction is informative and original, chances are that an editor or publisher predicted the market just wasn't there: They intuit that not enough people will buy the book to compensate for the efforts and expense required to produce and sell it. Maybe they are shortsighted or dead wrong; an impressive tradition of self-published writers, from Thomas Paine to Zane Grey to James Joyce, is testimony to the frequent initial myopia of commercial publishers. Maybe they are right. What if under ideal conditions your book of poetry would only sell 500 to 750 copies? Even then it doesn't follow that you should automatically forgo attempts to get it into print.

The alternatives to commercial book publishing have been in existence for a long time. The university press, for example, identifies an esoteric biblical commentary published by Oxford University Press in 1478 as its first publication. Small-press publishing, self-publishing, and vanity or subsidy publishing constitute, in a sense, the origins of book publishing. During publishing's infancy, books were produced either by small local printers or by individual authors and were usually financed or subsidized by the author or a patron. (The poet William Blake took all matters into his own hands and wrote, designed, printed, and sold his books.)

One of the problems in discussing the alternatives is defining them clearly and locating their boundaries: Small presses may overlap with trade publishers; subsidy publishing is sometimes a component of small-press (and even university press) publishing; and a self-publisher can become a small press merely by assigning an imprint to its first publication. Three major factors help to distinguish the alternatives: who pays the costs, who owns the book, and who distributes it. Since the small presses *in most cases* finance, distribute, sell, and license rights for the books they publish, and since they are initial logical alternatives for a writer, let us examine them first.

The Small Press

"A small press is a state of mind." In the course of interviewing small-press publishers and in gathering information about these presses—that now are more commonly called "independent presses"—this definition evolved as the only one that was even vaguely accurate. Certain characteristics generally hold true for most of them, but an all-embracing definition is impossible. These characteristics are: publishing fewer than 15 titles a year, a list that has a narrow focus (such as cooking, regionalia, travel, or poetry), small first-print runs (generally 2,000 copies or less), limited publicity and advertising, separate distribution channels, and reduced sales expectations. Today it is more difficult to state the differences between a small press and any other book publisher, because many small presses publish significant numbers of books, publish them profitably, and, allowing for differences in number of employees and lavishness of office space, generally carry on business in ways that are not much different from the big houses. *LMP* will list any company as a publisher (with the exception of vanity presses, a discussion of which appears later in this chapter) as long as they produce three or more books a year; even though many small presses are not listed in *LMP*, there is no distinction made between ones that are. Red Dust, Inc., and Random House are listed in the same section. *LMP* does have a section in which publishers that put out fewer than three books a year may pay to be listed. (While we are constructing definitions, *Books in Print* will list as a book any publication it receives that is available for sale to the public, not a periodical, and has 48 pages or more somehow bound together; children's books, poetry, and drama need not meet the page-length criterion.)

At one time small presses could be divided into regional publishers and "counterculture" publishers. The counterculture, of course, has gone mainstream (as with New Age titles) and, although some small presses publish regional books only, many publish regional books and others as well. In one sense, what separates small presses from regular commercial book publishing is that, in the various processes we have described so far, they tend to forgo traditional methods, either in favor of truncating them (such as in reducing expenditures for publicity and advertising) or in devising alternate methods of marketing (such as in forming their own distribution cooperatives). Depending on which sources you wish to quote, and which criteria you use to define a small press, there are as many as 30,000 publishers of books out there, with newcomers cropping up as fast as others are disbanding. For a representative sampling, see the *International Directory of Little Magazines and Small Presses*, the current edition of which contains more than 1,000 pages of listings.

Regional Publishing. Some of these companies prefer to be called "niche" publishers, since they publish books in marketing niches not ordinarily filled by mainstream houses. The methods and motives of these publishers are quite traditional, closely resembling those of commercial publishers, and they generally make a living if not a great profit for their efforts. Typically, a company consists of about a half-dozen employees, and the publisher him- or herself may perform the majority of the tasks, such as acquiring, editing, estimating, designing, and preparing catalog and flap copy. She will often farm out to freelancers such tasks as copyediting, proofreading, and jacket design. The yearly list, about 8 to 12 titles, will contain a high percentage of regional interest titles, such as *The Big Tomato: A Guide to the Sacramento Region* published by Lexicos Press or *My Pamet*, a book about Cape Cod published by Moyer Bell. Regional poetry and fiction, regional histories, regional flora and fauna, and regional crafts are the mainstays of the typical list.

Computer books are one area in which small presses have found a niche. *The Macintosh Bible*, which has sold more than 400,000 copies, was published by its author (who had already been published by other companies, and who started his own company to publish his own book) and distributed by Publishers Group West. PeachPit Press in California, which has a full-time staff of seven people, specializes in books about desktop publishing. Ventana Press in North Carolina specializes in books for computer beginners.

In addition to regional books, these publishers will frequently fill out their lists with small market "bread and butter" titles, ranging from bottle collecting to quilt making to a manual on making maple syrup. The diversity of the list is subject only to the interests and whims of the publisher, and many of the titles might be suitable for a commercial trade house. The publisher's only constraint is a modest sales expectation: Can the book sell more than 1,000 copies? Her costs and her overhead are geared to return a profit on as small a sale as 750 copies, and 7,500 copies is a best-seller. On rare occasions a commercial house will buy the rights, either cloth or paper or both, if the initial sales figures are impressive and the book is brought to their attention.

The publisher usually acquires manuscripts from local authors, either over-the-transom, by word of mouth, or by initiating book ideas and then locating a writer. As a one-person editorial board, the publisher's decision-making process is quite simple: If she likes both the idea and the sample chapters or manuscript, if she thinks it is suitable for her list, and if her preliminary estimate of the costs indicates that she can make a profit on a sale of roughly 1,000 copies, she will sign the book up. A contract may consist of a simple one- to two-page form or just a letter of agreement. Generally, no advances are given, though some regional publishers can be persuaded to part with $250 to $1,000. Royalties tend to be a flat 10 percent of list price for clothbound books and 6 or 7½ percent for paperbacks. Occasionally the publisher will request or be offered a subsidy for a specific book. For instance, if a local historian has produced a town history for which sales expectations do not exceed 400 copies, either the author, the Chamber of Commerce, or even a local patron may subsidize part of the production costs.

In the production of the book, from copyediting to design to typesetting to manufacturing, the publisher can reduce a portion of the normal direct and indirect costs by doing much of the work herself. She may, for instance, in working closely with a local printer, paste up the production proofs by herself. A personal computer gives her the ability to set her own type, and she can even, for a modest investment in hardware, produce her own repro, camera ready for a printer. Computer typesetting allows her (and any publisher, for that matter) to skip the galley stage and go directly to pages. She can cut corners by maintaining close personal control over every stage of the book, and by performing many of the tasks herself, she lowers the conventional break-even point to make a small printing feasible. This is not to imply that the final book looks like a homemade or cottage-industry product. Many regional presses will produce books that are indistinguishable in quality and appearance from their commercial trade counterparts.

In marketing the book, the publisher generally follows traditional procedures, though specific elements are reduced in scope. Working with an author's questionnaire, the publisher will solicit blurbs and send out advance review copies to trade magazines. Using the same kinds of lists as a trade house, promotion and review copies are sent to major review media, though the publisher will concentrate on regional media and specialized magazines and journals and will mail out an average of 50 rather than 100 review copies.

Advertising expenditures are equally reduced, but simple fliers as well as press releases are frequently employed, and most publishers will prepare a yearly general catalog that is sent to mail-order customers, individual bookstore accounts, wholesalers, and libraries. Though reviews in national media are rare, the trade magazines such as *Publishers Weekly* and *Library Journal* will occasionally review worthy titles, and an enthusiastic notice there may result in as many as 1,200 copies sold to regional libraries—a market that is particularly vital to the small publisher. Feature articles and even radio and television appearances by authors are not infrequent.

A few small presses have their own sales reps, but most depend on master distributors. These wholesalers, which distribute the books of many publishers, do shipping, billing, and collecting for dozens of small presses. Companies like Publishers Group West, National Book Network, the Tallman Company, and others (many started in the last decade) have given small presses access to an efficient distribution network that they would otherwise lack. Some of these distributors still specialize—Inbook, for example, is known for distributing women's titles and gay and lesbian books—but a company such as Publishers Group West handles titles for almost 150 small presses of all kinds. Nationwide commercial wholesale distributors, such as Baker and Taylor, often carry regional press books, too, though only in that specific regional office.

The regional press augments these sales efforts by mailing catalogs or individual fliers to libraries, lists of previous customers—both individuals and bookstores—and to mailing lists purchased from magazines, journals, or organizations. They also put in appearances at regional book fairs and exhibits.

Subsidiary rights or international sales are generally a very minor source of income and are not pursued with any consistency or aggressiveness.

In sum, the regional press resembles the commercial trade house and differs primarily in the limited scope and size of its list, its expectations, its overhead and expenditures, its ability to gain attention for itself in national media, and in its cumulative sales record. For the author whose book may have a limited audience, the regional press may be an ideal solution. While the publisher may not be a prestigious one or a household name, you will not feel that you or your book have been lost in the shuffle or that the book was taken to fill a slot on some publisher's semiannual list only to be summarily dumped on the market to sink or swim.

The Independent Press. While there have always been a number of small presses to accommodate "noncommercial," avant-garde, or radical writers, the true flowering, or more accurately, mushrooming, of these presses dates from the early 1960s, coinciding with the eruption of political and social activism that characterized the period. Lacking access to national media or commercial book publishers, except for lurid, newsworthy, or dramatic events, the members of the New Left began to print their own broadsides, pamphlets, and newspapers. Their immediate literary forerunners, the Beats, had already signaled the renaissance in the 1950s: Writers such as Kerouac, Ginsberg, and Corso began to see print from new "alternative-press" (so called through the 1960s and 1970s) publishers such as City Lights Books, founded in 1953 by poet Lawrence Ferlinghetti. Thus the ingredients out of which the alternative presses brewed this reincarnation—a voice for society's dissidents, political and social ferment, lack of an establishment platform from which to be heard—continue to infuse the rhetoric of alternative publishing, even though much of its current output is by no means radical, controversial, or even innovative. Today New Age, feminism, and gay rights seem to be the major social movements that guide the editorial policies of many independent publishers.

The belief among independent publishers that commercial publishing is publishing at its worst and small-press publishing is publishing at its best has faded in recent years and given way to a belief that independent publishers and commercial publishers fill different roles. While most small presses are in business to make money (and go out of business when they stop making money), some literary presses still operate as nonprofit-making organizations, dedicated to disseminating, at a reasonable price, literature or information that is either truly innovative, unavailable elsewhere, or which documents political and social problems and grievances: They do provide an alternate voice. And it must also be said that many of these presses also publish poetry and fiction, ranging from bad to mediocre to excellent, the authors of which are motivated primarily by the desire to see their work in print, rather than to reform society. Some authors prefer the intimacy of a small press, but just as many would welcome the opportunity to publish with Putnam, for instance, as a chance to have their work widely read and to provide them with the financial means to write at greater leisure. Equally so, most of these presses, if the sales figures warrant, will readily move into that gray area of production, sales, and distribution in which commercial and small presses overlap.

The diversity of independent-press methods of operation and range of publishing interests—from abortion to Zionism—are too numerous to catalog here. *The Small Press Record of Books* (22nd edition, 1993, available from Dustbooks, P.O. Box 100, Paradise, CA 95969 for $42.95) lists more than 25,000 books from more than 5,000 publishers. Most of the independent presses can also be found in the *International Directory of Little Magazines and Small Presses*.

What primarily distinguishes the independent presses from the regional presses are editorial policy and book content, methods of sales and distribution, and lack of profit. Though virtually any category of books can be found in browsing through a list of independent-press titles, there tends to be an emphasis on certain topics and genres. Foremost are poetry and fiction, which constitute more than 50 percent of the total output. One could safely say that there is no famous American poet of the twentieth century, from Pound and Williams to Lowell and Rukeyser, who doesn't have at least one volume that has been published by one of these presses. Many distinguished poets, novelists, and prose writers have been, and continue to be, published by independent presses. Capra Press, for example, has titles by Henry Miller (including his posthumously published study of D. H. Lawrence), Anaïs Nin, Lawrence Durrell, and Ross MacDonald. Often these presses will publish the less commercial works of successful trade writers—their poetry or collections of short stories or essays. "Chapbooks," small hand-bound pamphlets averaging 48 pages, selling for a modest price, and usually consisting of poetry, are as commonly published as books; they may be the most suitable format for publication of a first book of poems. For the poet, novelist, or short-story writer who does not, for one reason or another, scale the walls of commercial publishing, the independent press is the ideal option.*

In nonfiction, the emphasis is on militancy and social

---

*Poets and Writers Magazine, published bimonthly, is the most informative and professional magazine for this audience. Subscriptions are available for $18 a year from: Poets and Writers, Inc., 72 Spring St., New York, NY 10012. They also publish a handful of extremely useful books for their audience, including *A Directory of American Poets and Fiction Writers, Literary Bookstores: A Cross-Country Guide*, and *Contracts and Royalties: Negotiate Your Own*. Write and ask for a catalog.

change—feminism, Third World movements, gay liberation, peace movements, etc.; alternate or improved life-styles—back-to-the-land, pollution and ecology, gardening and farming, health, etc.; mental, physical, and spiritual self-help—from astrology and acupuncture to vegetarianism and Yoga; and how-to's of all types. But virtually any topic can be found in the subject index of the *A.I.P.* and is grist for the small-press mill.

Some of the independent presses, such as the Black Sparrow Press, have a long, stable tradition and reputation for publishing only first-rate work. By virtue of consistent high quality and staying power, Black Sparrow and others like them now occupy a position in the publishing hierarchy that straddles the small-press/commercial press world. Their books can be found in many standard trade bookstores and are carried by many of the commercial distributors. The majority of these presses, however, operate within a framework that is the outgrowth of small-press history, development, and custom.

The primary clearinghouse and professional organization for the little magazine and small-press field is COSMEP: The International Association of Independent Publishers.* Membership (currently more than 1,400) is also open to self-publishers—or even "just-interested" parties. Through its monthly newsletter, COSMEP keeps members informed of grant opportunities, new developments in production and distribution, lists of stores and libraries that carry small-press publications, and pertinent regional and national fairs and conferences. It also lobbies for small presses, both in Congress (against rising postal rates, for instance) and in national review media for greater small-press coverage.

Lack of money is obviously one of the small presses' biggest problems. Undercapitalized to begin with, the income from book sales rarely manages to cover the costs and overhead. Most of the literary small presses are subsidized either out of pocket by their owners, by contributions solicited from their own authors,

---

*Send for details and a sample newsletter to: P.O. Box 420-703, San Francisco, CA 94142-0703.

by private grants (including patrons, among whom are a number of successful and best-selling authors, some of them originally published by small presses), or by federal grants. In fiscal year 1993, the National Endowment for the Arts gave out 69 grants totaling more than $1.1 million to small presses and literary magazines. Small presses garnered 23 of these grants—more than $560,000. N.E.A. grants range from $2,000 to $30,000, and they are given for specific projects, not general support; however, they are given for promotion and distribution projects as well as for book production.

Virtually all literary small presses operate at a deficit, and most can finance only about 50 percent of their operating costs from the sales of books. One reason is that in an effort to reach as wide an audience as possible, most books are published as paperback originals, and sold at list prices somewhat lower than comparable books from commercial trade houses. The other 50 percent of their operating costs comes from grants, donations, "family money," or the publisher's own pocket(s). Making a profit is the exception, not the rule. Grantsmanship, then, often becomes a crucial factor in keeping a number of the better literary presses afloat, and grant "politics" is an ongoing game. Grants are sought not only from the N.E.A., but from state arts councils, the Coordinating Council of Literary Magazines, various government agencies, and from successful authors, most of whom remain anonymous donors (how would you like to have 1,000 small presses asking for a donation?).

Some of the manuscripts are acquired through local supporters and friends, and a small percentage of the titles are the works of the staff of each press, but "casual acquaintance" is the most common entry to small presses. As each press grows, however, the range of manuscripts published broadens to include over-the-transom submissions. A typical literary press may receive as many as 2,000 manuscripts a year, out of which it may choose to publish three to five books (so you can expect a high rate of rejection slips here too). The ability or inclination of the author to promote, publicize, and sell his or her own book (as at poetry readings) is sometimes a key factor in deciding whether or not to take on a book. Small presses are quirkier in their decisions, since their own tastes rather than commercial considerations generally determine their choice of what to publish. Good work may be turned down only because it doesn't suit the tastes of the editors. And with 2,000 submissions a year and an average yearly list of ten books, writers must be as persistent, and as careful in their selection of houses, as they should be with trade houses. Many small publishers are looking to discover new writers, rather than publish small-press "professionals," even those with good track records. So the novice may have a step up on the pro. Prospective authors can consult the *International Directory* or *A.I.P.* catalog to decide which presses might be suitable for their books, or can write directly to these publishers for current catalogs or fliers.

Authors accepted for publication should be prepared for very informal contracts or letters of agreement. You may get a token advance of $50 to $250, but no advance at all is more common. The royalty terms range from the conventional to the conditional; for example, royalties will be paid only after a requisite number of copies are sold to recoup expenses. More common as a royalty is to give the author 10 percent of the books from the first print run and 10 percent of any reprints. For authors who expect to give readings, this can add up to a 10-percent-of-list royalty (also a conventional royalty for small presses). In fact, these two rates are not only recommended in the N.E.A. "Grant Guidelines," but are now required of houses that receive their grants. If you hope or expect to generate sales on your own, as from poetry readings, you should ask to buy copies at 10 percent above the cost of printing, with no royalty paid on these copies; this, of course, adds up to a hefty royalty if you sell them. While a handshake is as common as a contract, you should at least expect or ask for a letter from the press, stating its intention to publish a book ("within one year," preferably), what kind of royalty it will pay, and what your share of the subsidiary rights are.*

Sub-rights sales are still rare (though more common than they

---

*A small-press "Book Publishing Agreement" is available from Dustbooks for $2.

were before small presses started sending galleys to book clubs and mass market reprinters) and very few books are sent overseas. In compensation, many small presses will only take 10 percent of these unexpected rights sales, or will gladly let you keep—and spell out in the letter—first serial, performance, British, and foreign translation rights, and even second serial rights (for a short story or a poem to be reprinted in an anthology or magazine is obviously not as remote a possibility as a film option or even a book-club sale).

Even if your publisher doesn't mention subsidiary rights, you should; there is always the possibility of a sale, and there is usually nothing to stop you from initiating it yourself. Provided the press doesn't object, you might try selling the sub-rights on your own, or at least recommend to the publisher where a sale is a possibility; there are several hundred small book clubs, for example, that are particularly receptive to nonfiction, even from obscure presses.

The appearance and quality of the bound book can be of prize-winning stature, or it can look like a mimeographed broadside handed out on a street corner. Tight budgets, however, are frequently compensated for by loving care: Many of the small-press publishers have a strong and abiding interest in the aesthetics of book production, which is reflected in the final product. The in-house labor, of course, whether editorial, production, or marketing, is donated. No profits also generally mean no salaries.

The average first printing for a novel, book of poems, or collection of short stories is in the range of 1,200 copies, but it may go as low as 500 or as high as 2,500. This is calculated to cover the first 18 months' to two years' sales (in contrast to trade houses, which rarely print for more than one year's sales, and now often print for only the first six months' estimated sales). Books from small presses sell more slowly, and it takes more time to get them publicized and distributed.

Though restricted by small budgets, the majority of independent presses will carry out traditional publicity functions. Review copies (though maybe not advance page proofs, but up to 10 percent of the first print run) will be sent to trade magazines such as *Publishers Weekly*, *Library Journal*, and *Choice*, which are increasingly taking note of small-press books. Review copies will also go out to local and regional newspapers, as well as to a variety of special-interest magazines, though only a few optimistic presses will gamble on sending copies to national consumer media such as the *New York Times*, even though they do occasionally review small-press books. The most receptive review media are the "little magazines," the small-circulation literary journals and reviews that are the magazine counterparts to the small presses. Many of them review small-press books regularly, and a few are devoted almost exclusively to the small-press industry and book reviewing, such as *Small Press Review*, which "seeks to study and promulgate the small press worldwide."*

Press releases are common, as are active attempts to get local coverage, whether in newspapers or on radio or television. Some small presses are quite successful in arranging local lecture tours or poetry readings. Catalogs are produced, usually once a year, and are sent to libraries, bookstores, and mail-order lists of previous individual customers. Individual fliers for specific books are often sent to lists of potential customers provided by the author, and also to relevant special-interest groups and specific magazine and journal subscribers.

Advertising is minimal, but ads in little magazines and literary quarterlies, local newspapers, library publications, and even national media are not uncommon, while ads for appropriate nonfiction titles may be placed in classified sections.

The major problems for alternative presses are sales and distribution. For poetry, for example, even a sale of 500 to 750 copies can be considered a success. (Curiously, there seem to be more writers of poetry than buyers or readers.) Ideally each book requires and will get a separate sales strategy. Within a radius of 100 miles or so, the publisher may make direct calls on and service the local bookstores. This is especially true in col-

---

*For a free sample issue of this monthly, write to Dustbooks, P. O. Box 100, Paradise, CA 95969, or subscribe for $23 per year.

lege towns. Cities such as Austin, Berkeley, Cambridge, Iowa City, New Orleans, and Northampton are heavily populated by students and professors, who are a prime audience for literary presses. One successful ploy in developing new bookstore accounts is to give away a free copy of one or two or more titles. Assuming they sell—and the bookstore has been able to pocket the entire amount—the store will now presumably be more receptive to stocking new titles from that press. Another promotional device is to give a store 100 or more copies of a slow-moving book, which the store will use as a free premium in its Christmas catalog. Most stores send these catalogs to their charge-account customers, and the free copy is sent out with any order. A key salesperson, however, in any marketing strategy is the author, who is usually expected to sell a hefty number of copies of his or her work, since many poets, novelists, and short-story writers teach, lecture, or give readings at colleges, coffee houses, YMCAs, and other localities.

The more financially successful small presses are those that prepare individual marketing plans for each book, carefully identify and seek to reach a specific audience, try to sell subrights, and concentrate on nontraditional markets; for example, publishing regional trail guides and then selling them directly to "outdoor" and sporting-goods stores, such as Eastern Mountain Sports.

Since many independent-press books will not be carried by commercial jobbers and distributors, nor in most bookstores, a variety of solutions has evolved. At one extreme are the very few presses that have made sales and distribution arrangements with a commercial publisher, such as has Ecco Press, which is distributed by W. W. Norton & Co. (it also distributes eight other independent presses; a number of commercial houses have such stables). In recent years, a number of small-press regional associations have sprung up to provide collective distribution facilities; membership numbers range from roughly 15 to 50 publishers. Half are full-service distributors—that is, they will stock, bill, and ship titles—and the other half act as clearinghouses that forward orders to the individual presses. These collectives are eligible for grants, and some are even eligible for nonprofit, tax-exempt status. Member presses, if geography permits, share in the work; otherwise, one member coordinates and the rest contribute operating capital. The value of collective or wholesale distribution, aside from the obvious benefits to the individual publishers, is felt more strongly by the bookstore and the library. The abundance of publishers and small-press titles, their limited sales potential and audience, and the occasional here-today-gone-tomorrow syndrome discourages libraries and bookstores from stocking titles or dealing individually with any but the top 10 percent of the field. But the professionalism, stability, and convenience of dealing with distributors makes buying books more attractive and less complicated.

Nevertheless many independent presses have often been cavalier about—if not downright disdainful of—the sales and distribution side of publishing. A sign of change in attitude is evident in the growing number of publishing seminars on marketing for small presses sponsored by COSMEP, Knowledge Industries, and others. After all, sales + grants = survival. Three problems that continue to plague some small-press distributors are "anti-business" prejudice, which still permeates much of the small-press world; the meager amount of income actually generated by their sales; and the difficulty in collecting on bills to bookstores, which are now either paying in 90 to 120 days, making heavy returns, or not paying bills at all. This last set of issues is a problem that now extends to trade book publishing as well.

The production and distribution of a joint mail-order catalog is the most effective tool of both the wholesale and cooperative distributor. Libraries and lists of individual consumers are as much a target as bookstores, since few of the latter stock titles on a regular basis. Many of the larger bookstore chains, however, such as Waldenbooks, and B. Dalton, are becoming less resistant to ordering individual titles, though poetry and fiction are still the lowest priority genres. The larger small-press wholesalers, such as Publishers Group West and Inbook, employ sales representatives, follow up catalogs with individual mailing pieces and fliers, and exhibit at major publishing industry meetings. The collectives are less rigorous: If there are salespeople, they may be working part-time or they may be individual small-press publishers who voluntarily rotate sales calls. As collectives, with very low budgets, the necessity for communal cooperation and free voluntary services are vital to their continued existence.

The experimental, on-again, off-again distribution schemes of the 1970s and 1980s have given way to a much more professional system for small-press distribution. With COSMEP acting as a professional and educational organization, and the growth of distributors that specialize in small presses, it's much easier for small publishers to put worthy books in the hands of readers.

Authors who have published with the better small presses are generally surprised and delighted by the quality of book production, but are frequently frustrated and disappointed by the length of time it takes for books to appear in the stores or to get reviews, and by the modest sales. Keep in mind that the operation of almost all small presses is a labor of love, and that the motives of those who run them are rarely found in commercial publishing today. Small-press people are often juggling full-time jobs and raising families and are usually not rewarded for all their efforts with so much as a bus token. They generally deserve your gratitude, no matter how many copies of your book they sell.

Though shoestring budgets and other problems remain, the independent presses are growing, thriving, and developing new techniques for overcoming their inherent limitations. Fed up with what many writers and small-press impresarios feel is the growing bottom-line mentality of the publishing industry—"Make your living at anything *except* with the biggest literary cesspool called commercial publishing"—the independent presses are providing an opportunity for a growing number of unpublished or disillusioned writers.

The University Press

The primary goal of a university press is to publish scholarly works that contribute to the advancement of knowledge in specific fields. In general, it has not been their objective to make a profit. But even for university presses, times are changing, subsidies from the university's budget are more difficult to obtain, and many university press directors are under pressure if not to make a large profit, at least to break even and not cost the university too much money. In response to this, some university presses have begun to publish books, both fiction and nonfiction, that were once considered—if not exactly commercial—at least more suitable for trade houses. When the Naval Institute Press published *The Hunt for Red October*, when John Hopkins University Press sold more than 250,000 copies of *The Thirty-Six Hour Day*, and when Indiana University Press put more than 80,000 copies of a book about basketball, *Beyond the Brink*, into chain stores around the country, these presses were acting in ways that were almost indistinguishable from their counterparts in the trade book part of the industry. Indiana University Press even has its own book club, which offers discounts on selected Indiana titles.

Still, these are the exceptions for university presses. The University of Chicago Press, for example, the largest university press in the country, publishes many books that have a trade audience, none more successful than Norman Maclean's classic *A River Runs Through It*, which was boosted to the best-seller lists in 1992 by Robert Redford's movie adaptation (and which the Press followed with yet another Maclean best-seller, *Young Men and Fire*). But even so, the trade books on their list account for only 20 percent of their publishing program, with the rest devoted to scholarly works. A handful of other large university presses—Oxford, Harvard, Yale, Princeton, the University of California, and several others—account for most of the trade books published by these houses.

Many smaller university presses, particularly those connected to public universities, specialize in regional titles of a scholarly or at least "serious" nature. The University of New Mexico Press, which is well known for its books of photographs of the American West, sells 30 percent of its books within the state of New Mexico, and the University of Washington Press gets a similar percentage from its regional sales in the Northwest. Translations, poetry, and a small amount of fiction, especially short stories, are now also the domain of university presses, and there are those previously mentioned examples of university press novels that have made their way into the mainstream and even onto best-seller lists.

University presses operate with varying levels of subsidies from the university, from state government, and from grants. They also frequently enjoy below-market rents and lower labor costs. These advantages allow them to carry on their primary mission of publishing works of scholarship that are rarely profitable in the marketplace.

These houses have editorial staffs like any publisher, but they are usually encumbered by faculty boards consisting of from 6 to 12 professors who must approve publishing projects. Because of the outside academic critiques that are solicited for each manuscript (usually two or three) as well as the faculty board review, the presses often take from two months to a year to make a final decision about signing up a book—a factor to be weighed carefully before submitting your manuscript.

Because most scholarly books generally sell modestly, first printings average only 2,000 to 2,500 copies, and there is little money to spare for advances, though the larger, more solvent, or commercially oriented UP's will sometimes pay advances of from $1,000 to $10,000. Royalties are similar to those for trade books, although about a third of presses pay on net receipts rather than list price. Some presses now consistently require a subsidy to help defray the cost of production. It may come from out of the author's pocket, from private or federal grants, or from university research funds. Other presses may require a subvention only on occasion, but particularly when a project requires years of preparation and results in a multivolume set, such as Princeton's collected papers of Albert Einstein, which garnered more than a million-dollar grant.

The quality of design and production is consistently good and frequently superb: The books are usually a delight to hold, to look at, and to own. Due to financial pressure, some of the presses are now cutting corners, but the list prices of the books nevertheless remain very high.

With regard to publicity and advertising, most UP's follow the conventions of commercial presses, although on a reduced scale. Rarely is enough money spent on advertising and publicity to "manufacture" a market for a book, and the average press spends approximately $10,000 advertising each list (twice a year). This means that the ads appear in specialized journals their audience is likely to read: scholarly journals, library publications, and special-interest magazines.

University presses carry on marketing in much the same way as commercial houses do. Most of them have their own sales reps, commission reps, or both. Some go further: Princeton, for example, has a commission sales force for England and Europe. There are also distribution consortiums that take care of the warehousing, sales, and distribution of groups of university presses. Most presses attend academic conferences, and many attend the Frankfurt Book Fair where they do a lively business in subsidiary and foreign rights. Direct mail is more commonly used in university presses than in commercial houses, mostly to reach academics and libraries. Short discounts discourage bookstores from handling most university press books, but the larger stores, particularly those in academic communities, do stock titles from these houses, and a certain percentage of UP titles are sold to bookstores at a normal trade discount. Foreign export sales represent a considerably higher percentage of sales than in commercial houses—about 10 percent of sales, as opposed to about 5 or 6 percent in trade houses.

A decision to submit a manuscript (proposals with samples are frowned upon, except from scholars with previous publications) to a university press must be based on the specific interests and informal guidelines each press maintains. The *A.A.U.P. Directory*, which can be found in most libraries, contains a list of its 111 members (which include, in various categories of membership, museums that publish books, like the National Gallery of Art, and scholarly organizations that publish journals, like the Modern Language Association) with a description of their publishing interests. Several of the presses are known for their poetry contests, such as "The Yale Series of Younger Poets," whose awards consist of book publication, occasionally supplemented by nominal advances of $500 or $1,000. The competition is very keen, and the standards are very high: The criterion for publication is excellence, not salability. A listing of these contests can be found in the *Grants and Awards Available to American Writers.** This publication, incidentally, is an invaluable resource for writers seeking scholarships, grants, and awards; more than 500 are listed.

In general, the presses will only consider "serious" nonfiction and literary fiction; before submitting a manuscript, it would be advisable to write the individual presses for a copy of their current catalog, to determine the kinds of books they publish as well as the audience they target. Although the presses are not opposed to signing up books that might have an impressive (for them) sale, they are usually more concerned with the quality of the writing, the originality of the research data, the contribution to the advancement of knowledge in a particular field, and the regional potential.

The 111 members in the Association of American University Presses together publish about 8,000 titles a year.

Publishing for Hire

There are several instances in which a writer might decide to pay for the cost of publishing his or her book. Foremost is the blunt fact that no commercial house, small press, or university press will take on the manuscript. But there are other sensible reasons for considering this option. A writer could spend a lifetime canvassing publishers (*LMP* rents several mailing lists, including one that contains the names and addresses of more than 32,000 publishers) and most are unwilling to do so. If seeing your work in print is the primary goal and you are fully prepared to write off the investment—since the odds are that you will recoup only a small portion of it—then you might as well consider

---

*Copies can be purchased for $8 (18th edition) from PEN American Center, 568 Broadway, New York, NY 10012.

taking the plunge. Perhaps you have written a history of your family, a book of light verse, a novel, or even a polemical denunciation of capital punishment. You may have an avocation or vocation from which you collected a considerable body of specialized or technical data or information that might interest only a few hundred readers, or even more. Incidentally, this is the most appropriate genre for self-publishing, and the one most likely to earn you back your investment. You will not be in isolated company paying for book publication: The so-called vanity presses alone publish about 2,000 books a year.

There are two basic choices for the writer who travels this route, and the decision of which to make should hinge on two simple factors: time and money. Now that you have been exposed to the fundamental operations of publishing, it should be clear that there are a limited number of skills and procedures that, with a certain amount of patience and effort, can either be learned or purchased, or a combination of both. You may not want to learn how to set your own type, but you can, for instance, learn how to prepare your manuscript for composition, how to design the interior of the book, and how to assemble or buy mailing lists for review copies and library sales. If you have the time, the inclination, and the confidence, and wish to keep your costs to a minimum, you should seriously consider publishing your own book. If money is no object, or if you cannot spare the time or are intimidated by the thought of tackling the job on your own, then you may want to look into the vanity presses. One reason the decision is a simple one is that there is no indication that the vanity press will sell more copies of the book—all claims notwithstanding—than you can.

The Vanity Press. There are about a dozen nationally known and advertised companies, such as Dorrance and Vantage, that actively solicit or advertise for authors. They refer to themselves as subsidy publishers, shunning the designation *vanity*, although that is the term people in the publishing industry continue to employ. They advertise their services frequently in writers' magazines and national media, and a headline such as "Publisher Seeking Authors" will serve to identify them. The larger companies will often also advertise in local newspapers, stating that a publisher's representative will be in town for several days to talk to prospective authors, and so forth.

Practically everyone in publishing wrinkles his nose when you mention vanity presses; unfortunately, that includes reviewers, bookstore buyers, distributors, and libraries. One of the major reasons for the conventional disdain (aside from the generally poor quality of the writing) is the variety of misleading claims purveyed by these presses. The Federal Trade Commission has censured these companies several times during the last three decades, so that their ads, brochures, and contracts are now no more misleading than those of used-car dealers. Since in a capitalist society we are all exposed to the hawking of services or wares that do not quite measure up to our expectations, there is really no reason to single out the vanity press for an extra dose of condemnation. Just remember that if you are going to consider doing business with them, you are well advised to keep your eyes wide open, read contracts and other documents very carefully, and make sure not only that you understand exactly what goods or services you think you are buying, but that you have a written document to detail them. (It might be wise to have an attorney vet the contract.)

Vanity presses will publish virtually *any* manuscript for a fee, provided that it is not racist, pornographic, excessively violent, patently subversive, or so out of bounds that for one reason or another the publisher might expose itself to a lawsuit. In preparation for this book, I sent copies of an unpublished manuscript of roughly 300 pages to two of the leading vanity presses. Within ten days I had a glowing report from each publisher, praising my work in superlatives and indicating that it had been accepted for publication. Within less than a week after that, I received a contract from each company—very complicated ones, I might add—along with catalogs and fliers with testimonials from satisfied customers. There were numerous case histories of books that had gone into multiple printings, sold in huge quantities, and had earned their authors thousands of dollars. One book had actually made the best-seller list of the *New York Times* (in 1954), one author had allegedly published 300 books (none of which are currently listed in *Books in Print*), one book was written by a Nobel Prize winner, and another author had gone on to become a Pulitzer Prize winner. Very impressive! Both the contracts and the author's questionnaires (which were included) looked infinitely more professional than the ones I normally get from commercial publishers. In order to appreciate the optimistic and enthusiastic vapors with which these documents intoxicate the potential customer, you will have to send a vanity press a copy of your manuscript and receive your own set of blandishments. The only apparent thorn in this bouquet of roses was on the last page of the contract: "In consideration of the advantages to accrue to the author . . . he agrees to pay $9,000" (the other read $7,700).

Vanity presses will only accept a completed manuscript, since they cannot calculate the actual costs of your fee without it. Simply put, they will publish your manuscript in a cloth or paper binding at a cost to you which enables them to make a very handsome profit whether or not they ever actually sell a single copy of the book. According to all the literature on vanity presses, about 10 percent of their authors recoup their entire investment. For the other 90 percent, the average return is roughly 25 percent of the total payment. In other words, out of my $9,000 investment, I could expect to kiss $6,750 goodbye.

Some of the conditions and services pertinent to the vanity press agreement are worth considering here. Obviously the cost of publication will depend on the size and complexity of your manuscript, as well as on the number of copies printed. The manuscript I submitted was 300 pages long; a 64-page book of poems in a paperback edition would have cost considerably less. According to the terms of the contract, the publisher generally sends the author 50 to 75 free copies and mails out approximately 75 review copies. Yearly catalogs are produced and sent to distributors, bookstores, and libraries, and a press release is also produced. A mailing piece will be sent to a list of potential customers provided by you and to "any other appropriate list" (you would want some clarification here). On all copies sold of the first printing (roughly 3,000, although only about 400 to 600 are actually bound—the rest remain in "sheets" unless sales warrant binding), the publisher pays a royalty of 40 percent of the list price; for subsequent printings, 20 percent. Some of the contracts stipulate that the publisher will spend 10 percent of your payment in direct mail, space, or cooperative advertising. While the quality of the design, the print, the jacket, the binding, and the paper will not win any awards, they are practically indistinguishable from many trade books. The presses work fast: They will generally bring the book out in six months or less. Books of a certain ilk, such as local histories or technical manuals, will receive more promotional attention if the publisher actually feels that the sales potential is there.

So far, so good, but here's the rub. The author receives virtually no editorial guidance; only gross grammatical and spelling errors are corrected. Reviews, whether in trade or consumer magazines, are as common as needles in haystacks, and space ads do not pull many orders, even though the largest houses frequently run list ads in the *New York Times Book Review* to impress you. Sales prospects are dismal: In most cases only local bookstores will carry the book; distributors or chains will rarely touch them. Aside from copies purchased by your own friends and acquaintances, mail-order sales and library sales are minuscule. In other words, if the book is going to sell, you will have to be the salesperson. A final drawback is the stigma attached to publishing with a vanity press. If you ever hope to publish a second book with a commercial press, you would only damage your chances by referring to your first (unless the sales were extraordinary, say, over 3,000 copies).

Two conclusions to be drawn are that vanity presses stimulate unrealistic expectations, and for the goods and services they offer, they charge a higher price than they should. If they actually bound all the copies of the first printing and then turned the remaining stock over to the author after, say, a year, the arrangement would be almost equitable. But in fact, when and if the contract is terminated (usually after two years), the author must purchase the remaining stock, if he or she wants it, though most of it will still be in unbound sheets. Nevertheless there are a number of satisfied customers, particularly among the 10 percent who recoup their investment. Shop around. Submit a copy of the manuscript to several companies and see who offers the best deal. Be sure not to negotiate for more than a 1,000-copy first printing, and keep in mind that a paperback may cost a lot less than a clothbound edition.

Self-Publishing

There are many famous and successful self-published writers—more than any vanity press would care to admit. In this country, one of the best-sellers of the eighteenth century, Paine's *Common Sense*, has ultimately sold more than half a million copies. Whether you consider reference books, such as Bartlett's *Quotations* or *Robert's Rules of Order*; novelists, such as Twain and Crane; poets, such as Whitman, Pound, and Sandburg; or inspirational writers such as Mary Baker Eddy (whose estate of more than $2 million was derived from numerous editions of *Science and Health*) there is a long tradition of self-published stalwarts willing and determined to take a chance.

Some current phenomena suggest that the tradition is still alive and well: the unusual success of *The Original Publish-It-Yourself Handbook: Literary Tradition and How-To*,* edited by Bill Henderson, which has received national media attention and has sold more than 50,000 copies to date; the publication of several recent how-to's on self-publishing (the best of which are listed in the Bibliography); and some current success stories of self-publishers. Craig I. Zirbel, for example, the author/publisher of *The Texas Connection*, saw his book on the Kennedy assassination spend more than two months on the *New York Times* best-seller list, and *What Color Is Your Parachute?*, a career guide self-published by Richard Nelson Bolle (later picked up by Ten Speed Press) has now sold more than 2.5 million copies.

Obviously we do not present these exceptional cases as the rule. Most self-published books are not successful economically,

---

*The third edition is available in paperback for $11.95 from Pushcart Press, Box 380, Wainscott, NY 11975, or from Pushcart's distributor, W. W. Norton, 500 Fifth Avenue, New York, NY 10110.

and self-publishing is not a step to be taken lightly. A number of time-consuming, detailed, and expensive tasks are involved, and the rewards are more likely to come from a job well done than from high sales figures and large profits. Essentially, the author takes on all the tasks that are usually the publisher's domain: final preparation of the manuscript, copyediting, design, typesetting, proofreading, manufacturing, registering copyright, publicity, advertising, sales, and distribution. Personal computers and publishing software have made some of these tasks easier (although sophisticated hardware and software is not necessarily a good substitute for the skills of an experienced copyeditor or book designer), and of course freelancers can be hired to do some of the jobs involved in publication. For starters, though, you will want to look over Henderson's book, which contains an excellent reference section with names and addresses and various other how-to tips.

There are three basic procedures for publishing your own book. The easiest is to work with one of the printers and manufacturers that are willing not only to print in short runs, but also to "midwife" your book from manuscript to bound books. *LMP*, under a section called "Complete Book Manufacturing," lists more than 150 companies, most of which have been recommended by the production departments of book publishers. The services these companies offer vary—some may not be willing to work with single titles in small print runs—but many of them are full-service operations which will print and manufacture books from manuscripts. This includes some of the major vanity presses, which offer these manufacturing services as a sideline, at competitive prices.

A more complicated and expensive method is to freelance separately most of the tasks involved, from copyediting to advertising. Refer to *LMP*, which contain listings of virtually every kind of service the self-publisher might require. One advantage of this method is that you can procure the highest quality professional work, and your final product will be indistinguishable from that of a commercial press.

Finally, you can work with a local printer who will provide some advice and help, but on most phases of the process you will be on your own, and the amount of time, care, and effort you expend will determine how handsome the final book is. This can be the most inexpensive method if you do most of the work yourself, shop around carefully for supplies, such as paper, and services, such as binding (as all commercial publishers do), and publish a small first-print run. You can do your own typesetting and page layout on a home computer. For most straightforward books with relatively simple designs, the latest versions of the standard word processing programs—Word, Wordperfect, Ami Pro, Wordstar, and some others—are sufficient to do this. For fancier books, desktop publishing packages like QuarkXPress, Aldus Pagemaker, or Ventura Publishing can be used. These packages cost more than $500, require a home computer of some power and sophistication, and are fairly complex to use, but they can be mastered by a diligent amateur. The results, of course, are dependent on your skills, and a professional book designer will almost always do better than a first-time amateur, even one who is adept at the computer keyboard. Submitting a book on a floppy disk to a printer can save money, and most printers are equipped to handle this. Though the plant costs are the same whether you print 100 or 1,000 copies, you can save a considerable amount of money on your first printing by binding only a portion of the print run, say 500 out of a 1,000-copy print run. If sales warrant, you can always bind the remaining sheets and then reprint.

The hardest and most frustrating part of the process may be the marketing and distribution of your book. Ingram, one of the large book wholesalers, receives as many as 100 self-published books per day, but stocks very few of them. Whatever the enthusiasm of the author for his or her book, wholesalers and booksellers have to look more realistically at the salability of a given title in a crowded market. If you are hoping that your book will be noticed and picked up by a commercial publisher, the chances are just as slim. Occasionally this happens: Joseph Girzone's *Joshua* was picked up and published very successfully by Macmillan, but only after the author had found a literary agent to submit the title to a number of publishers. And success at self-publishing may not be what it appears to be: In 1992, when Craig Zirbel's *The Texas Connection* had 77,000 copies in print and had been on the best-seller list for more than two months, he found himself more in debt than ever—whatever profits he was making were going right back to the printer to pay for more copies. Unfortunately, printers and binders almost always demand payment on delivery, whereas bookstores and wholesalers can take up to 90 days and more to pay their bills.

Yet success stories emerge every year: 1994 will see the appearance of two *second* novels by African American authors, Lynn Harris and Anita Richmond Bunkley, published by Doubleday and Dutton respectively. Both writers self-published their *first* novels, selling, respectively, 10,000 and 7,000 copies (Harris's publisher, Doubleday Anchor, is reprinting his first novel, *Invisible Life*, in paperback, with a first printing of 15,000 copies). Their self-publishing tales are odysseys too intricate to relate here, but a fragment will show that true grit is usually required for a happy outcome: Harris reports that when his book was printed in late 1991, he had 5,000 copies in rented office space. "At the first book party we sold 42 copies, and I felt sick."

The number of choices to be made is large: where to send review copies, how to get a press release into the right hands, where and how to advertise, which mailing lists to rent. Selling your own book requires stamina and plenty of brass, especially if you are going to call on bookstores—and you should. But others have done it, and done it well and successfully. With a bit of luck, and the right book, you might be shocked one day to receive a letter from a commercial publisher that has discovered your book and decided to make an offer. Or maybe, because of reviews and ads, or by word of mouth, the book will somehow catch on, sell out several printings, and you will find yourself in business as a small-press publisher. But chances are, you will try publishing your own book mostly because you want to see it in print. No matter how many books you sell, nothing can surpass the feeling of triumph and pride that comes from holding that first copy in your hands.

A Sample Query Letter

March 1, 1992

Mr. Richard A. Balkin
The Balkin Agency, Inc.

Dear Mr. Balkin:

In France, a well-kept secret is that the most-congenial country inns are converted water mills. Along with fine food and lodging, they offer tranquility, tree-lined streams, duck-laden ponds, and numerous activities. The atmosphere is friendly and casual, and flavored with nostalgia. And the mills bewitch. There's magic in their sylvan setting, the murmuring water, the elegant rusticity, in the arcane machinery and archaic wheels.

I am writing *INNside French Mills*, the first guide devoted to these inns. It will introduce travelers to the mystique of mills, and lead them to charming inns in every part of France. With the increasing numbers of mill-inns, and increasing travel in provincial France (17 million in 1992), it's a book whose time has come.

Years ago, while my wife and I were on a wine-buying trip to Burgundy, a grower took us to the Hostellerie du Vieux Moulin, in the hillside hamlet of Bouilland. The inn and the village enchanted us. On later visits we came across more than 100 other mills, each with something special. We recently returned for four months to photograph them, interview their owners and chefs, and complete the research for the book.

For centuries, mills were the heart of rural France, performing an astounding variety of tasks. In 1810 there were 18,000 mills — one for every 300 persons. Today only a few continue working, but more than 120 operate as full inns, an additional 100 as restaurants.

The owners are usually a married couple (chef and host or hostess). Some, like the Moulin Fleuri, offer comfortable rooms at low cost; others, like the Moulin du Roc, provide luxury at moderate cost. All serve generous regional cuisine. Twelve even have one or more Michelin stars; the consummate Espérance and the Moulin de Mougins each have three.

INNside French Mills will feature 30 of the author's favorites —their facilities, personalities, activities, food and wine (including some recipes), plus things to see and do nearby —and briefly cover an additional 70. (A longer book could feature 50 favorites.)

I would like you to share my enthusiasm. May I send you a proposal?

Sincerely,

A Sample Book Proposal

HOW TO WRITE FOREIGN CORRESPONDENCE

A U.S. businessperson, negotiating with a prospective Japanese client, once remarked that "this is a whole new ballgame." Echoing a typical Asian response, the Japanese client was deeply offended that the American viewed the negotiations as a mere "game." So he killed the pending business deal and cast about for a more serious foreign partner. Such gaffes in international communications occur on a daily basis. However unintentional they may be, the damage that results is hard to repair and is often translated into a financial loss to U.S. business.

The world has become so interactive that communication with foreign firms is now commonplace in many organizations. How to Write Foreign Correspondence will be a guide to developing the elusive skill of writing effective messages to foreign recipients, to people who often use English only as a second or third language.

According to a study by the Parker Pen Company in the 1980s, the use of idiomatic English is devastating in foreign correspondence. In addition, Americans are so accustomed to using slang, jargon, buzzwords, and cliches that they are completely unaware of the confusion that occurs in foreign translations. Even brief, innocent expressions are a mystery to foreigners. A regional expression such as "you all come again" is likely to be interpreted as "next time we want more people to come."

To write successful foreign correspondence, we must unlearn many of the rules presented in letter books about domestic correspondence. In domestic letters, for example, we are told to be casual and conversational. This tone has proved to be very effective in local, state, and national contacts. But exactly the opposite is needed in international correspondence. We must be more formal (although still courteous and friendly) and more literal.

Punctuation usage is another area in which we need a reverse approach to international letter writing. In contemporary U.S. composition, the trend is to use less punctuation. This style, however, is a nightmare for foreign translators. Heavy punctuation is needed to guide foreign readers through each sentence to avoid misreading.

U.S. writers also pay too little attention to foreign customs. They forget about religious holidays and cultural differences, and they forget that foreigners have different rules concerning invitations, flattery, attitudes toward women, and other styles and customs. In spite of the heavy commercial activity between the U.S. and foreign countries, particularly Japan and other Asian countries, the U.S. business people often fail to do their homework and instead apply the same approach to foreign contacts that they apply to U.S. contacts.

SPECIAL FEATURES

How to Write Foreign Correspondence will include four prominent features to enhance the text discussion.

1. Numerous "good-bad" examples of words, sentences, and complete model letters for comparison

2. Extensive lists of troublesome words and expressions to avoid in international correspondence

3. Numerous descriptive examples of customs in foreign countries that must be respected

4. An appendix with important reference material such as sources of trade, cultural, postal, and other essential information; models of basic letter formats; and a table of correct forms of inside address, salutation, and complimentary close for men and women in various organizations

In addition to these features, anecdotal experiences of U.S. business people will be woven throughout the text to provide insights into the do's and don'ts of foreign correspondence.

THE AUDIENCE

Readers will include U.S. personnel in all types of organizations who occasionally or regularly write and set up (by computer or typewriter) letters that are sent to foreign recipients. The book will be useful to everyone involved in this process, from the chief executive officer, departmental manager, or sales representative who writes the letter to the secretary or word processing operator who formats, types, and transmits it.

COMPETITION

Books in Print, 1991-92, does not list any title on foreign correspondence. Numerous letter books are available, however, and I have written three such books myself (see "Credentials," below). But the letter books currently available focus primarily or exclusively on domestic letter writing. How to Write Foreign

<u>Correspondence</u> will focus exclusively on international correspondence.

The State Department and other governmental bodies have style manuals (such as Foreign Service style manuals) for their own use, and some limited information is available through private industry (such as "The Tower of Business Babel," an eighteen-page report by the Parker Pen Company, 1985). <u>How to Write Foreign Correspondence</u> will have an entirely different and more comprehensive coverage and treatment than such governmental and private-industry publications.

SPECIFICATIONS

The book will have 275-300 printed pages, including traditional front matter, appendix, and index, and will be suitable for hardcover publication in a standard size. The text will consist of discussion combined with numerous examples, lists, and model letters (no halftones). No special permissions requirements are expected.

A deadline of one year from the date of contract signing is recommended.

CREDENTIALS

I have written more than thirty business, professional, and reference books including three letter books:

The Prentice Hall Complete Book of Model Letters, Memos, and Forms for the Secretary (Prentice Hall, forthcoming, 1992)

The New American Handbook of Letter Writing (New American Library, 1988)

The Prentice Hall Complete Secretarial Letter Book (Prentice Hall, 1978)

and including other communication-oriented books that contain chapters on correspondence:

The Prentice Hall Style Manual (Prentice Hall, 1992)

The Office Sourcebook (Prentice Hall, 1989)

Complete Secretary's Handbook (revisor: Prentice Hall, 1988)

A Sample Reader's Report

One publisher to whom I submitted my original proposal and sample chapters for this book inadvertently enclosed his reader's report when he rejected the book and returned the materials to me. The contradiction evident here—the enthusiasm and then the suggestion to decline—is not uncommon.

To RL from SH
HANDBOOK TO PUBLISHING (Preface, two chapters, Contents)
by Richard Balkin
October 12, 1975

The author proposes a book which, if successful (very good likelihood as he has good background experience as both editor and agent), will cover every area for a prospective author from manuscript to printed book and after, in fact, with inclusion of material on subsidiary rights, expectation of reviews and sales.

Like:

Do I need/can I get an agent? How? What do they do?

How a publisher evaluates and makes a decision on one's proposal

How to read, understand and negotiate a contract (what an author can expect financially; what riders can be added to a contract)

How to prepare your manuscript for the publisher (not at all how to write, exclusively how to prepare: typing, style books suggested; front and back matter; permissions and copyright rules; who pays the fees for permissions; tables and illustrations; additional tips)

What happens to your manuscript at the publishers (a discussion of the various departments and functions in the house—why it takes the time it takes to publish a book)

What happens to your manuscript upon publication (sales, promotion, publicity, how and why a book gets remaindered)

Alternatives—university presses, vanity presses and self-publishing

Bibliography (books on style, various aspects of publishing, LMP)

I can see how this kind of book would be very helpful but I do personally see it as an agent's obligation to inform an author of his rights; an editor's to give his author a basic understanding of all the information contained above. I may be optimistic. To be truthful, if I were an author I think I would prefer to get it from my editor rather than from a book.

On the other hand, I do think that this book, in paperback form, would sell very well—and perhaps not only to prospective authors but to people involved in the publishing business itself.

I am not sure what information is contained in a new book, just out, an original paperback, entitled something like "How to Publish Your Own Book." The material in this proposal may overlap, but, as I say, I do not know.

My basic inclination is to decline.

A Sample Contract

Agreement made this———thirteenth———day of———January———1993 by and
between———————RONALD TAXXXI————————————————————————
of 1XXX TXXXX Avenue, BXXXXXXY, CA 94XXX—————————————————
xxx
sk———————————————————————————————the author(s)
or proprietor(s) (hereinafter in either case called the "Author") and XXXXXXXXX and
Company (Inc.), 3XX XXXX XXXX Rxxxx, XXXXXXXXX XXXX (hereinafter called the "Publisher"), with respect to the publication of a fxxxx/nonfiction work of between one hundred twenty-
five thousand (125,000) and one hundred———XXXXXXXXXXXXXXX seventy-
five thousand (175,000) words, and to contain between twenty (20) and
forty (40) black and white photographs, to be described as follows:

The Work

Tentative Title: Almanac of Int'l Body Building

Subject Matter: Historical account of body-building
competitions from 1946 to present

together with all photographs, illustrations, maps, charts, titles, indexes, and other non-
textual materials provided by the Author (hereinafter called the "Work"), which the Author
agrees will be in conformity with any manuscript, proposal, or other material for the said
Work submitted to the Publisher.

Now therefore, in consideration of the mutual promises hereinafter set forth, the Author
and the Publisher agree as follows:

Grant of Rights

Grant

1. The Author hereby grants and assigns to the Publisher, with respect to the Work (and
any revisions thereof), during the full term of the copyright the sole and exclusive right to
reproduce, distribute, license, and sell the Work in whole or in part in xxlxxxguxxgxx as set

forth in Section 8 hereof throughout the work in the English language in the United States of America and its dependencies, the Republic of the Philippines and Canada; and the non-exclusive right to sell or to license others to sell in any edition or editions in the English language for export to any country other than the United States of America and its dependencies and the Republic of the Philippines, and other than the countries listed in Schedule A, attached hereto and made part of this Agreement.

Author's Warranty and Indemnification

Warranty

2. The Author represents, warrants, and covenants as follows: (a) The Author is the sole author and proprietor of the Work; is the owner of all rights in the Work granted hereunder, free of liens and encumbrances, and has full authority to make this Agreement; (b) the Work is original, has not been previously published, and is not in the public domain except for any publication referred to in Section 7(c) hereof; (c) no part of the Work, including the title, contains any matter which is defamatory, unlawful, or which in any way infringes, invades, or violates any right, including privacy and copyright, of any person or entity whatsoever; (d) the Work contains no formulas, instructions, or advice which may cause harm or injury; (e) the publication of the Work shall not breach any oral or written agreement which the Author has made with any individual or entity; and (f) the representations and warranties of the Author hereunder shall remain in full force and effect on the date of each actual publication of the Work and at all intervening times.

The Publisher shall have no obligation to make an independent investigation to determine whether the foregoing warranties and representations are true, and any such investigation by or for the Publisher shall not constitute a defense to the Author in any action based upon a breach or alleged breach of any of the foregoing representations and warranties of the Author. However, if in the Publisher's reasonable opinion there appears to be a substantial risk of liability to third persons or entities or of governmental action against the Work, the Publisher with the Author's agreement may undertake an investigation, verification, and analysis of the Work and implement such revisions of the Work with the approval of the

Author which the Publisher believes may eliminate or lessen such risk. Notwithstanding anything contained herein to the contrary, in no event shall the Publisher be obligated to publish the Work if in its judgment the Work contains libelous material or its publication would violate the rights of privacy, the copyright, or any other rights of any person or entity.

Indemnity

The Author shall indemnify and hold the Publisher harmless from any losses, expenses, or damages arising out of or for the purpose of resolving or avoiding any suit, claim, or demand made or brought against the Publisher which, if sustained, would constitute a breach of any of the above representations and warranties; provided, however, that this indemnity shall only apply to losses, expenses, or damages which exceed three thousand dollars ($3,000) in the aggregate and which are not otherwise payable under any media perils insurance which the Publisher may have obtained for such purpose. However, the Author's liability under this indemnity to the Publisher shall be reduced by one-half (½) of the Publisher's said uninsured losses, expenses, or damages in excess of three thousand dollars ($3,000) in cases (a) in which, despite a settlement by the Publisher, the Author went forward independently and obtained a final judgment in his or her favor with respect to the claims which the Publisher had settled or (b) which were finally adjudicated in favor of the Publisher. In the event of a claim which is covered by the Publisher's media perils insurance policy, the Author shall not be responsible for the payment of more than twenty-two thousand dollars ($22,000.00) with respect to such a claim.

The Publisher shall have the right in its own discretion to extend the benefit of the Author's warranties and indemnities to any person, firm, or corporation, and the Author shall be liable thereon as if originally made to such person, firm, or corporation. Each of the foregoing warranties and representations shall survive the termination of this Agreement.

The Publisher and the Author agree to give each other prompt written notice before or after publication, giving the fullest information obtainable at the time, of any claim, threat, or demand of which either party obtains knowledge regarding the Work. The Publisher shall have the right to select counsel to defend itself and the Author. Subject to the limitations set forth above, the uninsured costs, allowances, and reasonable counsel fees arising out of the prosecution of said defense shall be the obligation of the Author under the terms of this Section. The Author agrees to cooperate fully in the defense of any claim and may select an associate counsel at the Author's expense.

Upon receipt of notice of any suit, claim, or demand which would obligate the Author under the above indemnity, the Publisher reserves the right to pay from monies due the Author an amount commensurate with the size of the claim into an interest-bearing escrow account pending the final resolution of such suit, claim, or demand.

Settlements

The following procedures shall apply to settlements:

(a) The Publisher may, in its sole discretion, settle any suit, claim, or demand against it or waive any appeal of any judgment of a trial court against it.

(b) If any suit, claim, or demand is also made against the Author and the Author disapproves of the settlement proposed by the Publisher, the Author, at the Author's own risk and expense, may proceed independently and assume responsibility for his or her defense including the bringing of an appeal in the event of an unfavorable judgment. Prior to proceeding, however, the Author must consult with any insurer with respect to possible loss of coverage (see reference in Notice of Insurance, if any) and must pay into an interest-bearing escrow account the full amount of the Publisher's uninsured losses, expenses, or damages exceeding three thousand dollars ($3,000). If the Author obtains a favorable final judgment in the matter, the Publisher shall return such payment to the Author, less an amount up to one-half (½) of such payment which is equal to any losses, expenses, or damages, arising out of the suit, claim, or demand, which the Publisher has incurred.

(c) If the Author disapproves of a settlement proposed by the Publisher and the Author desires to go forward independently, but the plaintiff(s) will not agree to settle with the Publisher unless the Author joins in such settlement, then the Publisher agrees to retain responsibility for the defense or the appeal and go forward, but only if the Author provides the Publisher in a timely manner with such security as the Publisher deems necessary to protect its interests (which may include a bond or some other equivalent assurance of payment).

Insurance

The Publisher shall seek to obtain, at its own expense, media perils insurance coverage for the benefit of the Author. A Notice of Insurance shall be attached to this Agreement where such coverage is obtained for the Author.

Manuscript and Delivery

3. (a) The Author shall deliver two (2) copies of the final manuscript of the Work, between twenty (20) and forty (40) black and white photographs** in length, content, and form satisfactory to the Publisher, in proper shape for the press, together with all permissions and releases required under Section 3(c), on or before the 1st day of October , 19 93, time being of the essence of this Agreement. The Author's failure to comply with any of the above delivery terms shall be just cause for the Publisher to terminate its obligations under this Agreement and to recover from the Author all amounts which it has advanced or paid to the Author. Until repayment in full by the Author to the Publisher of such amounts, all rights granted to the Publisher by the Author with respect to the Work in this Agreement shall remain in full force and effect, and except with the Publisher's prior written consent, the Author shall have no right to submit the Work or to grant rights with respect to the Work to any other person, firm, or entity.

** see attached rider #28, page 10

2

Other Material

(b) The Author shall supply promptly, at the Author's own expense, such photographs, illustrations, maps, charts, titles, indexes, and other materials in form and quality satisfactory to the Publisher as are in conformity with the original proposal for the Work. If the Author shall fail to supply such materials promptly or in proper form and quality, the Publisher shall have the right to supply the same at the Author's expense.

Permissions and Releases

(c) The Author, at the Author's own expense, shall have obtained from any person or entity from whom permission or licenses may be required, written permissions, releases, or licenses in form and content satisfactory to the Publisher and shall deliver such permissions, releases, or licenses to the Publisher on the date specified in Section 3(a) above. Any such permission, release, or license must grant at least the same rights to the Author as the Author has granted to the Publisher under this Agreement unless otherwise agreed.

Loss

(d) The Author shall retain one copy of the Work submitted to the Publisher. The Publisher shall take reasonable measures to preserve the original manuscript including any artwork, illustrations, and photographs submitted by the Author.

If the Publisher loses or damages beyond reasonable editorial wear and tear the original copy of the manuscript or any artwork, illustrations, or photographs, the costs of any copying or retyping from the copy of the manuscript retained by the Author or the mechanical or conventional reproduction of artwork, illustrations, or photographs deemed necessary by the Publisher shall be paid by the Publisher.

If the Author believes that the artwork, illustrations, or photographs to be submitted to the Publisher have value that exceeds the cost of mechanical or conventional reproduction or are irreplaceable, then the Author shall so notify the Publisher prior to submitting such artwork, illustrations, or photographs. In such cases, the Publisher shall supply the Author its standard Artwork Valuation Form. Upon approval by the Publisher of the completed form, the Author may submit the artwork, illustrations, and photographs to the Publisher, and the form shall be attached to this Agreement.

Style

(e) The Author authorizes the Publisher to make the manuscript of the said Work conform to its standard style in punctuation, spelling, capitalization, and usage.

Author's Inability to Deliver

(f) If the Author dies prior to delivery of the final manuscript of the Work, or if the Author shall be incapable of completing and delivering the final manuscript of the Work as specified in Section 3(a) of this Agreement, the Publisher with the consent of the Author or the Author's representatives or estate with respect to matters of content shall have the right but not the obligation to publish, edit, revise, or complete the Work upon giving proper credit to the Author for such portion of the Work created by the Author and the cost incurred by the Publisher for services performed by a third party in that regard shall be charged against any sums accruing to the Author or to the Author's estate under this Agreement. If consent is withheld by the Author or the Author's representatives or estate, or if the Publisher chooses not to exercise its right to publish, edit, revise, or complete the Work, the Publisher may terminate its obligations under this Agreement and recover from the Author or the Author's estate all amounts that it has advanced or paid to the Author.

Manuscript Correction and Revision

Proof

4. (a) The Author agrees to correct and promptly return the copyedited manuscript and all proof sheets of the Work. If the Author fails to do so within thirty (30) days of their submission to the Author, the Publisher shall have the right to publish the Work in the condition in which it was submitted by the Author, subject to the terms of Section 3(e). With respect to the first proofs, the Author agrees to pay the cost of alterations required by the Author, other than those due to the Publisher's or printer's errors, in excess of ten percent (10%) of the cost of composition. With respect to all subsequent proofs, the Author agrees to pay for all costs of alterations required by the Author, other than those due to the Publisher's or printer's errors. In either case, the Publisher, upon the written request of the Author, said request to be made within thirty (30) days of the receipt by the Author of the statement of the above-mentioned charges, shall provide the corrected proofs for the inspection of the Author.

Corrections

(b) In the event the Author believes corrections of the Work are necessary after publication, they may be made at the Author's expense in the next printing. If the corrections are so extensive that the Publisher believes a completely revised edition is necessary, the corrections shall be made at the Publisher's expense, but royalties to the Author shall be computed from the beginning of the schedules set forth in Section 8.

Use of Author's Name

Author's Name

5. The Author grants the Publisher and its licensees the irrevocable right to use the Author's name and likeness in the sale, promotion, and advertising of the Work as published or distributed under the terms of this Agreement.

Publication

Publication

6. The Publisher agrees to publish the Work at its own expense in such style and manner, and at such price as the Publisher shall deem suitable, within eighteen (18) months from the acceptance of the Work in accordance with the terms of Section 3.*In case of delays from causes beyond the control of the Publisher, or in case the Author fails to return proofs within thirty (30) days after they have been delivered to the Author, the period shall be extended to cover such delays. Should the Publisher fail to publish the Work before the expiration of said period, except as provided herein, its failure to do so may be deemed cause for the Author, if the Author so desires, to terminate this Agreement pursuant to the terms of Section 13.

Copyright and Copyright Infringement

Registration

7. (a) It is understood and agreed that the copyright in the Work shall be registered by the Publisher at its own expense in the United States of America and such other countries as the Publisher may elect as follows:

Copyright © - - - - by Ronald Takaki

The copyright in any artwork, illustrations, or other materials supplied by the Publisher shall be owned by the Publisher.

(b) The Author shall provide the Publisher, at its request, with such other documents as the Publisher may require in order to enable the Publisher to obtain or enforce copyright in the Work.

Other Publication

(c)   The Author agrees to notify the Publisher promptly of any prior publication or of any agreement made for future publication of the Work, in whole or in part, in any language and to provide the Publisher, at its request, with whatever documents shall be necessary in order to enable the Publisher to affix proper copyright notices and legally to discharge its obligations relating to publication hereunder.

(d)   The Author shall inform the Publisher in writing of the date of substantial creation of the Work if such date was prior to January 1, 1978.

Infringement

(e)   In the event that any copyright in the Work is infringed, and if no mutually satisfactory arrangement can be arrived at for joint action in regard thereto, either party shall have the right to bring an action to enjoin such infringement and for damages. If the parties arrange to proceed jointly, the expenses and recoveries, if any, shall be shared equally; if they do not agree to proceed jointly, the party going forward with such action shall bear all the expenses thereof and shall retain any recovery therein, and if such party shall not be the registered owner of the copyright, the other party hereby consents that such action be brought in its name. In no event shall either the Publisher or the Author be liable to the other for failure to take action.

Royalties and Advances

Advance

8.   The Publisher agrees to pay as an advance against and on account of all monies accruing to the Author under the terms of this section of this Agreement the sum of   twenty thousand dollars ($20,000.00)

to be divided and paid as follows:

--ten thousand dollars ($10,000.00) on receipt by the Publisher of one copy of this Agreement signed by the Author; and

—ten thousand dollars ($10,000.00) on delivery of the final, acceptable manuscript of the said Work including all illustrations and releases deemed necessary by the Publisher.

A. Book Sales

On sales of the Work in book form, less returns, but with no deductions for cash discounts or bad debts, the Publisher agrees to pay to the Author:

Hardcover   On hardcover copies sold, a royalty of ten percent (10%) of the catalog price on all copies sold in the United States of America up to and including five thousand (5,000) copies; twelve and one-half percent (12½%) of the catalog price on all copies so sold over and above five thousand (5,000) copies up to and including ten thousand (10,000) copies; and fifteen percent (15%) of the catalog price on all copies so sold over and above ten thousand (10,000) copies——————

*it being further understood that first publication shall be a hardcover edition of the Work. It is further understood that, except under circumstances unforeseen as of the date of this Agreement, the Publisher intends to publish, or to license the right to publish, a trade paperback edition of the Work to be published within two (2) years of the date of publication of the Publisher's hardcover edition.

Paperback   On paperback copies sold, a royalty of seven and one-half percent (7½%) of the catalog price on all copies sold in the United States of America ——————

hereinafter called the "Stipulated Royalty" except that:

Regular Quantity Sales   (1) On copies, either bound or unbound, sold to the regular bookselling market in quantity at a discount of fifty-one percent (51%) or more, a royalty based on the amount of the Publisher's charges of ten percent (10%) on hardcover and seven and one-half percent (7½%) on paperback;

Mail Order and Advertising

(2) On copies sold directly to the consumer by the Publisher as a result of solicitation by mail, radio, television, or coupon advertising, a royalty based on the amount of the Publisher's charges of five percent (5%);

Premiums

(3) On copies, either bound or unbound, sold as premiums, or otherwise in quantity to organizations outside regular bookselling channels, a royalty based on the amount of the Publisher's charges of seven and one-half percent (7½%) on hardcover and five percent (5%) on paperback;

Canada

(4) On hardcover copies sold in Canada by ~~Entwhistle~~ & Company (Canada) Limited, a royalty of six percent (6%) of the U.S. hardcover catalog price and on paperback copies so sold a royalty of three percent (3%) of the U.S. paperback catalog price;

Export

(5) On copies, either bound or unbound, sold outside the United States, other than sales made by ~~Entwhistle~~ & Company (Canada) Limited, a royalty based on the amount of the Publisher's charges of ten percent (10%) on hardcover and five percent (5%) on paperback;

Small Reprintings

(6) On hardcover copies sold from a reprinting of twenty-five hundred (2500) copies or less, made after one (1) year from the date of first publication, and provided the regular sales in the six (6) months' royalty period immediately preceding such reprinting do not exceed seven hundred fifty (750) copies, and on paperback copies sold from a reprinting of twenty-five hundred (2500) copies or less, made after one (1) year from the date of first publication, and provided the regular sales in the six (6) months' royalty period immediately preceding such reprinting do not exceed one thousand (1000) copies, one-half (½) of the Stipulated Royalty;

Overstock

(7) On copies of overstock which the Publisher deems it expedient to sell or otherwise dispose of a royalty based on the amount of Publisher's charges of ten percent (10%) on hardcover and five percent (5%) on paperback when such copies are sold at a discount of more than fifty percent (50%) but less than sixty percent (60%), and five percent (5%) on both hardcover and paperback when such copies are sold at a discount of sixty percent (60%) or more. If said copies are sold or disposed of at or below cost, no royalty shall be paid. In no event shall the amount paid the Author exceed the difference between the amount received by the Publisher from sales and the Publisher's bound cost;

Special Media

(8) ~~On copies of the Work sold or rented by the Publisher in those media set forth in Section 9(B)(9), a royalty to be negotiated between the parties;~~

Packages and Sets

(9) If the Work is sold as part of a package or a set for a single price, the amount received shall be determined by prorating the revenues received from the sale of the package in proportion to the suggested catalog prices established for the separate items contained in the package, whether or not such works are sold separately;

Review Copies

(10) No royalties shall be payable on copies furnished for review, promotion, sample, and like purposes, or on copies supplied by the Publisher in payment for advertising.

All references to catalog price shall mean the Publisher's catalog invoice price for the Work which does not include any freight pass-through increment. Said increment shall not exceed five percent (5%) of said catalog price. All references to Publisher's charges shall mean the Publisher's catalog invoice price for the Work less any discount.

B. Subsidiary Rights

On sales or licenses of related book rights in the Work the Publisher agrees to pay to the Author:

Book Clubs

(1) On sales or licenses of rights to book clubs, including Reader's Digest, fifty percent (50%) of all royalties accruing to the Publisher;

Reprint Editions

(2) On sales or licenses to other U.S. publishers of the right to publish a paperback or hardcover edition or editions of the Work, fifty percent (50%) of all royalties accruing to the Publisher. No such edition may be published earlier than one (1) year from the date of the Publisher's first edition of the Work, except with the consent of the Author;

No sale of mass market or trade paperback rights under the terms of this clause shall be made without consultation with the Author.

Foreign Editions

(3) On sales or licenses to ~~British,~~ Canadian (other than sales made by ~~Kisk; Baw~~ & Company (Canada) Limited), Philippine ~~or Australian~~ publishers of the right to publish editions of the Work in the English language ~~or of translations of the Work,~~ seventy-five percent (75%) of all royalties received by the Publisher after the deduction of any taxes on royalties levied in the country in which the sale was completed or any bank fees or subsidiary agent's fees;

First Serial

(4) ~~On sales of the right, before the publication of the Publisher's first edition of the Work, to publish, or to authorize others to publish, the Work in whole or in part in magazines or newspapers, ninety percent (90%) of all sums accruing to the Publisher,~~

Second Serial

(5) On sales of the right, after the publication of the Publisher's edition of the Work, to publish, or to authorize others to publish, the Work in whole or in part in magazines or newspapers, fifty percent (50%) of all sums accruing to the Publisher;

Other Works

(6) On sales of the right, after the publication of the Publisher's edition of the Work, to publish the Work in whole or in part in other works, fifty percent (50%) of all sums accruing to the Publisher;

Condensations

(7) On sales of the right, after the publication of the Publisher's edition of the Work, to publish, or to authorize others to publish, either as part of a book (as distinguished from a periodical) or as a separate book publication, an abridgment or condensation of the Work, not exceeding two-thirds (⅔) of the original Work in length, such abridgment or condensation to be approved in writing by the Author, fifty percent (50%) of all sums accruing to the Publisher;

Licensed Special Media

(8) On sales or licenses of the right to use material from the Work in whole or in part for ~~phonographic, tape, wire, magnetic, light wave amplification, photographic, microfilm, microfiche, electronic, audiovideo, or audiovisual recording, slides, filmstrips, transparencies, programming for any method of information storage, reproduction or retrieval, and for any other forms or means of copying or recording (now known or hereafter devised), including~~ reproduction of the Work for the physically handicapped, fifty percent (50%) of all sums accruing to the Publisher.

Motion Picture

(9) ~~On sales or licenses of the right to use, or to authorize others to use, the~~ Work in whole or in part in any language to produce a motion picture for theatrical or educational distribution and exhibition both to live audiences or to produce an audiovisual cassette or diskette for home viewing, eighty percent

(80%) of all sums up to twenty thousand dollars ($20,000) and eighty-five percent (85%) of all sums thereafter accruing to the Publisher;

Radio

(10) On sales or licenses of the right to use, or to authorize others to use, the Work in whole or in part for AM or FM radio or other means of transmitting sounds to receivers, now known or hereafter devised, eighty percent (80%) of all sums up to twenty thousand dollars ($20,000) and eighty-five percent (85%) of all sums thereafter accruing to the Publisher;

Television

(11) On sales or licenses of the right to televise, or to authorize others to televise, the Work in whole or in part by means of over-the-air, closed circuit, cable, or any other method of transmitting sounds and images to receivers, now known or hereafter devised, eighty percent (80%) of all sums up to twenty thousand dollars ($20,000) and eighty-five percent (85%) of all sums thereafter accruing to the Publisher;

Dramatization

(12) On sales or licenses of the right to use, or to authorize others to use, the Work in whole or in part in any language for a dramatic work for performance to live audiences, eighty percent (80%) of all sums up to twenty thousand dollars ($20,000) and eighty-five percent (85%) of all sums thereafter accruing to the Publisher;

Merchandise

(13) On sales made by the Publisher or on sales or licenses of the right to exploit, or to authorize others to exploit, commercial or merchandising rights in and to the Work, a royalty based on the amount of Publisher's charges of ten percent (10%) on all copies so sold if said right is exercised by the Publisher and fifty percent (50%) of all sums accruing to the Publisher if said right is licensed by the Publisher.

The Publisher shall have the sole right to negotiate and sign contracts in regard to all Subsidiary Rights granted herein. The Publisher shall also have the right to publish or permit others to publish, free of charge, such brief selections as it thinks proper to benefit the sale of the Work.

Statements and Payments

Statements and Payments

9. The Publisher agrees to render semiannual statements of account and to make payments on or before April first and October first of each year covering sales (less returns, actual or estimated) to the preceding January first and July first respectively. The Publisher may withhold from payment to the Author a reasonable reserve for return copies. When as of any first day of January or July a sum less than twenty-five dollars ($25.00) shall have accrued to the Author, the Publisher shall be under no obligation to make payment or render a statement, unless it be a final payment or statement.

All royalties or other sums accruing to the Author in accordance with the provisions of this Agreement shall be reported as of the accounting periods in which the Publisher receives them.

Overpayment and Other Sums Due Publisher

Overpayment

10. Whenever the Author has received an overpayment of monies or otherwise becomes obligated for sums due the Publisher under the terms of this Agreement or any other agreement with the Publisher, the Publisher shall deduct the amount of the overpayment or other sums due the Publisher from any sums that accrue to the Author from this or any other agreement with the Publisher, it being understood an unearned advance shall not be considered either an overpayment or a sum due the Publisher, unless the Author is in default under this Agreement.

Author's Copies

Author's Copies

11. The Publisher agrees to give the Author on publication ten (10) copies of the Work **
and to sell to the Author further copies for the Author's personal use at a discount of forty
percent (40%) from the Publisher's catalog price. If the Author wishes to purchase copies on
a nonreturnable cash basis in quantities of one hundred (100) or more, said copies shall be
sold at a discount of forty-eight percent (48%) of said catalog price.

** and four free copies to the author's representative

Reserved Rights

Reserved Rights

12. All rights in the said Work now existing, or which may hereafter come into existence,
except those hereby specifically granted to the Publisher, are reserved to and by the Author.

Termination and Reversion of Rights

Discontinuance of Sales

13. (a) If at any time after the expiration of two (2) years from the date of first publication, the Publisher shall determine that there are not sufficient sales for the Work to enable
the Publisher profitably to continue its publication and sale, the Publisher may, at its election,
after written notice to the Author's last known address, dispose of the copies remaining on
hand as it deems best, subject to the provisions with regard to royalties set forth in Section 8
of this Agreement.

Out of Print

(b) If the Work is out of print or unavailable and if within six (6) months of written
demand upon the Publisher by the Author, the Publisher does not bring out a new printing
or make the Work available, then upon repayment of any overpayment of royalties or other
sums due the Publisher and upon expiration of such six (6) month period, this Agreement
shall be terminable by the Author pursuant to the provisions of Section 13(d) hereof. The
Work shall be considered in print or available if it is available from the Publisher or its
licensees as provided herein. In case of delays from causes beyond the control of the Publisher, the period shall be extended to cover such delays.

Bankruptcy

(c) In the event of a judgment of bankruptcy of the Publisher, the Author shall have the right to buy back the rights granted herein at fair market value and thereafter this Agreement shall terminate, except for the Publisher's right to complete production for work in process and dispose of inventory.

Rights Reversion

(d) In the event of a termination of this Agreement by the Author based on the Publisher's failure to publish the manuscript as provided in Section 6 of this Agreement or because the Work is out of print as set forth above, all rights herein granted to the Publisher shall revert to the Author and neither party shall have any further obligation to the other, subject to the exceptions that (i) the Publisher or its successors in interest shall have the right to sell or otherwise dispose of any remaining copies of the Work, plates, film or binders' dies, at the best price it can obtain therefor if, within thirty (30) days after such termination, the Author has not elected to buy at cost any or all of such items from the Publisher or its successors in interest; (ii) the Publisher and the Author shall each continue to have the right to receive their respective shares of sums due them from all licenses or contracts executed prior to such termination; (iii) the Author shall continue to be bound by his or her representations, warranties, and indemnification obligations set forth in this Agreement; (iv) the Author and the Publisher shall continue to be obligated to pay any sums due pursuant to any section of this Agreement; and (v) if termination occurred because the Work was out of print, the Author shall continue to be bound by any option the Author may have granted the Publisher and the Publisher shall continue to have all rights with respect thereto as are set forth in this Agreement.

Related Works

Related Works

14. The Author agrees that the Work shall be the Author's next published book-length work and that during the term of this Agreement the Author shall not, without the written permission of the Publisher (a) act in any capacity, such as writer, consultant, owner, or distributor with respect to other materials or works on the same or a similar subject which might materially impair the sale of the Work or lessen its value, (b) authorize the use of more than a total of twenty percent (20%) of the Work in magazines or newspapers if the Author

has reserved first serialization rights to the Work, and (c) grant publication rights in connection with any motion picture, radio, television, or dramatization rights if the Author has reserved such rights.

Option

Option

15. The Author agrees to submit the Author's next work in the form of ——————————a sample chapter and outline—————————— to the Publisher. The Publisher will have sixty (60) days from the date the submission is received in which to make a publishing proposal to the Author but in no event shall the Publisher be required to exercise this option prior to sixty (60) days following the Publisher's acceptance of the Work which is the subject of this Agreement. Should the Publisher and the Author be unable to agree in good faith on contractual terms for this option work, the

Author shall be free thereafter to submit such work to other publishers. ~~However, no contract shall be made with another publisher on terms equal to or less favorable than those offered by the Publisher and the Publisher shall have the option to publish the option work on the terms and conditions contained in any arm's length bona fide offer of another publisher.~~

Miscellaneous

Remedies

16. The parties agree that a breach of this Agreement would cause irreparable harm which could not be compensated with money damages. Accordingly, the parties agree that in addition to their remedies at law, they shall be entitled to injunctive relief in the event of a breach of, and in order to enforce the intent of, this Agreement. In no event shall either the Author or the Publisher be liable for consequential damages.

Binding Effect and Assignment

17. This Agreement shall be binding upon and inure to the benefit of the executors, administrators, and assigns of the Author and upon and to the successors and assigns of the Publisher. No assignment by either party of the rights or obligations under this Agreement may be made without the express written agreement of the other party.

Duration

18. Regardless of any termination of the rights granted herein which may be effective with respect to the United States of America and unless previously terminated as provided herein, this Agreement shall continue in force, with respect to any copyright obtained under the laws of any foreign country covered by this Agreement, for the term of the original copyright and for the term of any other copyright, renewal, or extension thereof which relates to the Work and which may accrue to the owner of said copyright under the present or any future law of said country.

Multiple Authors

19. If there are multiple authors as parties to this Agreement, their obligation shall be joint and several. The Publisher reserves the right to exercise any or all of its remedies solely against the author failing to perform this Agreement.

Applicable Law & Jurisdiction

20. This Agreement shall be deemed to have been made in Boston, Massachusetts, regardless of the order in which the signatures of the parties shall be affixed and shall in all respects be interpreted and construed in accordance with the laws of the Commonwealth of Massachusetts, regardless of the place of execution or performance. Author and Publisher consent to the jurisdiction of the state and federal courts located in the Commonwealth of Massachusetts and agree that any process or notice of motion or any application to a court, including application for judgment upon an award, may be served outside the Commonwealth of Massachusetts by registered mail or by in-hand delivery, provided a reasonable time for appearance is allowed.

Entire Agreement

21. This Agreement represents the entire agreement between the Author and the Publisher and supersedes all prior negotiations, representations, or understandings, either written or oral, and may not be modified or amended except by a writing executed by both parties.

Severability

22. If any one or more of the provisions contained in this Agreement should be invalid, illegal, or unenforceable in any respect, the validity, legality, and enforceability of the remaining provisions contained herein shall not in any way be affected or impaired thereby.

Waiver

23. The waiver or indulgence of any breach of any provision of this Agreement, regardless of the number or extent of the same, shall not be construed as a modification of this Agreement or as a waiver of any other breach of the said provision or any other provision of this Agreement.

Notices

24. Any notices permitted or required hereunder shall be deemed sufficient if sent registered or certified mail, postage prepaid, in the case of the Author addressed to the Author ~~xx~~ c/o Richard Balkin, ~~850 West 176th Street, New York, New York~~ ~~XXXX~~ and in the case of the Publisher addressed to it at ~~31 Beacon Street, Boston, Massachusetts~~ ~~02106~~, or in either case to any address which either party may subsequently specify by like notice.

Paragraph Headings

25. Descriptive words and statements used in the margin of this Agreement or as section headings to describe the contents of certain sections thereof are not to be deemed a part of the Agreement.

26. Advertisements may not be inserted or printed in any edition of the Work, whether issued by the Publisher or its licensee, without the Author's written consent. Such consent may be withheld in the Author's sole discretion, and he may require that a share of the advertising proceeds be paid to him, as a condition for his consent, if he so elects.

Any license granted by the Publisher to reprint the Work in book club or paperback editions, or in any other medium except newspapers and periodicals, must explicitly prohibit the licensee from inserting advertisements in its edition of the Work without the written consent of the Author as provided herein.

27. All sums of money due under the terms of this Agreement shall be paid to the Author's agent, Richard Balkin, ~~850 West 176th Street, New~~

XXXXXNXXXXXXX, who is hereby authorized by the Author to collect and receive such money, and the Author declares that the receipt of the said Richard Balkin shall be a good and valid discharge in respect thereof, and the said Richard Balkin is hereby empowered by the Author to act on his behalf in all matters arising out of this Agreement.

For services rendered and to be rendered, author does hereby irrevocably assign to said agent a sum equal to 15% (20% on British & Foreign rights) of all gross monies accruing to the author with respect to this work.

28-31 -- see below

IN WITNESS WHEREOF, the parties have executed this Agreement, or caused it to be executed, as a sealed instrument as of the day and year first above written.

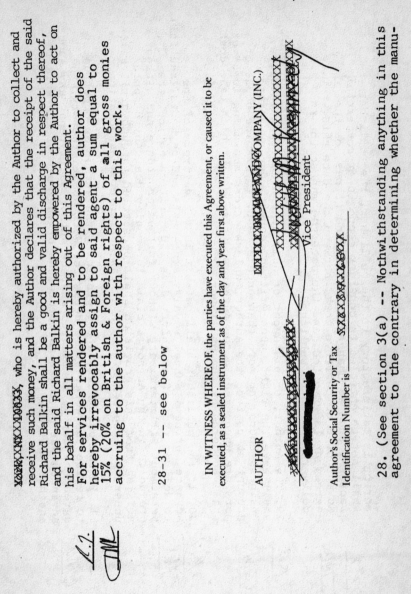

AUTHOR   XXXXX XXXXXXX XXX COMPANY (INC.)

                                XXXXXXXXXXXXXXXXXX
                                XXXXXXXXXXXXXXXXXX
                                Vice President

Author's Social Security or Tax
Identification Number is   XXXXXXXXXXX

28. (See section 3(a) -- Notwithstanding anything in this agreement to the contrary in determining whether the manu-

script is satidfactory to the publisher, the publisher shall not be entitled to consider economic or commercial factors, such as changes in market conditions, or the advent of a competitive work, between the date this agreement is executed, and the date the manuscript is delivered or to be published.

29. The Author, or his agent or duly appointed representative, shall have the right, upon written request, during normal business hours, no more than once a year, to examine books of account at cost to the Author, unless errors amounting to 5% or more are uncovered in the Author's disfavor, in which case cost shall be borne by the publisher.

R.7.
CMM

30. If the publisher shall default in the delivery of the advance, or semi-annual royalty statements and payments, and fail to deliver them after thirty days (30) written notice, the agreement will terminate without further procedure and without prejudice to the Author's claim for monies due. Any dispute arising from this provision shall be settled through arbitration under the auspices of the American Abritration Association.

R.7.
CMM

31. If the publisher, after providing the Author an opportunity to revise the Work, still deems the Work unsatisfactory, the agreement may be terminated and the author shall repay any sums advanced out of the first proceeds of the sale of the Work to another publisher.

R.7
CMM

A Publishing Fable

The Author's Tale—"The editor was so enthusiastic and supportive, I never thought there would be so many problems with getting the book out and getting it into the stores. Before it ever came out, she quit the publishing house and opened her own literary agency. I wrote her and called long distance, but she never calls back. I feel I was romanced."

The Editor's Story—"It was a good idea, with some fresh scenes, but the line editing took forever and the author didn't follow some suggestions that were crucial. Nevertheless, we went to press on schedule, and I'm sorry the house didn't follow through after I left. They're so disorganized. I still love the book and if X ever does anything more I want to see it, but. . . ."

The Publisher's Story—"She was recommended by one of our investors, you know, and she was good at grammar and spelling and punctuation even if she didn't have the editorial background. But she made these crazy deals. I think she was having a breakdown. We didn't let her go; it was her decision. And the book was one of a half-dozen we were left with. We put it out and gave it a push, but nothing happened. Have you seen the new book on running we have out?"

The Production Manager's Story—"It was a great design and seemed like an interesting subject, but the manufacturer made a last-minute switch in the text stock, and there were bindery errors, and the shipment was two days late. You can't be looking over the vendor's shoulder every minute. . . ."

The Printer—"If the book was selling well, you wouldn't hear a murmur. But when it bombs in the bookstores, they look around for someone else to sell the books to, and the first person they think of is the printer. So they want credit for 23 cases of books because it was two days late and one page was out of order in two dozen copies. This happens every day. . . ."

The Promotion Director—"The ads and the reviews and the promo were right on schedule, but we didn't have books in the stores because of the late delivery. And the author didn't proof it right, so there was a glaring error on page 93, and one page was out of order. That killed us for TV."

The Reviewer—"I never heard of the book before. Do you know how many books come in here in one day? I'll look for it, but why not send me another copy; it may be too late to write anything, but at least I'll look at it."

The Chain Buyer—"We'll fill any orders that come in, but we can't stock new titles just now. Things are just too tight. Try after the ABA, after Christmas, after you get a Book Club sale, after you get on the Tonight Show, etc. etc."

The TV Show Talent Coordinator—"If it isn't in all the stores, we can't touch it."

The Mom & Pop Stores—"Is it a local author? Will you leave, uh, one, on consignment? Can I have a reading copy?"

The Author's Mother—"It looks nice. I put it on the coffee table. You were always so good with words. Not like your brother, but it seems all he can do is make money, no matter what he touches it turns to...."

Moral: Really, we are all good people ... but we each have our own ways of doing things ... and explaining them ... and it all adds up to the publishing business we would rather be engaged in than anything else. If any of the foregoing seems like looking in the mirror ... let's try in the future to be a little more helpful, more responsible, and more aware of the other person's story.

Selected Bibliography

Book Publishing—General

Appelbaum, Judith. *How to Get Happily Published*. New York: HarperCollins, 4th ed., 1992. Chatty and supportive advice—though sometimes too upbeat and overly optimistic—geared to novice writers. Covers how, what, and where to break into print, with an elaborate and useful "resource" section of books, places, people and programs, and so on.

Curtis, Richard. *Beyond the Bestseller*. New York: NAL Books, 1989. If a writer wants to read only one other book about book publishing, this is it. Informative, streetwise, witty, and great fun to read. This book tells you exactly how it is, how this industry works, and how best to navigate most book-publishing minefields.

Dessauer, John P. *Book Publishing: The Basic Introduction*. New York: Continuum, 3rd ed., 1993. A thorough and authoritative survey of the components of the book-publishing industry and its practices.

Greenfield, Howard. *Books: From Writer to Reader.* New York: Crown Publishing, 2nd ed., 1989. This standard work about the publishing process has been updated to incorporate recent technologies that affect the industry. One of the best books available to offer a short, accessible explanation of what happens to a work after it has been accepted for publication.

Henderson, Bill, ed. *The Art of Literary Publishing.* New York: Pushcart Press, 1980. A lively collection of essays, by a mix of editors from trade houses, literary journals, and small presses, which blends personal recollections with practical advice.

Plotnik, Arthur. *Honk If You're a Writer.* New York: Fireside Books, 1992. The perfect book for creative writing majors and other writing wannabes. A knowledgeable, sympathetic, informal chatty book—it's sometimes a little too cute—with excellent advice on how to write and how to break into print.

Potter, Clarkson N. *Who Does What and Why in Book Publishing.* New York: Birch Lane Press, 1990. A detailed, realistic, and elegantly written explanation of how the key participants make decisions in book-publishing houses, by a longtime publisher. Excellent and lengthy bibliography.

Finding a Publisher

Burack, A. S., ed. *The Writer's Handbook.* Boston: The Writer, Inc., 1992. Seven hundred sixty pages of useful articles by writers and experts in publishing on how to write books and articles and then where and how to place them, followed by a listing and brief description of more than 2,500 markets for the writer. Second to *Writer's Market* in utility.

Collier, Oscar, and Frances Spatz Leighton. *How to Write and Sell Your First Nonfiction Book.* New York: St. Martin's Press, 1990.

————. *How to Write and Sell Your First Novel*. Cincinnati: Writer's Digest Books, 1986. An experienced agent and the author of more than 30 books team up to give realistic and detailed advice on how to write and then to sell a manuscript.

Curtis, Richard. *How to Be Your Own Literary Agent*. Boston: Houghton Mifflin, 1984. Savvy insider dope and advice on the entire range of author/publisher relations; couldn't be better, and still as pertinent and valuable as it was ten years ago.

Garvey, Mark, ed. *The Writer's Market*. Cincinnati: Writer's Digest Books, annual. The most complete and up-to-date listing of markets for writers, interspersed with tips on how, what, and where. A fair number of suitable trade book publishing houses are not listed, but the magazine section can't be beat.

Gee, Robin, ed. *Guide to Literary Agents and Art Photo Reps*. Cincinnati: Writer's Digest Books, annual. Detailed listing of U.S. and Canadian agents, but not as complete as Orrmont and Rosensteil (see below). Does have subject index (listing which agents are interested in which genres), and ten very informative essays by and about agents. *Literary Market Place* has the most complete listing of literary agents but no subject index.

Literary Market Place. New York: R. R. Bowker, annual. The most comprehensive directory of commercial publishers and personnel, as well as of all other ancillary publishing services. But at $140, so overpriced! *LMP* contains unexpected treasures for writers: a list of publishing courses and prizes, fellowships, and grants for writers; a huge bibliography of reference books about publishing; an up-to-date listing of writers' conferences and workshops, and many other useful sources for writers. It's well worth browsing through.

Orrmont, Arthur, and Leonie Rosenstiel, eds. *Literary Agents of North America*. New York: Author Aid Associates, 5th ed., 1993. Complete and detailed listing of most U.S. and Canadian agents, with very useful indices: subject (especially useful), agent policy, geographical, and agency size.

Turner, Barry, ed. *The Writer's Handbook*. London: Macmillan Press, Ltd., annual. The British version of our *Writer's Market*, but more thorough, detailed, and useful. Lists book publishers, magazines, agents, and so forth in the U.K. and Canada. Gives some information on the United States, too.

Writers' & Artists Yearbook 1993. London: A & C Black, Ltd., annual. This is Tweedledum to the preceding title's Tweedledee; almost as long and just as good.

Contracts and Copyright*

Andorka, Frank H. *A Practical Guide to Copyrights and Trademarks*. New York: Pharos Books, 1989. A useful but very brief primer on current copyright and trademark law, and on how to protect copyright and trademarks. Not detailed enough for nuances and gray areas.

Bunnin, Brad, and Peter Berens. *The Writer's Legal Companion*. Reading, MA: Addison-Wesley, 2nd ed., 1988. Unquestionably the best book available on negotiating all sorts of publishing-related contracts, including collaboration agreements and author/agent agreements. Also offers authoritative advice on libel, taxes, and the like. A gem. Copyright information updated in 1993.

Clark, Charles. *Publishing Agreements*. New York: New Amsterdam Books, 3rd ed., 1988. A British import. Publishing and media contracts of all different sorts, such as book club and translation, with boilerplate on the recto and interpretations, negotiating tips, variations, and so forth on the verso. Most of the contracts and advice are suitable for either side of the Atlantic. Extremely useful for a do-it-yourselfer.

---

*The free "Copyright Information Kit #109" is available from the Register of Copyrights, Library of Congress, Washington, DC 20559. It contains copyright forms for books and articles, as well as several circulars on various aspects of basic and current copyright provisions.

Crawford, Tad. *Business and Legal Forms for Authors & Self-Publishers*. New York: Allworth Press, 1990. Seventeen photocopyable publishing contracts and forms, with negotiating tips for all of them. Extremely useful for the experienced full-time writer.

Fishman, Stephen. *The Copyright Handbook*. Berkeley: Nolo Press, 1992. Complete, thorough, reader-friendly, extremely practical and useful, and all you'd want to know about copyright and related issues. A terrific job; Nolo's self-help books for lay people are uniformly superb.

Madison, Charles A. *Irving to Irving: Author-Publisher Relations, 1800–1974*. New York: R. R. Bowker, 1974. The evolution of contracts, copyright agreements, and other arrangements between authors and publishers.

The Tenth Annual Seminar on Negotiating Contracts in the Entertainment Industry. Annual, New York: Law Journal Seminars Press, 1993. Photocopies of actual negotiated contracts reprinted in their entirety for almost every possible publishing and media deal a writer might encounter. For agents, lawyers, and high-powered writers who negotiate on their own.

Editing and Copyediting

Barzun, Jacques. *On Writing, Editing, and Publishing*. Chicago: The University of Chicago Press, 2nd ed. (expanded), 1986. A discursive and timeless selection of essays by one of America's foremost *hommes de belles lettres;* worth reading for its stylistic elegance alone.

Gross, Gerald. *Editors on Editing*. New York: Grove Press, 3rd ed., 1993. Forty articles and miscellanea by well-known and successful editors describing how they feel about their work and how they do it. Thoroughly revised, and a gem of a collection.

Plotnik, Arthur. *The Elements of Editing*. New York: Macmillan, 1982. Still a must-read primer for book editors, but any career author should know and will appreciate learning about the other side of the fence.

Reference Books

All three of the following style manuals are comprehensive and authoritative classics.

Jordan, Lewis. *New York Times Manual of Style and Usage.* New York: Times Books, 1982.

The Chicago Manual of Style. Chicago: University of Chicago Press, 14th ed., 1993.

Skillin, Marjorie E., and Gay, Robert M. *Words into Type.* Englewood Cliffs, NJ: Prentice-Hall, 3rd ed., 1986.

Design and Production

Black, Alison. *Typefaces for Desktop Publishing: A User Guide.* London: Phaidon/Architecture Design and Technology Press, 1990. A handbook for designers familiar with traditional typesetting who are adapting to desktop; it also contains basic information for the computer-literate novice designer.

Hunter, David. *Papermaking: The History and Technique of an Ancient Craft.* New York: Dover reprint ed., 1978. A historical survey of interest to anyone who cares about literature, the evolution of writing, or the book as a physical craft object.

Lee, Marshall. *Bookmaking: The Illustrated Guide to Design/ Production/Editing.* New York: R. R. Bowker, 2nd ed., 1979. Still the book designer's classic ABC. Comprehensive instruction on book design and production.

Other Categories of Publishing

Children's Books*

Children's Books: Awards & Prizes. New York: The Children's Book Council, 1992. Almost 200 major U.S., U.K., and international book awards and prizes.

Shulevitz, Uri. *Writing with Pictures: How to Write and Illustrate Children's Books.* New York: Watson-Guptill Publications, 1985. Especially good for apprentice illustrators; the one most frequently cited by professionals as the best and most useful.

Woolley, Catherine (A.K.A. Jane Thayer). *Writing for Children.* New York: Plume, 1991. A brief but thorough A to Z on both the techniques and business of writing children's books. The author of 87 children's books gives sound, down-to-earth, specific advice that is authoritative and reader-friendly. Highly recommended.

Zinsser, William, ed. *The Art and Craft of Writing for Children.* Boston: Houghton Mifflin, 1990. A collection of six very charming essays—based on a series of lectures given at the New York Public Library—by distinguished writers of children's books (Sendak, Prelutsky, Krementz, Fritz, Wells, and Paterson), with a thoughtful introductory overview of their work by Zinsser. Long on reminiscence, these offer almost as much pleasure as their books.

University Press

The Association of American Universities Directory 1993–1994. New York: A.A.U.P., 1993. A listing of all current U.S., Canadian, and foreign university presses, including—

---

*For two brochures, *Writing Children's Books* and *Illustrating Children's Books* (both of which include a bibliography), plus an annotated list of publishers of children's books, send $1 plus S.A.S.E. to: The Children's Book Council, 568 Broadway, Room 404, New York, NY 10012.

among other useful information—genres of interest to each press.

Luey, Beth. *Handbook for Academic Authors*. New York: Cambridge University Press, 2nd ed., 1990. An excellent and thorough exploration of all aspects of scholarly publishing. Includes how to get published in journals, revise a dissertation, find the right scholarly or textbook publisher, prepare a final manuscript, and work with an editor. For an academic author, this is the one to read.

Small Presses and Self-Publishing

Burke, Clifford. *Type from the Desktop: Designing with Type and Your Computer*. Chapel Hill, NC: Ventana Press 1990. Clear, concise, and encouraging. For the impecunious do-it-yourselfer.

Fulton, Len, ed. *International Directory of Little Magazines and Small Presses*. Paradise, CA: Dustbooks, 29th ed., 1993. As complete a listing of alternative/independent publishers and magazines as can be found, with descriptions of what they publish, what they pay (if anything), and how to submit a manuscript.

Henderson, Bill, ed. *The Publish-It-Yourself Handbook*. Wainscott, NY: Pushcart Press, 3rd ed., 1987. An anthology comprised of articles by those who did it themselves. Good reading, filled with reminiscences, and a must for the tyro self-publisher.

Huenefeld, John. *The Huenefeld Guide to Book Publishing*. Bedford, MA: Mills & Sanderson, 4th ed., 1990. A reference book for small publishers; complete, detailed instructions on how to run a small press.

Holt, Robert Lawrence. *How to Publish, Promote, and Sell Your Own Book*. New York: St. Martin's Press, 1985. Just what it says, and very detailed and useful (but out of date on the use of the computer in self-publishing).

Poynter, Dan. *The Self-Publishing Manual: How to Write, Print and Sell Your Own Book*. Santa Barbara, CA: Para Publications,

7th ed., 1992. On most topics, as much detail as you would need to do it yourself. Sometimes oversimplified or overly optimistic, but essentially an ideal handbook. Poynter has become the doyen of self-publishing, and publishes a kitful of books on the topic, as well as a newsletter. Write for a free catalog: Para Publishing, P.O. Box 4232, Santa Barbara, CA 93140.

Miscellaneous

The ASJA Handbook: A Writer's Guide to Ethical and Economic Issues. New York: ASJA, 2nd ed., 1992. A nuts and bolts pamphlet on crucial business issues for writers, such as collaborating, dealing with corporate clients, tax tips, analyzing contracts, dealing with book packagers and more. Frank and filled with real-life examples from A.S.J.A.'s voluminous files. Best to become a member and get it for half-price.

Book Publishing Career Directory. Detroit: Gale Research Co., 1987. Essays by pros on what specific publishing jobs are like, from all different departments in book publishing. Somewhat outmoded, but invaluable if you're considering a career in book publishing.

Congrat-Butler, Stefan, ed. *Translation & Translators.* New York: R. R. Bowker, 1979. An exhaustive and thorough encyclopedic work for translators. Contains sections on associations, conferences, awards, contracts, and so on, together with a register of professional and accredited translators. Out of print and outdated in many areas, but the only reference of its kind available at most academic libraries.

Grants & Awards Available to American Writers. New York: P.E.N. American Center, 18th ed., 1994. The title says it all.

Kremer, John. *1001 Ways to Market Your Books.* Fairfield, IA: Open Horizons, 4th ed., 1993. "All the answers you'll need to sell your books." Kremer offers a newsletter and ten books on marketing, publicity, and promotion for commercial as well as self-publishers, and is highly respected. Write for a free catalog and sample newsletter: Open Horizons, P.O. Box 205, Fairfield, IA 52556.

Spiker, Sina. *Indexing Your Book: A Practical Guide for Authors*. Madison, WI: Univ. of Wisconsin Press, 1954. The oldest, the only, and yet still an extraordinarily useful 28-page pamphlet ($3.95 plus .52 handling; a bargain!), even though the "C" word (computer) doesn't appear in this book. Well worth it.

Index